Karen Spear

ADAPTIVE COACHING

ADAPTIVE COACHING

COACHING

The Art and Practice of a

Client-Centered Approach to

Performance Improvement

TERRY R. BACON • KAREN I. SPEAR

Davies-Black Publishing
Palo Alto, California

Published by Davies-Black Publishing, a division of CPP, Inc., 3803 East Bayshore Road, Palo Alto, CA 94303; 800-624-1765.

Special discounts on bulk quantities of Davies-Black books are available to corporations, professional associations, and other organizations. For details, contact the Director of Marketing and Sales at Davies-Black Publishing, 3803 East Bayshore Road, Palo Alto, CA 94303; 650-691-9123; fax 650-623-9271.

Visit the Davies-Black Publishing web site at www.daviesblack.com.

07 06 05 04 03   10 9 8 7 6 5 4 3 2 1
Printed in the United States of America

Library of Congress Cataloging-in-Publication Data
Bacon, Terry R., and Karen I. Spear
        Adaptive coaching: The art and practice of a client-centered approach to performance improvement / Terry R. Bacon and Karen I. Spear.— 1st ed.
        p. cm.
Includes bibliographical references and index.
ISBN 0-89106-187-8
        1. Coaching. 2. Performance improvement. I. Title.

FIRST EDITION
First printing 2003

CONTENTS

ACKNOWLEDGMENTS

A book of this nature is not merely the product of two minds but is the result of years of accumulated experience and the thoughts and contributions of hundreds of people, not least of whom are the countless professionals, executives, and students we have coached in the course of nearly three decades of experience as coaches, educators, and managers. We therefore begin by thanking the many coaching clients with whom we have worked during the course of our careers. Without their problems, questions, challenges, and faith in us, we would know very little about coaching. The plain fact is that without the thousands of dialogues we have had with them, we would not have understood what successful coaching looks like or how critical it is to be adaptive to our clients' needs and preferences.

We also acknowledge the help we've received from our many colleagues in the Lore Division of Heidrick and Struggles. The fine men and women of Lore, who coach thousands of executives every year, are a source of inspiration and wisdom. One of the values of working in a collegial environment of professionals is the sharing of insights and experiences, which makes each of us more effective in our individual roles with clients. In this regard, our experiences at Lore have been invaluable. We are especially grateful to Andrew Ackemann, Nancy Atwood, Caroline Ballantine, Ben Cannon, Heather Connelly, Sean Darnall, Chick Davis, Richard Eidinger, Greg Elkins, Carol Emmott, Rene Fernandez, Michael Flagg, Mike Franzino, Gregor Gardner, Steve Gilman, Dick Gustafson, Glo Harris, Jean Hauser, Linda Heagy, Melodie Hicks, Michael Hume, Thomas Kell, Jory Marino, Rafael Mora, Jack Nederpelt, David Pugh, Karen Quint, Wes Richards, Gale Roanoake, Colette Ruoff, Monte Sher, Linda Simmons, Les Stern, Andy Talkington, Alex Trisoglio, Rick Troberman, Kathy Uroda, Laurie Voss, Wolfgang Walter, and others who have helped us practice and develop our craft through the years.

We are especially grateful to Barbara Spencer Singer, whose landmark work on recovering executives who are at risk of derailing was instrumental in our thinking about how to coach executives. Barbara has done a considerable amount of thinking about how to coach effectively and is responsible for the Lore Division's coaching certification program, which is one of the most rigorous in the world. Her criteria for professional coaching are the standard by which we measure the quality and value of a coach.

We also thank our friends and colleagues at Fort Lewis College who graciously spent precious time reading drafts of several chapters and who offered insightful criticism and unfailing support and interest: anthropology professor Kathleen Fine-Dare, communications professor Carol Smith, and English professor Mary Jean Moseley. Psychology professor Mukti Khanna, now at Evergreen College, also deserves our thanks for her help in identifying key issues and resources in cross-cultural psychology.

A number of people played important roles in the creation of this book. We particularly thank Donna Williams, who managed the book's production, did a considerable amount of research and proofing, and helped us gather permissions; Tom Fuhrmark, who is the graphic artist responsible for the book's visuals; and Sheri Lightenburg, who proofread the book and helped us avoid many embarrassing mistakes. Finally, we offer our deepest appreciation to Connie Kallback, our editor at Davies-Black Publishing, who believed in this project from its inception and offered us considerable latitude, guidance, and encouragement along the way. It is fair to say that this book would never have existed without her assistance and support and that its form and content are due in part to Connie's editorial judgment.

The idea of coauthoring a book with one's spouse raised many eyebrows and predictions of impending divorce. So we end these acknowledgments by thanking each other for practicing what we preach about being good coaches, particularly for being good thought partners. We're still speaking, still sharing, still married.

PERMISSIONS

We would like to thank the authors and publishers who have granted us permission to include lengthy quotations from their works: Larissa MacFarquhar (2002), "The Better Boss," in *The New Yorker;* Steven Berglas

(2002), "The Very Real Dangers of Executive Coaching," in *Harvard Business Review;* Charles A. O'Reilly III and Jeffrey Pfeffer (2000), *Hidden Value: How Great Companies Achieve Extraordinary Results with Ordinary People;* David Bohm (1996), *On Dialogue;* Lester Tobias (1996), "Coaching Executives," in *Consulting Psychology Journal;* Deborah Flick (1998), *From Debate to Dialogue;* Fons Trompenaars and Charles Hampden-Turner (1998), *Riding the Waves of Culture: Understanding Diversity in Global Business;* Alan Roland (1988), *In Search of Self in India and Japan: Toward a Cross-Cultural Psychology;* and David Bohm, Donald Factor, and Peter Garrett (1991), "Dialogue: A Proposal."

A WORD ABOUT PRONOUNS

Throughout this book, we have tried to avoid the awkward use of dual pronouns: he/she, his/her, him/her, and himself/herself. Although these constructions attempt to be inclusive, they are a clumsy use of English. Instead, we have varied our pronoun use, sometimes referring to coaches or clients as "he" and sometimes as "she." Our pronoun choices are random and are meant to illustrate that, insofar as our discussion of coaching is concerned, the gender of the coaches and clients is largely irrelevant.

ABOUT THE AUTHORS

Terry R. Bacon is founder and chairman of Lore International Institute, a professional development firm specializing in solving business problems through integrated systems, tools, and training in these critical business areas: leadership development, strategic account management, proposal development, sales and marketing, communication skills, and interpersonal skills. Consulting services include organizational and skills assessments, program and curriculum design, process/systems development, change management, business development system audits, and proposal consultation. His clients include Putnam Investments, American Express, General Electric, Ford Motor Company, and Fluor Corporation.

Bacon's unique background has enabled him to formulate and demonstrate particular insight regarding the skills necessary for an exceptional team leader. While completing his B.S. degree in engineering at the U.S. Military Academy at West Point and then later in Vietnam, he developed an aptitude for understanding group dynamics and communication and for mediating conflict. Following his army career as an intelligence analyst and personnel officer, he earned a Ph.D. degree in English from The American University. After teaching at the university level for a short period, he joined a consulting firm specializing in business communication where, as Vice President for Research and Development, he created more than fifty programs for industry and government clients and won numerous awards for program design. He also created and managed a strategic business unit offering a broad spectrum of specialty client services.

Bacon's interest in professional development led him to dedicate his new firm to the concept of developing today's more highly educated professionals, who often have greater responsibility in many different areas and require new skill sets to meet the challenges of working more productively individually and in teams. Through awareness and skills building, supported by tools and innovative learning methodologies, Bacon has demonstrated that "tapping the resources of the team" is a significant component for success in our team-oriented society. A prolific author and popular speaker, his most recent books include *Winning Behavior* and *Selling to Major Accounts*.

Karen I. Spear is a senior researcher for the Lore Research Institute and director of the institute's peer review program, which involves coaching Lore's professionals on all phases of their research and writing efforts. She has been a consultant to Lore International Institute informally for the past ten years and formally for the past two. Her areas of specialization include women's leadership, interpersonal leadership skills, executive coaching, and adult learning, particularly the question of how professionals respond to change and growth needs throughout their careers. She has provided coaching for consultants at all levels, from business analysts to directors, for McKinsey and Company and for Egon Zehnder International, including coaching in Europe on inspirational leadership. She has also served other Lore clients including the World Bank, Chase Bank, and the Gartner Group.

Spear holds a B.A. degree in English from the University of Maryland and a Ph.D. degree in literature and psychology from The American University. Recently retired from her first career after twenty-five years in higher education, she has served as a professor, researcher, and administrator at the University of Utah, Utah State University, the University of South Florida, and Colorado State University. She served for a year as interim CEO of the University of South Florida's St. Petersburg campus. Most recently, she was Professor of English and, for nine years, Dean of Arts and Sciences at Fort Lewis College in Durango, Colorado. As a teacher of writing, an executive, and a consultant on program design and review, her entire higher education career involved coaching and mentoring students and colleagues on a range of sensitive developmental issues.

Author of two books on collaboration in the teaching of writing that are widely used by secondary and higher education faculty, Spear has published a wide variety of work on liberal education, cognitive development, writing development, and collaboration. She has consulted with colleges and universities throughout the United States on faculty development and program design in writing and liberal education, and had an interesting stint working in Hungary following the fall of the Communist government to aid in the reorganization of the higher education system in that country. The report that came out of that study was disseminated to universities throughout eastern Europe.

INTRODUCTION

Consider these facts:

- Ninety-nine percent of corporate officers believe that their pool of managerial talent will need to be stronger three years from now.

- Fifty-four percent of corporate officers report that their inability to cultivate strong executive leadership from their people is a "huge" or "major" obstacle to their success.

- Fifty-seven percent of managers believe that their company does not develop their people quickly and effectively.

- Fifty-seven percent of managers who intend to seek new jobs with new companies name insufficient development and learning opportunities as "critical" or "very important" reasons for leaving.

We learn these facts in the recent book *The War for Talent* (Michaels, Handfield-Jones, and Axelrod 2001), which is based on a series of Mc-Kinsey-sponsored studies conducted in 1997 and 2000 with more than one hundred large and midsized U.S. companies. The ten thousand respondents in these studies included corporate officers, senior managers, midlevel executives, and HR executives (pp. 4, 97–98). The real war for talent is not so much a war among corporate combatants raiding each other's fiefdoms for executive plunder, although it is often practiced as such. It is really a war of the imagination and the will to envision and implement new and better ways to develop and retain existing talent. Businesses are coming to recognize that they cannot simply recruit their way to victory. Winning the war for talent means winning on the home front by developing more skillful, more sustained, more effective means of helping good people grow into their current assignments and into the challenges of their next assignments and the ones after that.

To wage the war for talent largely outside your organization is to chase a chimera. In *Hidden Value: How Great Companies Achieve Extraordinary*

Results with Ordinary People, authors Charles A. O'Reilly III and Jeffrey Pfeffer (2000) offer a compelling, commonsense argument for talent development:

> *Of course, companies that want to succeed need great people, and recruitment, selection, and retention are obviously important. But companies need something else that is even more important and often more difficult to obtain: cultures and systems in which these great people can actually use their talents, and, even better, management practices that produce extraordinary results from almost everybody. The unfortunate mathematical fact is that only 10 percent of the people are going to be in the top 10 percent. So, companies have a choice. They can all chase the same supposed talent. Or, they can do something even more useful and much more difficult to copy—build an organization that helps make it possible for regular folks to perform as if they were in the top 10 percent.* (pp. 1–2)

While exciting work at a great company with good compensation and work-life balance all contribute to getting good people, a key element in keeping them is development—opportunities to stretch and grow in an environment that communicates its commitment to employees.

As the war for talent continues, companies are increasingly turning to coaching as a principal means of developing their existing people in an effort to produce extraordinary results from almost everybody. Coaching has become one of the hottest movements in professional development in the last decade. By some estimates, there are now more than forty thousand individuals in North America and Europe who call themselves executive coaches—more than ten times the number of coaches who hung out a shingle just a decade ago—and that number pales beside the hundreds of thousands of executives, managers, supervisors, and other professionals in thousands of companies worldwide whose jobs include coaching others. This extraordinary burst of coaching activity has generated an accompanying explosion of coaching literature. A look at the Amazon.com listing under "business coaching" reveals 135 books on coaching, most written since the mid-1990s and many written by sports coaches, military leaders, and others with only a peripheral connection to business.

Businesses moved to coaching as the limitations of traditional classroom training became more and more obvious. Lack of transfer in learning and lack of sustained behavioral change pointed toward the need for more individualized, more engaged, more context-specific learning. Coaching seemed to provide a solution to the human and systemic challenges posed by the new business paradigm:

- Real-time, on-time learning

- Individualized learning

- Integrated learning to help people negotiate the demands of their work with the demands of their lives

- Sustained attention to progress and development to foster genuine change

- Accelerated learning for a rapidly changing business environment

- A changed role for managers in the new learning organization

The coaching literature that emerged both responded to and drove these expectations—in many cases to absurd extremes. The literature is replete with grandiose claims about personal growth and transformation, improved quality of life, spiritual renewal, wildly enhanced productivity, unleashed human potential, enhanced creativity, heightened self-confidence, and having it all faster and easier with the help of a devoted coach. Leading the charge are sports coaches like Don Shula and Rick Pitino, who are cashing in on their fame. Pitino, coach of the Louisville Cardinals men's basketball team and formerly coach of the Kentucky Wildcats when they won the NCAA title, wrote a 1998 book called *Success Is a Choice: Ten Steps to Overachieving in Business and Life.* The blurb on the back cover reads, "Make Rick Pitino your personal coach and achieve more than you ever thought possible." Shula coauthored two books with Ken Blanchard titled *Everyone's a Coach* (Blanchard and Shula 1995) and *The Little Book of Coaching: Motivating People to Be Winners* (2001). While some readers may enjoy the sports anecdotes, these books offer little beyond the standard platitudes about leadership and motivation. They reduce coaching to cheerleading and the coach to a dynamic dispenser of wisdom. Moreover, they misplace the responsibility for successful coaching interventions. In *Everyone's a Coach,* Blanchard and Shula argue that ". . . beliefs are what make things happen. Beliefs come true. Inadequate beliefs are setups for inadequate performance. And it's the coach's—the leader's—beliefs that are the most important; they become self-fulfilling" (p. 29). In their perspective, coaching is all about leading and motivating others, and the people being coached change through the strength of a paternalistic coach's vision, energy, and charisma. In this reductio ad absurdum, which shows little insight into human development, clients simply follow the leader. They accept the coach's direction because the coach knows best and bear no responsibility for their own development. As such, these books are works of staggering oversimplification.

There is only the loosest affiliation between athletic coaching and business practice, and a number of better works on coaching are quick to dissociate the meanings they attach to coaching in business from what is practiced in sports. While applications of coaching vary widely depending on the context and the client, coaching in business contexts can generally be defined as *an informed dialogue whose purpose is the facilitation of new skills, possibilities, and insights in the interest of individual learning and organizational advancement.* Coaching is anchored in a trust relationship best characterized by listening, observing, questioning, joint problem solving, and action planning. Business coaching is largely not about the processes more commonly associated with sports coaching—advice giving, training, instruction, exhortation, rewards, and punishments—although, to be sure, *some* business clients *do* want advice, direction, and motivational speeches.

As the coaching boom gained momentum, the literature began to reflect a shift from its roots in the organizational changes of the late 1980s when managers saw the need to let go of their old command-and-control styles and become more developmental in their orientation. Companies needed and expected more of their employees, and coaching emerged as a way to get it. However, as outsourcing became more prevalent in the nineties, the locus of coaching shifted away from managers—at least in the literature. Though it is often not clearly specified, the most recent coaching literature is more geared toward the external executive coach, the coach-for-hire whose functions range from extended one-on-one coaching with a high-level executive to coaching of an entire executive team. As the demand and cost for such services escalated, so did the claims about what coaching could achieve.

So why one more book on coaching? The truth is that in spite of all the excitement, there is still a huge gap between rhetoric and reality. First, the McKinsey studies indicate that coaching, combined with performance feedback, ranks among the most significant drivers of talent development, yet respondents in the 2000 "War for Talent" survey rate only 35 percent of the coaching they receive as *good* to *excellent.* Research on coaching effectiveness conducted by Lore International Institute also shows a significant gap between what companies and clients expect from coaching and what it actually does for them. From 1996 through 2002, Lore conducted an extensive survey of coaching effectiveness within Fortune 500 companies. Lore's database includes assessments from more than two thousand coaching clients. Here are some of the data that indicate the need for dramatic improvements in alignment between the expectations for coaching and its effectiveness:

- Fifty-seven percent of clients say they would like *more* coaching than they are currently getting.

- Sixty percent of clients say they would like *better* coaching than they are currently getting.

- Fifty-six percent of clients report that the coaching they receive is often not focused on the right things and does not help them learn exactly what they should do differently to be more effective.

- Forty-five percent of clients report that coaching sessions with their current coach have not had much positive impact on their work performance.

For all the vaunted claims about the potential of coaching advanced in the hundreds of books on the topic, these outcomes are dismal. How many of us would purchase a product that had only a 45 percent likelihood of doing what it was purported to do?

Second, who receives coaching from whom? Companies can afford outside coaches for senior executives, but the need for developmental coaching extends throughout the entire organization. External coaches should be used at executive levels where objective outside help can be most beneficial, as well as for special cases at lower levels. However, *everyone* deserves the opportunity to improve his or her skills, so education and coaching should be part of the fabric of a company. In most companies, managers throughout the organization provide the bulk of the coaching, but, as our research on coaching effectiveness reveals, the grassroots work of developing managers as coaches remains far from finished. Furthermore, many of the people who sell themselves as coaches do a poor job of it. We hear time and again from companies that they have been disappointed by much of the coaching their leaders have received from external coaches. Coaches of both sorts—internal and external—need to continue to refine their skills to adapt to the coaching situations in which they find themselves.

Coaching holds much promise, but there is a serious need to improve on what it currently delivers. Improvement will come only from a sober and realistic look at what coaching can and cannot do, not from hyperbolic and suspect claims. Coaches must be clear and realistic about what they are offering and why. They must hold the line about what coaching is and is not. And clients must be encouraged to be thoughtful in defining what they want and need. Once the ground rules are set, clients and coaches can determine what falls in the realm of coaching and what may more properly belong in other kinds of helping situations, such as psychotherapy, family therapy, formal education, spiritual guidance, human resources functions, or even legal intervention. The coach can often serve quite usefully as a conduit to other kinds of helping interventions. The coach can also define fully what coaching *can* provide, such as gathering and interpreting performance feedback; career planning for personal and professional development; improving interpersonal and leadership or management skills; mediating team relationships; analyzing career roadblocks and setbacks; uncovering blind spots and assumptions that limit the client's abilities; helping clients stick with and assess progress on an agenda; and serving as a confidential, disinterested sounding board to deliberate on alternative courses of action and business strategies.

In spite of this vast potential for coaching, in reality there is only the skimpiest of empirical evidence for what happens in the relationship, why it happens, and what makes it effective or ineffective. Most of the published research can be found only within the relatively narrow confines of doctoral dissertations. Instead, most coaching theory and practices reside in the vivid anecdotal accounts of successful practitioners, where all kinds of variables from personal charisma to the halo effect of receiving special attention from a coach cloud a genuine understanding of the dynamics and techniques of good coaching. In a lengthy literature review in his book *Executive Coaching*, Richard Kilburg (2000) concludes that only two of the research studies he uncovered "can be said to be even tangentially related to what is now being extensively marketed and practiced in the field. This lack of an empirical foundation has not inhibited practitioners or authors from advocating their approaches or from publishing their views" (p. 59). If coaching is to capitalize on the promise it holds, we need to understand more specifically what constitutes effective coaching in the eyes of the client.

What we have learned over the last decade, by listening carefully to the wants and needs of coaching clients and analyzing their responses, is that effective coaching must first and foremost be *adaptive*. By this we mean that coaches must be skilled at adapting their methods, techniques, and approaches to the needs of their clients—both personally and contextually. Throughout this book, we will report some of the tens of thousands of responses we've heard from coaching clients to the question, "What could your coach do to be more effective?" Their answers indicate a crying need for coaches to be more adaptive. Here are a few representative responses:

- *Use different coaching styles; ask more questions.*

- *Become more patient during coaching sessions and take more time for the concerns of those who are being coached.*

- *Release your own agenda.*

- *Be more open in helping the coachee develop his ideas rather than providing him direction.*

- *Help the person being coached to consider the culture and what will actually work in the organization rather than a pure view of what is best in a vacuum but may not fly in practice.*

- *Take more time to find out the history of the individual (what he has done, good and not so good, his experience).*

- *Be more open in helping me develop my ideas rather than providing me with direction.*

- *In my opinion, it is important to view coaching more as a part of a long-term development process, instead of a way to solve specific performance problems.*

- *Ask the coachees more where they see improvement potential by themselves. Match their point of view with her observations and work out individual development plans with defined tasks, milestones, and feedback loops together with the coachees.*

Although the first principle of coaching espoused in most of the coaching literature is to do all the things these respondents call for, coaches consistently fail in the fundamentals of listening, empathizing, probing, and contextualizing even when they think that's what they are doing. Instead they revert to advice giving, problem solving, and theorizing. This is not simply a coaching shortcoming as much as it is a human tendency in all kinds of helping situations, a tendency to want to fix the problem. All of us have grown up with an implicit model of coaching that is fundamentally flawed. We have learned how to help others while receiving instruction, advice, and guidance from our parents, schoolteachers, religious leaders, scoutmasters, dance teachers, music instructors, friends—and athletic coaches—who, for the most part, take a highly directive and authoritarian approach. John Goodlad's (1984) research, in *A Place Called School,* established clearly that teachers teach the way they were taught, not the way they were taught to teach. The same can be said about the difficulties anyone faces in a helping relationship. The challenge is to unlearn that deeply embedded, directive model of helping in favor of one that is more mutual, more collaborative, and more centered on the needs and preferences of the other person. Our research tells us that most corporate coaches prefer to use a directive approach, whereas most clients want their coaches to use a nondirective approach. Furthermore, in training coaches through role plays, we have found that many coaches prematurely decide what the client's issues are, direct the conversation according to that assumption, and frequently discover later that they were wrong.

What many coaches lack are frameworks for understanding what it means to adapt to the client. The admonition to adapt is clear enough, but absent a sense of what the alternatives are, coaches revert to the style and approach with which they are most comfortable. To elaborate further, we will frame our approach to adaptive coaching with three concepts: the two-minds model, a taxonomy of coaching styles, and the use of dialogue, each of which will be explored more fully in subsequent chapters.

THE TWO-MINDS MODEL

At the outset of a coaching relationship, there are enormous differences between the coach's perspective and the client's perspective. As figures 1 and 2 illustrate, each has a very different set of experiences, expectations, assumptions, and perhaps values and beliefs. For the coach to build trust with the client, there must be enough alignment in their mind-sets for the client to feel that the coach understands him and his circumstances, is sympathetic toward him, is genuinely interested in helping him, is credible as a helper, is on his side, and can be trusted. This is a tall order, especially when the coach and client are members of the same organization, when the coach has some role relationship with the client (such as his

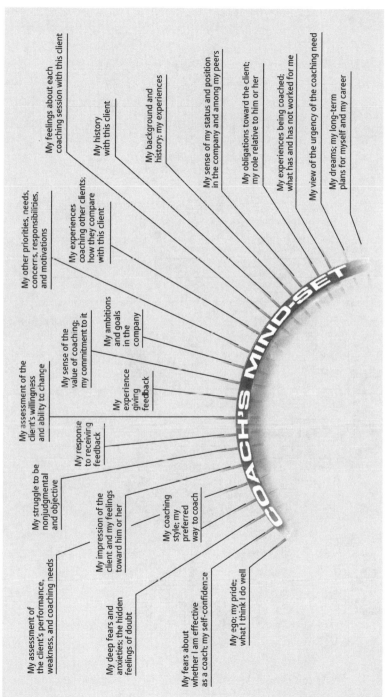

Figure 1 The Coach's Mind-set

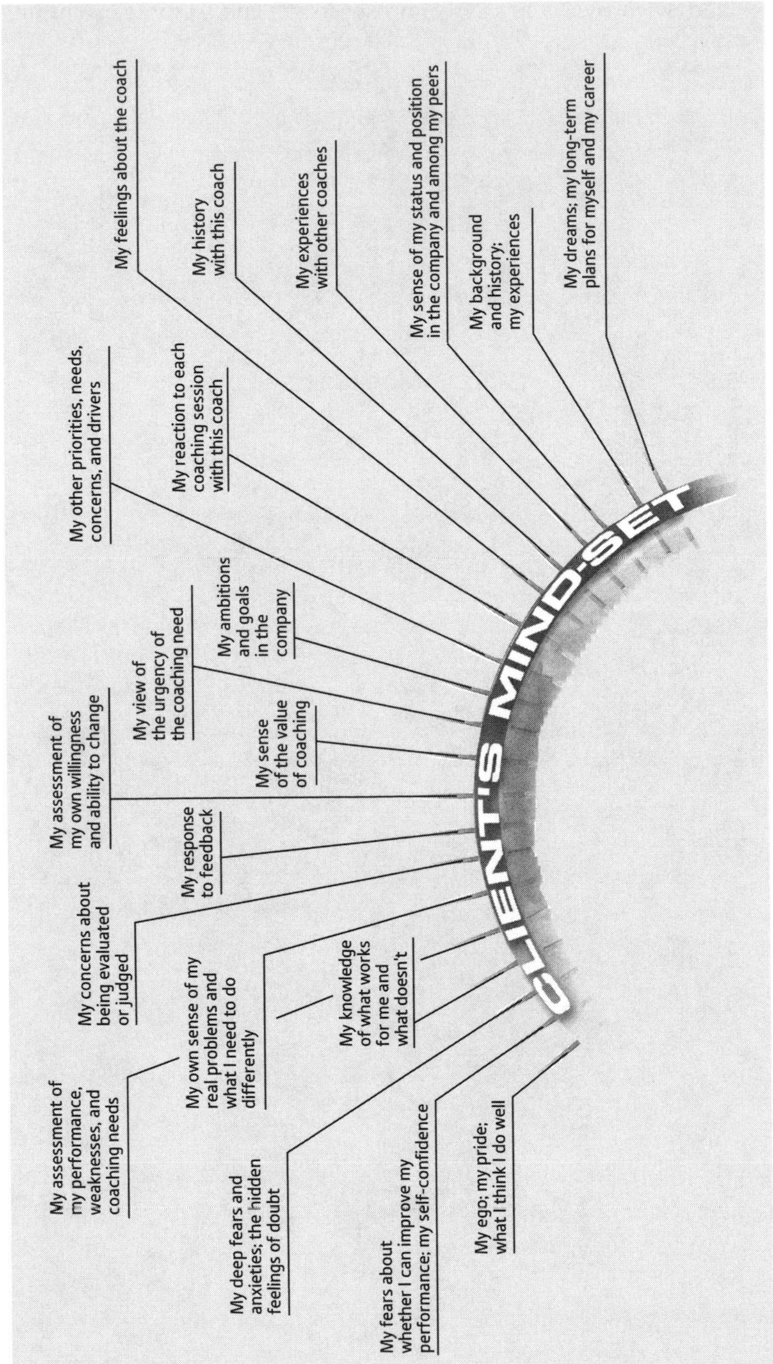

Figure 2   The Client's Mind-set

boss), and when the client's career prospects depend to some extent on the outcomes of the coaching.

It's fair to say that most of the coaching that takes place in business organizations is boss (coach) to direct report (client). To achieve successful coaching, the boss has to work hard to establish a coaching relationship that is productive and useful in the client's eyes. Because of the power difference, this is not easy. Recognizing how difficult it is, some companies have set up coaching programs where the coach is not a client's boss but is instead a peer, an unrelated manager, an HR professional, or an outside coach. Even under these conditions, however, coaching will only be effective to the extent that the coach can understand and reflect the client's mind-set. The coach's first task in building a relationship is to gain alignment between her mind-set and the client's. Metaphorically, this means moving the two minds closer together.

How do coaches do this? Essentially, through a nonthreatening discussion—asking questions, clarifying assumptions, listening carefully, and sharing their own perspective. Coaches have to know how to open and sustain coaching relationships through the right kinds of questions, suggestions, and observations. They have to be aware of the two minds' differences and aware that they need to gain alignment on some fundamental things—like how the client wants to be coached, what has worked for the client in the past and what hasn't, and so on. Too often, coaches short-circuit this phase of the coaching relationship and fail thereafter to create a space in the dialogue for the two minds' differences and alignment to emerge. In the next chapter, we will examine more fully how coaches can adapt to a client's context in order to gain alignment between their mind-set and their client's.

COACHING STYLE PREFERENCES—A TAXONOMY

In our coaching experience, we have noticed that some clients want to be given advice and direction; others (most others, in fact) prefer the coach to ask questions and guide but not direct them. We came to see this as a fundamental distinction in coaching preferences, and we labeled these diametrically opposed approaches *directive* and *nondirective*. We also observed that most coaches naturally used a more directive approach;

however, most clients prefer a nondirective approach, which may explain why so many clients felt that the coaching they were receiving was not helpful.

We also noticed that some clients want to be coached only when a particular need arises; others want a longer-term relationship with their coaches and to be coached regularly, with development plans guiding what amounts to a program. As we explored these differences in preference, we called them *circumstantial* versus *programmatic*. Finally, we observed that some clients want coaching only about specific, task-related work issues, like how to conduct a meeting, how to use a piece of equipment or software, or how to build stronger relationships with customers. Other coaching clients want their coaches to take a more holistic view of their development and help them think about their careers and perhaps even personal problems. We came to call this distinction *specific* versus *holistic*.

As we explored these distinctions, we realized that they formed different coaching approaches or styles, and this led us to create the coaching styles taxonomy that we explore in chapter 5. The coaching effectiveness survey we developed to test this model showed that it was a valid way of understanding how different coaches approached coaching and how different clients responded to coaching. We learned that the most effective coaching occurs when coaches adapt their approach to their clients' preferences. In chapters 3 through 5, we explore how to assess a client's needs and coaching style preferences and adapt to them.

Dialogue

What drives adaptive coaching is the ongoing dialogue between a coach and a client. The term *dialogue* acquired a specialized meaning in the early 1990s when British physicist and philosopher David Bohm used it to describe a multifaceted process that helps groups of people explore their perceptions and assumptions and deepen communication and understanding. Bohm felt that many of the world's problems occurred because people talk at cross-purposes, don't examine their assumptions, are unaware of how their perceptions influence their thought processes, and try to prevail in conversations by imposing their "truth" on others. Bohm's concept of dialogue pushes against popular understandings of the role of empathy in coaching. While we tend to think about the outcome of empathy as a merger of one person's perspective with another's (the cliché of walking in another person's shoes), dialogue elevates the importance of difference as a key to reaching new understandings:

> *When one person says something, the other person does not in general respond with exactly the same meaning as that seen by the first person. Rather, the meanings are only similar and not identical. Thus, when the second person replies, the first person sees a* difference *between what he meant to say and what the other person understood. On considering this difference, he may then be able to see something new, which is relevant both to his own views and to those of the other person. And so it can go back and forth, with the continual emergence of a new content that is common to both participants. Thus, in a dialogue, each person does not attempt to make common certain ideas or items of information that are already known to him. Rather, it may be said that the two people are making something* in common, *i.e., creating something new together.* (Bohm 1996, p. 2)

Bohm's concept of dialogue puts the coaching relationship at the center of the activity. It suggests that every coaching situation involves the co-construction of a narrative of the client's experience in terms of the issues that are the focus of the coaching. The narrative is constructed to make sense of the client's experience in a more coherent way than the client felt it at the time. The coach doesn't know the ending of the story. In fact, at the beginning of a coaching relationship, the coach doesn't really know the beginning. The coach can't know everything about the client; can't know what the real issues are; and can't know how the client will respond, how hard the client will work, what exigencies will help or hinder the client, or how the story they construct will turn out. However, the coach has the ability to influence the outcomes, which gives the coach a unique role as both a character in the story and a co-creator of its meaning. The coach can't dictate the outcome—but through the dialogue, the coach and client attempt together to influence the outcome through the meanings they attach to the story. Actually, the art of coaching is to exert only enough influence to help the real participants in the story tell their own tales and shape their own destinies. We will explore Bohm's concept of dialogue more fully in chapter 7 to show how managing the ongoing dialogue is a coach's most fundamental skill.

AN OVERVIEW OF THE BOOK

To help readers explore adaptive coaching, we have divided the book into three parts. Part 1, Assessing Clients' Needs, explores how coaches discover what their clients really need and adapt their coaching style and approach to their clients. As you will see, this is no trivial matter. Clients often don't know what they really need, and coaches who jump too quickly to conclusions about what clients need are often wrong. Determining clients' real needs requires patience, multiple sources of information, and skillful exploration. In this part of the book, we also discuss the differences between coaching and therapy, and we introduce a taxonomy of coaching style preferences that can help coaches adapt to the needs and wants of the people they are trying to help.

Chapter 1 discusses the various contexts of coaching and how those contexts are important in establishing a coaching relationship, creating a "contract" between coach and client, and assessing the client's real needs.

Chapter 2 introduces several fundamental adaptive coaching concepts and illustrates how you and your clients can negotiate your expectations of the coaching process and intended outcomes so that you are both comfortable with the process and your roles in it.

Chapter 3 presents a concept we call the *needs compass*. There are four primary sources of information about clients' needs. To uncover someone's *real* needs, you should seek information from all four sources.

Chapter 4 addresses how you discover the client's real issues—the problems or opportunities that often lie below the surface of the "presenting problem." Surfacing the real issues—and therefore handling the real problems—is one of the art forms in effective coaching. A lengthy coaching dialogue in this chapter illustrates this process.

Finally, chapter 5 elaborates on our coaching styles taxonomy and explores how coaches can adapt to different client preferences. We elaborate here on the differences between directive versus nondirective coaching, programmatic versus circumstantial coaching, and specific versus holistic coaching. This chapter includes many of the responses we received from coaching clients when we asked them what their coaches could do to be more effective.

Part 2, Practicing Adaptive Coaching, addresses the art and skill coaches need to initiate coaching, manage the coaching dialogue, and conclude coaching successfully. The aim of these chapters is to help coaches increase their flexibility in using a range of coaching skills.

Chapter 6 discusses how you initiate a coaching relationship, prepare for the first coaching ses sion, conduct the first session, explore the client's needs, initiate a personal development plan, and open subsequent sessions. The beginning of a coaching relationship is critical. As Alexander Clark said, "Let us watch well our beginnings, and results will manage themselves."

Chapter 7 elaborates on the art of managing the coaching dialogue and includes a lengthy illustration of dialogue in action. Few coaching skills are as important as managing the dialogue. As we observe in this chapter, coaching can be powerful—indeed, life changing—if the journey is interesting, the discoveries unexpected, and the insights actionable. Or the journey can be dull, uninspiring, and empty. The art and skill of the coach makes the difference.

Chapter 8 discusses two fundamental coaching skills—listening and questioning. Although this will be familiar territory for many readers, we offer some insights on listening and questioning that may be new to some readers, including using "Columbo" questions, listening with your eyes and your heart, following the bread crumb trail, and going through the open doors. These are critical skills for anyone who coaches others.

Chapter 9 talks about how you should share your observations with clients, including how to give effective feedback; how to solicit feedback on clients from others; how to reframe your client's perceptions, including how to differ with them; and how to reflect your perceptions of clients in ways that can be insightful for them.

Chapter 10, Pushing and Pulling, describes effective means of telling clients what you think by advising or teaching them, by confronting them, and by encouraging them. The chapter also discusses a crucial adaptive coaching technique—the process check. Effective coaching is often a combination of pushing clients by asserting your point of view and pulling clients by encouraging them and continually involving them in the management of the dialogue.

Finally, chapter 11 discusses how you close individual coaching sessions and bring closure to the coaching relationship itself. As there must be good beginnings, there must also be good endings. The most satisfying coaching relationships end with a sense of accomplishment and quiet celebration.

Part 3, Coaching Special Populations, shifts the focus from coaching skills to the needs of specific populations of coaching clients. Almost without exception, the coaching literature assumes a genderless, non-age-specific, racially, culturally, and ethnically neutral coach and client, and thus fails to acknowledge the special needs of diverse coaching populations and the challenges to the coaching relationship once these inevitable realities enter the room. Chapters 12 through 15 discuss how coaches can be adaptive in situations where they are coaching across cultures, coaching women and minorities, and coaching across generations. With the heavy emphasis of the more recent literature on coaching executives, this population is about the only group whose characteristics have been discussed. However, the unique situations and coaching needs of C-level executives have not been adequately addressed in the literature, so in chapter 15 we discuss the special challenges of coaching C-level executives and the important role coaching plays in helping executives transition into C-level positions and preventing derailment once they are in those positions.

As its name implies, our epilogue, Helping Clients Change, discusses how coaches help clients change. As we argue throughout this book, coaching is about change: improving skills, building better relationships, overcoming performance problems, and so on. Much of the change clients seek is behavioral, and it is notoriously difficult for adults to alter their behavior significantly. A lifetime of habits is difficult to alter. So in this chapter, we present a framework for guiding change. This framework is an effective way to gauge what will be required for clients to make significant and lasting changes—and to identify what is getting in the way when they can't or won't change.

For all the talk about change in business, politics, and global events, and for all the evidence we see daily of sweeping change in all these arenas, human change at the micro level of the individual is among the most difficult challenges we face. The aim of coaching is to facilitate constructive, self-initiated change one person at a time—not just to ward off catastrophic change imposed from without, but to help individuals maximize their potential and the contributions they can make to the businesses with which they have chosen to invest their passions and their energies. For change of this sort to occur, coaching must become a vastly more adaptive, responsive enterprise. In short, if the clients we coach are to change in the ways they hope, we as coaches must be masters of change as well, starting with ourselves. This book seeks to help in that most personal of transformations.

PART

1

ASSESSING CLIENTS' NEEDS

The most effective coaches adapt their coaching style and approach to *every* client because *every* client is different. We became acutely aware of this fact in our research on coaching effectiveness. As we noted in the introduction, from 1996 through 2002 we surveyed hundreds of coaches and many thousands of clients (the people receiving the coaching) in large and smaller corporations in a variety of industries and countries. From these surveys, we learned that different clients prefer to be coached in different ways. We also learned that coaches tend to coach the way they *prefer to coach,* rather than the way their clients *prefer to be coached.* The resulting misalignments in coaching preference mean that a large number of clients are frustrated with the coaching they are getting. In fact, nearly half of the clients we surveyed said that their coaching sessions with their current coach have not had much positive impact on their work performance.

In the first part of this book, we discuss the foundations of adaptive coaching, namely, understanding the context in which coaching takes place, understanding clients' expectations about the coaching and negotiating a set of shared expectations, using the four primary sources of information to discover clients' needs, triangulating among these sources to uncover the underlying issues that must be resolved for the client to make progress, and, finally, adapting to clients' coaching style preferences.

The purpose of coaching is to help people change. If there is no change, then the coaching has not had any impact. However, coaching does not occur in a vacuum. To facilitate change, you must understand the context in which that change needs to occur, including peoples' job situations, the organizations they work in, the urgency of their needs, their psychological readiness to change, their history with and expectations of coaching, and their view of and respect for the coach. Clients' openness and willingness to change is shaped by this context. If you fail to understand it, you may use the wrong approach at the wrong time and focus on the wrong issues, which is a formula for failure.

To help clients change, you must not only consider the context in which they work; you must also uncover and address the root causes of their problems. But this raises an important issue: How is coaching different from therapy? In chapter 1, as we discuss the contexts of coaching, we also address this thorny question. In chapter 2, we describe an effective process for understanding clients' expectations about coaching and then negotiating a set of shared expectations. To coach adaptively, you have to be transparent about how the coaching will occur, what you will focus on, how you will help clients, and so on. Surfacing their preferences and changing your approach accordingly is obviously a crucial part of being an adaptive coach. You have to start where your clients are and then continuously adapt to their needs or preferences.

Chapters 3 and 4 address the difficult challenge of discovering your clients' real needs. In our coaching experience, we have found that the *presenting problem,* what clients say they need help with, is rarely the real one. To discover what clients *really* need, you have to explore all four points of what we call the *needs compass:* your own observations of clients, clients' perceptions of themselves, others' observations of clients, and clients' work products and performance metrics. The client's real needs emerge through a process of co-discovery in which all sources of information are explored within the context of the client's life and work. Themes and patterns emerge as coaches triangulate from these different sources, and coaches use them to form and test hypotheses about the real issues.

Part 1 ends with a more detailed discussion of the taxonomy of coaching preferences introduced in chapter 1. In chapter 5, we describe the client comments and research findings that helped us distinguish between directive versus nondirective coaching, programmatic versus circumstantial coaching, and specific versus holistic coaching. This chapter includes suggestions for coaching clients who prefer each of the eight possible coaching styles.

1

The Contexts of Coaching

Take more time to explore the backgrounds of the people you coach and the situational constraints on their behavior.

Help the person being coached consider the culture and what will actually work in the organization rather than [taking] a pure view of what is best in a vacuum but may not fly in practice.

Find out the history of individual coachees (what they have done, what experiences they've had, what they've done well and not so well, what education they've had, and so on).

SUGGESTIONS TO COACHES FROM THE "COACHING EFFECTIVENESS SURVEY," LORE INTERNATIONAL INSTITUTE, INC.

We have found, in our studies of coaching effectiveness, that the comments above are representative of how clients expect coaching to reflect the various personal and organizational contexts that define their work. It is, of course, impossible to coach anyone without knowing enough about the client to know which questions to ask, what avenues to follow, what suggestions make sense, and which options are appropriate and relevant for the client. Coaching without considering the context would be no more accurate or useful than following the astrological advice in the Sunday newspaper. This point seems self-evident, yet in the coaching world a debate is raging about the importance of context and the kind of background and personal information the coach should consider. On the opposite ends of this debate are Marshall Goldsmith, a professional executive coach, and Steven Berglas, a psychiatrist who was formerly at Harvard Medical School and is now at UCLA's John E.

Anderson School of Management. It's useful to view their opposing ideas as bookends in a debate that raises several important questions: What is coaching? How does the context of coaching influence its outcome? What are these contexts? How does coaching differ from therapy? And how important to the coaching process are a client's past, a client's feelings, influences on a client's perceptions and behaviors, and motivations, past and present? The sharp differences between Goldsmith and Berglas allow us to map out a reasonable middle ground for coaches who seek neither exclusion of the client's perspective nor psychotherapeutic specialization.

THE COACH AS DIRECTOR

In a profile of Goldsmith in the *New Yorker*, we learn that Goldsmith "tells his clients that he doesn't care about their past, doesn't care how they feel, doesn't care about their inner psyche—all he cares about is their future behavior. He provides them with a tightly structured program of things to do and a money-back guarantee that, if they do exactly what he tells them, they will get better" (MacFarquhar 2002, p. 120). Goldsmith's metaphor of the outcome of coaching as "getting better" evokes a medical model of treatment in which the doctor diagnoses the illness and prescribes the proper treatment. This approach represents one bookend, emphasizing coaching as prescription and the coach as the director.

Other elements of Goldsmith's approach are described as follows.

> Goldsmith has turned against the notion of feedback in favor of a concept he calls "feedforward." "How many of us have wasted much of our lives impressing our spouse, partner, or significant other with our near-photographic memory of their previous sins, which we document and share to help them improve?" he says. "Dysfunctional! Say, 'I can't change the past—all I can say is I'm sorry for what I did wrong.' Ask for suggestions for the future. Don't promise to do everything they suggest—leadership is not a popularity contest. But follow up on a regular basis, and you know what's going to happen? You will get better." (p. 115)

What is the ultimate aim of coaching? According to this profile, it is not about changing behavior:

> Coaching, [Goldsmith] had recently realized, was not, ultimately, about changing his client's behavior so much as changing percep-

tions *of the client's behavior. He had observed that his clients had to change a hundred percent to get ten percent credit, partly because people could be ungenerous, but mostly because they simply didn't notice. And in leadership, as he liked to say, it doesn't matter what you say—only what they hear.* (p. 120)

Taken the wrong way, this could imply that real change is less important than impression management. Should clients really not worry about their own behavior and its consequences and effects on others but instead only about how they are perceived?

Finally, according to the *New Yorker* profile, Goldsmith's approach to coaching is pragmatic and antipsychological: "Goldsmith . . . has no patience for the psychological approach. 'My attitude is, it's easier to get unf---ed up than it is to understand why you are f---ed up, so why don't you just get un-f---ed up?' he says" (p. 120). This approach suggests that clients don't need insight; they just need direction (the right "tightly structured program of things to do"). And while it is certainly true that clients cannot change the past, it is equally true that they cannot escape it.

As portrayed in the *New Yorker* profile, Goldsmith represents one approach to coaching—the coach who disregards the client's past, his psychological state, and apparently his perspective, as indicated in this quotation from the article: "There was one guy I coached who spent hours on 'Marshall, you don't understand, let me explain why I have these issues, let me explain my mother, my father.' Whine, whine, whine. I tell clients, 'Here's a quarter—call someone who cares.' They don't need empathy. They need someone to look 'em in the eye and say, 'If you want to change, do this'" (p. 120). In this view, change is as easy as receiving the right direction from a coach who can show clients the way. In the real world, argues Steven Berglas, things are more complex.

THE COACH AS PSYCHOTHERAPIST

In a *Harvard Business Review* essay, Berglas (2002), who is an executive coach with a doctorate in psychology, argues that "in an alarming number of situations, executive coaches who lack rigorous psychological training do more harm than good. By dint of their backgrounds and biases, they downplay or simply ignore deep-seated psychological problems they don't understand. When an executive's problems stem from undetected or ignored psychological difficulties, coaching can actually make a bad situation worse" (p. 87). Berglas exemplifies the opposite bookend from Goldsmith. He stresses a regimen of extensive psychological evaluation as a prelude to coaching and an in-depth coaching relationship that is in some ways difficult to distinguish from therapy. Berglas believes that today's popularity of executive coaching reflects a desire for quick fixes. The problem, he argues, is that these quick fixes often don't fix anything and may in fact do damage.

> *To achieve fast results, many popular executive coaches model their interventions after those used by sports coaches, employing techniques that reject out of hand any introspective process that can take time and cause "paralysis by analysis." The idea that an executive coach can help employees improve performance quickly is a great selling point to CEOs, who put the bottom line first. Yet that approach tends to gloss over any unconscious conflict the employee might have. This can have disastrous consequences for the company in the long term and can exacerbate the psychological damage to the person targeted for help.* (pp. 88–89)

In Berglas' view, every executive who is about to participate in coaching should first undergo a psychological evaluation to ensure that he or she is psychologically prepared for it and does not have any conditions that require more competent help than a coach who is not psychologically trained can provide. He cites several cases to support his position. One is a narcissistic manager, who Berglas concludes cannot benefit from coaching (and we concur). He also cites an executive who is driven by a fear of failure and another whose apparent assertiveness problem masked an inability to form intimate relationships with men. Clearly, these are cases where the clients would benefit more from therapy than from coaching. However, in our experience, the more common issues coaches face are difficulty balancing life and work, being somewhat insensitive to others, failing to delegate enough to empower and inspire subordinates, not being appreciative enough of others' contributions, and so on.

The most common issues can be handled through feedback, awareness building, skill building, goal setting, and discussion with a coach who is competent in managing the dialogue. In our opinion, Berglas' solution—having *every* candidate for coaching be psychologically screened—is impractical and expensive. It also sends the signal that coaching is a psychological process and the people receiving coaching may have a psychological problem. In many company and country cultures, this conclusion would automatically kill a coaching program because of the stigma attached to anyone who needs psychological help. This is less true in the United States as a whole (although the attitude exists in some companies), but it is a widespread attitude in southern Europe, some Latin American countries, and Asia.

Nonetheless, Berglas raises three cautionary red flags. First, in their zeal to create change programs for clients, coaches may fail to see warning signs of deeper psychological problems that may exist. Second, coaches may grasp that there are deeper psychological problems but lack the skill or credentials to deal with them and the integrity to withdraw from the assignment. Third, coaches may believe that these issues are irrelevant and focus on changing behavior without regard to any underlying dysfunctions. Berglas calls this the trap of treating the symptoms rather than the disorder, much like a doctor treating an internal injury by applying a Band-Aid. In all three cases, coaches may do more harm than good.

We believe that coaches do not have to be licensed psychologists, but they should be trained and certified in coaching (even if they are employees of a company and only coach internally). They must know the ethical and professional boundaries of coaching and adhere to a code of ethics that prohibits them from delving into matters they are not trained to deal with. They must know the warning signs when deeper psychological issues exist and be able to refer their clients to competent professionals. And they must beware of becoming arrogant, trying to supply all the answers, or dispensing advice in homespun homilies or clever turns of phrase and assume that this passes for wisdom.

The danger implicit in therapists acting as coaches is that they may not be able to separate coaching from therapy—in their own minds as well as the minds of their clients—and we have worked with many organizations where even the hint that coaching is therapy would doom the coaching program. As Berglas warns, however, problems may arise when coaches act as directors and ignore their clients' past, feelings, motivations, and beliefs. Like it or not, we are psychological creatures. Our brains are hardwired with powerful emotional as well as cognitive responses to stimuli, and our behavior is shaped to a significant extent by our personal and cultural history and experiences as well as our hopes, dreams, fears, and goals. Coaches who are either unaware of or have no patience with their clients' psychology risk ignoring a substantial amount of the context of people's lives that affects how responsive they will be to coaching and what they can reasonably—and permanently—change.

There is danger, too, in assuming that coaching is all about giving clients the right program for them to follow. What if you're wrong? What if you have ignored (or simply been unaware of) an important but hidden constraint on their ability to effect this program? What if an unintended consequence of this program is that it exacerbates a psychological condition you did not or could not see? When you presume to know exactly what your clients should do to become better (however *better* is defined), you place an awful burden on yourself. You had better be right! If human beings were simple creatures, this might work. You might be able to diagnose the problem precisely, give clients the right corrective program, and send them on their way. But we humans are not simple creatures, so this approach is fraught with peril. Furthermore, it places the responsibility for change and growth on you, the coach, rather than on the client. When it's over, all clients can say is, "Thank God I had such a wise coach." They may not have learned anything other than how to follow directions. We believe that a more satisfying conclusion for clients is for them to realize that they have found most of the answers themselves and that their coach was a helpful guide.

COACHING VERSUS THERAPY

The contrast between Marshall Goldsmith's approach and Steven Berglas' concerns about coaches who lack rigorous psychological training raises some significant questions: What is the difference between coaching and therapy? Do good therapists make good coaches, and vice versa? These have been topics of considerable interest in the past decades as more psychologists and others have joined the ranks of executive coaches. In an essay focused on the differences between coaching and therapy, Vicki Hart, John Blattner, and Staci Leipsic (2001) observed that in *therapy* "the focus is often on interpersonal health and an identifiable issue, such as acute depression or relational discord, that interferes with the client's level of functioning and current psychodynamic or psychosocial adjustment. The focus is typically retrospective, dealing with unconscious issues and repair of damage from earlier experiences. . . . It may even involve medication, adjunct therapies, and coordination of services" (p. 230). The most rigorous forms of psychological therapy are psychiatric treatment (which often involves medication) and psychoanalysis, followed by psychological counseling. All are performed by highly trained, licensed professionals whose goal is to help patients deal with chronic and traumatic psychological problems and illnesses. Coaching *should* be conducted by highly trained, licensed professionals, too, but the lamentable fact is that anyone can hang out a shingle as a coach (and a lot of unqualified people do).

In contrast, a recent literature review of executive coaching defines the practice this way:

> *Executive coaching appears in the workplace with the intention of improving the executive's interpersonal skills and ultimately his or her workplace performance. It is more issue focused than therapy is and occurs in a broader array of contexts— including face-to-face sessions, meetings with other people, observation sessions, over the telephone, and by e-mail—and in a variety of locations away from work.* (Kampa-Kokesch and Anderson 2001, p. 210)

The symbolic trappings of therapy as opposed to coaching convey some of the critical distinctions. In therapy, clients, still often called patients, typically visit the therapist's office, where credentials are prominently displayed and other elements of the setting convey the authoritative role of the therapist in providing treatment. A therapeutic relationship begins with the requisite medical insurance paperwork being completed. The relationship is a therapeutic one, heavily modeled on the doctor/patient relationship of medical practice. In coaching, the coach typically comes to the client's office, where the client's home turf conveys quite a different locus of power. The relationship is a business relationship. Subsequent sessions may be conducted by telephone, by e-mail, or in some informal location. There is no insurance benefit; fees are negotiated with the company. Sometimes coaches are paid by the client, not unlike students making tuition payments for continuing education.

Coaching is intended to improve skills and ultimately workplace performance. As Kampa-Kokesch and Anderson noted, it is more issue focused than therapy, and it includes more types of interventions. Furthermore, coaching is typically more finite. A coaching program should last a specified amount of time and should be focused on specific work-related goals (such as improving an executive's ability to work with a board). A coaching contract, or action plan, is typically formulated quite early in the relationship, often by the end of the first or second meeting. This plan serves as the measure against which to assess progress. Therapy is usually not bounded by time, and its goals are less defined. Both coaching and therapy may touch on all aspects of a person's life. In coaching, however, life issues may be relevant but are usually not central; in therapy, life issues are central but business issues may be relevant. Coaching is usually more pragmatic and practical in its application. In coaching, the focal point is the person's performance; in therapy, the focal point is the person.

These are some of the differences. There are also similarities. Both involve trust-based relationships and are intended to help clients build their skills and capabilities. Both rely on feedback, assessment, and observation of clients. Both use dialogue as a primary tool. As part of dialogue, the coach or therapist must listen well, know how to ask insightful questions, know when and how to offer suggestions or advice, and know how to synthesize key points in the dialogue and identify or create memorable insights. Finally, though Marshall Goldsmith might disagree with us, both depend on insights from various parts of clients' lives (including the past) to help them better understand themselves, their patterns of behavior, their options, and their roadblocks. In therapy, questions about the past might include "When was the first time you remember feeling this way? How did you get along with your older sister? How would you describe your parents' relationship?" In coaching, questions about the past are typically different: "How have you handled this kind of situation before? What have been your toughest management challenges? Who were your mentors early in your career, and what did you learn from them?" In both coaching and therapy, these kinds of questions are intended to develop a context, to understand the environment and circumstances in which the person works and lives, decides what is important and what's not, and makes decisions that affect not only his or her life but the lives and work of others with whom the person associates.

Coaching is about change, and it's impossible, as Lester Tobias (1996) observes, to foster change unless you get at the root causes of problems and consider the context in which the person works: "To achieve lasting and fundamental change, people need to alter their perspectives, to see things in a new light, or to overcome internal resistances that may be unrecognized and habitual. Therefore, the [coach] needs to help the person get to root causes, whether the apparent problem is organizational or one of personal style" (p. 88). If coaching and therapy occupy opposite ends of a continuum, it's in the middle of that continuum that distinctions become blurry. Ultimately, maintaining distinctions between them is *the* fundamental ethical obligation for the coaching practitioner. The coach must be unhesitant about where to draw the line between coaching and therapy and must exercise appropriate tact and persuasiveness to direct a client to therapy, particularly in situations where the surfacing of issues in coaching pushes the client into dangerous psychological territory. A clearer distinction between coaching and therapy lies in the very different contexts that bring one person into therapy and another into coaching.

THE CONTEXTS OF COACHING

Clients' openness and willingness to explore their attitudes, perspectives, behaviors, decisions, alternatives, and operational effectiveness are shaped by the context in which coaching occurs. The most important element of the coaching context is the client's perspective, which includes the client's situation, the organizational context, the urgency of the need, the client's psychological readiness, the client's view of and respect for the coach, and the client's expectations.

The Client's Situation

Our research on coaching effectiveness told us repeatedly that coaches don't pay enough attention to the most important contextual element of coaching—the client's situation. It's not that coaches don't understand objectively what makes up the client's situation; it's that they don't fully appreciate and don't fully probe the subjective meanings the client attaches to that situation or the nuances of the organizational environment in which the client works, including the political, social, and cultural environment of the executive's organization. From an organizational standpoint, some cultures not only support personal and professional development (including coaching), they practically demand it. Other cultures pay lip service to development, even if they invest in it. Some treat coaching, and other forms of professional development, as just that—development, particularly at key transition points in an executive's career. Some can conceive of coaching only as a form of remediation, a last-ditch effort to save someone the company has invested too much in to lose. Still others do not invest the resources required to develop executives and almost openly disdain coaching. Clearly, the more supportive the organization is, the more likely it is that clients will be open to and accepting of coaching help.

From an individual standpoint, clients bring all sorts of predispositions and presuppositions to coaching, even in the most supportive business environments. Most coaches collect basic information about the client's background, such as level of education, years with the company, employment history, interests, family, and so forth. These form the safe territory for introductory conversation. On deeper levels, though, the client's situation has to do with understanding the person the client becomes at work and how the work environment tends to construct that person. It includes understanding how factors such as gender, age, race, social class, ethnicity, and nationality define the client and the client's experiences at work. These factors in the client's context are discussed at length in chapters 13–15 and in the epilogue.

For instance, clients who are transitioning into executive positions of increasing responsibility have to manage the persona they must take on—either because the client assumes such a persona is called for or because the organization has expectations about who and what this new executive must be. Relationships with former peers who are now subordinates must be renegotiated. Former friendships can become strained as the new executive holds power that the old colleague did not. As much as there is a sense of achievement in these kinds of career shifts, there is just as often a sense of loss. Too frequently, new executives discover these issues only in hindsight and only after costly mistakes have been made. Coaching executives through such a transition phase means a heavy emphasis for both parties on understanding the context: helping clients distinguish pressures that are self-imposed from those that are imposed from without in order to evaluate those pressures and find the self who is both personally authentic and publicly effective.

THE ORGANIZATIONAL CONTEXT

Since one of the key factors that distinguishes coaching from therapy is that coaching is a business relationship, coaches must understand the business or organizational context in which their clients work. This involves knowing about the business itself: its history, current issues and problems, key people and their expectations, and the nature of their relationship with the client. In "Business-Linked Executive Development: Coaching Senior Executives," Thomas Saporito (1996) argues that coaches need to investigate three areas before the coaching relationship begins: 1) the "organizational imperatives" that shape the expectations for the executive, 2) the "success factors" that define what the client must do to fulfill these expectations, and 3) the "personal qualities and behaviors" that will be required to achieve these success factors (pp. 96–103). Some of this information can be obtained by reviewing the organization's Web site, annual reports, and other documents; some will come from interviews with human resource managers and those more directly involved in working with the client.

Understanding the client in the context of the organization makes it possible to frame the coaching engagement more broadly than simply as a one-on-one relationship between coach and client. Lester Tobias (1996) observes that

> when coaching is done in isolation, the absence of organizational context will inevitably limit the coach's perspectives on the presenting problem. Furthermore, it may also limit the coach's options regarding interventions. . . . It is essential for the coach to keep in mind that relevant others may not only be potentially part of the solution, but that they are usually directly or indirectly part of the problem. However maladaptive an individual's behavior may be, it never occurs in a vacuum, even though the more outrageous the behavior is, the more people will attribute it to the individual's personality. (pp. 87–95)

Coaching may very well include other members of the organization so that issues such as unnecessary bureaucratic obstacles, unrealistic expectations, scapegoating, and other tensions that occur within relationships can be addressed. But such problems cannot be named, let alone addressed, unless the coach understands the larger organizational context in which the client works.

The Urgency of the Need

One of the most important psychological contexts is the client's sense of urgency and the threat of consequences or the benefits of success. That sense of urgency may arise from intrinsic needs or dissatisfactions or from extrinsic fears (of consequences) or hopes (for success). Psychological research suggests that intrinsic motives are more powerful and longer lasting, but extrinsic drivers can also be powerful. In any case, it's important for executive coaches to understand what motivates the client and whether the client feels that the need for coaching is urgent.

The Client's Psychological Readiness

We said earlier that the successful outcome of coaching depends in part on the client's openness and willingness to explore. While environmental factors certainly affect a person's openness, the most important factors are psychological. How mature is the client? In this case, maturity refers to the person's self-acceptance, willingness to admit mistakes, and openness to feedback. Each of us builds a self-concept, which Freud referred to as the ego, through which we define who we are. In less-mature people, that ego can be fragile and tends to be defended heavily. That's why some people won't admit that they are wrong or have made a mistake—to them, admitting error is an assault on their ego construct. Maturity tends to soften the edges as people develop a more realistic view of themselves and come to accept their foibles and weaknesses as part of their total being. With maturity come grace and forgiveness—toward oneself as well as others.

Central to this concept of maturity is the willingness to be vulnerable and imperfect, to acknowledge that one can improve, which leads to an awareness and acceptance of the need to change. Many executives never reach this point. They fear appearing imperfect, so they blame failures on others or on circumstances beyond their control and never admit to themselves or others that they need help or could do better and would benefit from coaching. These executives remind us of the observation said to have been made by Benjamin Franklin: "He that won't be counseled can't be helped."

Another aspect of maturity is resilience—the ability to rebound, pick oneself up, and march on despite adversity, roadblocks, criticism, and failure. In a recent study of resilience, Diane Coutu (2002) defines it as "the skill and the capacity to be robust under conditions of enormous stress and change" (p. 52). Resilient people share three characteristics: "an ability to face reality as it is, not as one thinks or wishes it should be; deeply rooted beliefs, sometimes reinforced by well-articulated values, that sustain a conviction that life has meaning; and the capacity to improvise with whatever is at hand, in particular to call on resources within oneself in unique and creative ways" (p. 48). Resilience is important because coaching may require clients to hold the mirror and see aspects of themselves they don't like. They need the ability to rebound from those experiences in order to make progress and stick with the program of change and improvement they have embarked upon. This may all sound familiar. It's what author Reuven Bar-On, Daniel Goleman, and others have referred to as emotional intelligence. An emotionally intelligent adult is emotionally self-aware; is able to manage his or her own emotions, read others' emotions, and use emotion productively; and is good at handling relationships. These psychological resources make emotionally intelligent executives better candidates than others for coaching because they are more open, more responsive to feedback, more motivated to change, more willing to admit their weaknesses, and more willing to accept responsibility for themselves and their behavior. Clearly, executives who lack these psychological resources are not good coaching candidates. No matter how much quality coaching they receive, they are unlikely to change.

The Client's View of and Respect for the Coach

An element of context that coaches often overlook—but clients never do—is the client's view of and respect for the coach. Early in a coaching relationship, clients may grant their coaches the benefit of the doubt, but they remain wary and will decide within the first few meetings whether this coach deserves their trust and whether they find the coach credible and helpful. For a productive coaching relationship to be established, as further explained in the text box "Building Coaching Relationships" on pages 16–17, the coach must earn trust and demonstrate credibility.

The Client's Expectations

Finally, an important element of context is the client's expectations. Clients will define for themselves what is useful in the coaching relationship and what they find helpful about the dialogue. They enter into a coaching relationship with a set of expectations, which may or may not be realistic. Their expectations are often based on their previous coaching experiences at work (both as coaches and clients) but may also be informed by their experiences as students, athletes, and children. They know how they learn best, how feedback should be given to them, what they're willing to try, and what is most helpful to them. The best way for coaches to discover their clients' expectations, of course, is to ask them.

It should be obvious how these elements of the context of coaching affect the dialogue between the coach and the client. They govern, among other things, the client's willingness to disclose his feelings, to trust the coach with confidential information, to explore uncomfortable areas, to open new avenues of possibility, and to experiment with new

BUILDING COACHING RELATIONSHIPS

Good coaching relationships are made, not born. You build them by establishing trust with people who want you to coach them. That trust usually consists of confidence, caring, and acceptance:

- Clients must have confidence in your coaching—that you know what you're talking about, that you are credible and experienced, that your guidance will be accurate and helpful, and that your coaching will help them.

- Clients must believe that you care about them—that you have their best interests at heart, that you care about them as human beings, and that your desire to help them is sincere.

- Clients must have confidence that you will not judge them—that you accept them for who they are.

You build confidence by being knowledgeable and resourceful, by walking your talk, and by being genuine. Ironically, admitting that you don't know something and admitting when you're wrong build credibility because they show that you're human and fallible. Pretending that you know everything, on the other hand, destroys credibility and confidence.

You show caring by being available, by taking an active interest in how clients are doing, by offering to help rather than waiting to be asked. Of course, you must maintain confidences, refrain from judgment or evaluation except in the spirit of being helpful, and follow through with the people you're coaching over a long period. Otherwise, your "caring" will seem transactional and superficial.

You accept clients and suspend judgment by monitoring carefully the tendency to judge, which may operate in other domains of your life, in order to convey what Carl Rogers called "unconditional positive regard." No matter how poor people's performance, you as their coach nonetheless regard them positively as human beings. Suspending judgment is difficult because many people, especially in management positions, are trained to be judgmental. But if you can't set judgment aside during coaching, you won't be an effective coach. Interestingly, our research on coaching effectiveness indicates that many coaches do not suspend judgment or demonstrate the degree of caring that inspires trust.

- Forty percent of clients say that their coaches are occasionally judgmental.

- Thirty-one percent of clients say that their coach is impatient and hurries to finish the coaching.

- Twenty-five percent say that their coach does not always recognize either excellent performance or superior effort, even if it fails.

  Effective coaching requires the right attitude about coaching and the right temperament. If people trust you, if they feel that you have their best interests at heart, if they find you credible, and if you take the time to be helpful to them, then you are more likely to develop an effective coaching relationship.

perspectives, ways of thinking, and behaviors. We've been focusing on the elements of the context that relate to clients and their environment and perspective, but there are also important contextual elements from the coach's perspective.

The Coach's Relationship with the Client

If the coach has an existing relationship with the client, then the dialogue will be informed by the nature of that relationship and the history of interactions between the two people. As a dialogue unfolds, it creates its own interactional history—a record, in each person's memory, of the ideas, insights, discussions, disagreements, and developments that have occurred since the dialogue began. Even if the coach and client have not previously had a coaching relationship, if they have known and worked with each other in any capacity, the dialogue will be affected by what each person knows about the other and what has transpired between them. That history can help or hinder the coaching process, so it's worth thinking about what impact the existing relationship might have.

The Coach's Experience As a Coach

The coach also brings to the dialogue her experience as a coach and the history of all previous coaching experiences—the memories of former and other current clients, reflections on what worked and what didn't, and a perspective on how to approach coaching problems and challenges. A coach's experience creates a kind of *expert system* for her, which she draws upon when she coaches any client. The richer and deeper her experience, the more likely she is to have seen similar issues before, and she will remember how she helped previous clients with those issues. New coaches have to rely more on their instincts, education, and training; more experienced coaches rely on their internal expert system. This expert system is a useful shortcut, but it can also be a straitjacket if it forces you to see all similar problems the same way or assume that a new client's problems are identical to what you've seen dozens of times before. Our brain forms new neural pathways when we encounter new problems and develop new solutions. When we see similar problems, we assume we should try similar solutions. If they work, these neural pathways are reinforced and strengthened. This phenomenon has been called *hardening of the categories,* and it's why older, more experienced professionals are typically less creative than their younger, less experienced counterparts.

So a coach's experience creates a great deal of the context in which she coaches. If she's careful, she uses her experience to make informed assumptions about each new client and new set of issues or challenges, but she also tests those assumptions and remains open to forming new opinions, exploring new avenues, and finding new solutions to problems that, within each client's unique context, are generally new to the client.

The Coach's Mandate As a Coach

If the coach has been hired or asked to provide coaching by someone other than the client, then the coach will have an assignment—along with some preconceptions about the nature of the problem and expectations regarding the desired outcomes of the coaching. For instance, the context could be that the client is part of a high-potential program in the company, and the coaching is being provided to help the client assess his skills and build them in areas that will help prepare him for his next assignment. Or the context could be that the client manages a division of the company and is in danger of derailing because she drives people relentlessly and is insensitive to their needs. She may not be aware that she's at risk of derailment, but it would not be unusual for the HR director who arranged for coaching to tell her coach of the risk—but not want the client to be aware of it.

In our own coaching experiences, few circumstances make us more uncomfortable than having a mandate from a company that the client is not fully aware of. However, for various reasons, companies sometimes find it necessary to arrange for coaching without being totally candid with the client about the reasons for it or the consequences to the client if the coaching doesn't help. We have been in situations where we wished there had been more candor and where, frankly, the company's unwillingness to be candid was a symptom of an underlying systemic issue. But resolving a company's systemic issues may not be feasible. If you can be helpful to clients, even though the company is not being candid with them, then you are still performing a useful service, however uncomfortable you might be with the context in which the coaching is taking place.

The Coach's Expertise

If the coach is an expert in the subject being discussed with the client, it is impossible not to bring that expert perspective into the dialogue, and in fact, coaches are appointed on the basis of their experience and expertise in particular business areas or specific levels of management as well as requisite coaching skills. This is not to say that the coach should start dispensing advice—merely that having the expert perspective will affect how the coach listens, interprets information, frames questions, and provides help.

The Coach's Objectivity

Finally, an important element of the context is the coach's degree of objectivity. Coaches who can avoid projecting themselves into the situation are generally better coaches because they can remain objective enough to recognize what is happening in the dialogue and steer it in a productive direction. Coaches who lose that objectivity often become too immersed in the content of the dialogue to recognize when it's becoming unproductive or is heading in the wrong direction.

Good coaches remain acutely aware of the context all the time. They take care to understand the departure point and establish the right context at the beginning of the coaching process. They try to understand how the context affects the client's openness and willingness to explore. They also use the context to help shape the dialogue as coaching continues. Even bad coaches are aware of the context, but they are often incapable of managing it or using it to their and the client's advantage. Instead, the context can become an impediment ("The culture doesn't support the kinds of changes he needs to make") or an excuse for lackluster results ("She wasn't willing to listen to feedback").

Beyond knowing and using the context effectively, coaches must be skilled at guiding and shaping the dialogue. As we said earlier, the two primary factors that determine whether executive coaching will be effective are the client's openness and willingness to explore and the coach's skillfulness in guiding the dialogue. The next chapter is the first of several that explore the special nature of the coaching dialogue.

2

Negotiating Expectations

Have a kickoff meeting with each person to be coached to get a common understanding of needs and expectations.

Try to determine the aspirations of the people you are coaching so that you can tailor your coaching to fit in with their goals.

Review each team member's goals for development and develop a game plan to get there. We've had discussions, but neither party committed to a real plan.

SUGGESTIONS TO COACHES FROM THE "COACHING EFFECTIVENESS SURVEY,"
LORE INTERNATIONAL INSTITUTE, INC.

In the introduction, we described the two-minds model, which illustrates the differences in perspectives between coaches and clients. When these perspectives are not aligned, coaches risk providing the wrong kind of coaching on the wrong issues at the wrong time and never building the kind of trust and confidence essential in a coaching relationship. When, as a coach, you negotiate expectations for the engagement, you are trying to understand the client's perspective and share your own so that you develop a mutual understanding of the coaching process, the client's needs, and the desired outcomes. As our opening quotations suggest, coaches need to spend more time exploring what clients expect and reaching agreement on processes and outcomes. In chapter 1, we discussed the contexts of coaching. In effect, setting expectations means *applying* multiple contexts and establishing the conditions in which the coaching will occur.

Throughout the book, we focus on the mind-set of the coach, but this is a good place to raise some cautionary flags about the mind-set of the client. While many clients will welcome the coach's guidance and appreciate the vote of confidence that the organization's investment in the coaching signifies, coaching is not something that appears risk free to many clients. For some, coaching may suggest failure to succeed on one's own or may even conjure up memories of visits to the principal's office. For others, developing intimacy with a coach as a thought partner or trusted advisor will take time and will come only as the client gains confidence that the coach can reliably contribute to both process and context. The client's mind-set is not a static thing; it will change as the relationship matures. Coaches who adapt successfully to new clients take time at the outset to explore the client's frame of mind about coaching. They monitor and adjust to changes throughout the engagement.

The two-minds model that we discussed in the introduction nicely illustrates the differences in perspective between coach and client, but in the real world even this seemingly complicated model is too simplistic because it ignores the organizational context in which coaching generally occurs. In large, sophisticated companies with well-established systems and procedures for developing people, the organization itself may have expectations about coaching that influence and even specify elements of the coaching process, such as when and how coaching will be conducted, how coaching fits in with the overall human development process, and how coaching effectiveness will be measured. Expectation setting, therefore, can involve not only the coach and the client but others in the organization who have a stake in the coaching process and its outcomes. Sometimes the goals and outcomes of coaching are syndicated with the client's manager, the relevant HR manager, and members of a leadership development task force or development group that oversees leadership development in the company. When CEOs are being coached, the stakeholder group may include the board of directors.

Negotiating expectations means bringing the coach's expectations and the client's into alignment within the organizational context in which the coaching is occurring. This is fundamental to our concept of adaptive coaching—starting where the client is and continuously adapting to his or her needs or preferences. While this may sound complicated, in practice it's a simple matter of knowing how to ask the right questions and taking the time to do so. Expectation setting, which should occur at the very beginning of the coaching process, is an activity that we often refer to as "contracting." The word *contracting* makes this part of the process seem very formal, but it doesn't need to be. Contracting can be as simple as saying, "What kind of help would you like?" The purpose is to reach a mutual understanding of what will most benefit the client and to ensure that you understand the client's needs and expectations from the coaching process. If you clarify the client's expectations about the kind of coaching you are going to provide, then you can be reasonably certain that you are being most helpful to him or her. If you aren't explicit about the agreement, then you run the very real risk of doing the wrong kind of coaching, which will frustrate both of you.

THE ELEMENTS OF THE CONTRACT

Some coaches prefer formal, written contracts or agreements with their clients. We tend to be more informal in our approach to coaching, but it isn't a bad idea to write down what you've agreed to and then send your statement to the client—or ask the client to write down the agreements and send them to you. Coaching is a jointly constructed journey, and mutually agreeing to the expectations up front is a reasonable and collaborative way to ensure that everyone involved clearly understands how the process will work. Furthermore, it's best to be explicit about these matters to reduce the risk that differing, unspoken assumptions on anyone's part will later derail the process or destroy trust.

Clearly, coaching contracts can include anything coaches and clients wish to include. The next several pages identify a range of issues and questions that should be addressed and resolved early in the relationship, whether they are explicitly named in the coaching contract or discussed in an initial meeting. What is the coaching about? Is its purpose performance improvement, leadership development, skill building, career development, life coaching, problem resolution? In many cases, clients will be asking for coaching and should have a clear sense of why they want help. Sometimes, however, their organization decides they need coaching, either to resolve problems or develop their skills. In this case, determining the purpose of the coaching may be tricky, especially if the clients don't know why the coach is there, haven't asked for help, or are unclear or resentful about the fact that "help has arrived."

Goals

What are the goals of the coaching? We are referring here to the intended outcomes of the coaching. If the coaching succeeds, what will that mean? What will be different or better? The more specific you can be about the outcomes, the more focused the coaching is likely to be. Sometimes the goals may not really be clear until the coaching process has begun and the client has discovered enough to know what the desired outcomes should be. In some of our coaching engagements, the goals have been negotiated, in effect, among the coach, the client, the client's manager, and the relevant HR manager. When organizations hire external coaches, they frequently insist on accountability for the process, and they often have ideas about how the clients should change. The coaching is therefore goal driven not only from the client's perspective but also from the organization's perspective, and the coaching will not be deemed successful unless the organization feels that its goals have been accomplished. The coach's job becomes one of balancing organizational expectations with the client's needs and preferences.

Type of Coaching

What kind of coaching does the client want (directive or nondirective)? What would be most helpful to the client: advice, counsel, teaching, feedback, a sounding board? It's often good to ask simple questions about coaching preference, such as "How can I be most helpful to you?" or "What kind of coaching has worked best for you in the past?" Clients typically have very individual preferences—no matter what the coach wants to do or what the organization prefers. Only the client can really determine what works for him or her, and frequently this must be discovered through trial and error (and ongoing process checking) as the coaching begins—hence another meaning for our term *adaptive coaching*: adapting occurs in situ as both coach and client discover what works best.

Client Reservations

What reservations, if any, does the client have about engaging in coaching? Is the client a reluctant participant, perhaps simply carrying out an order from above or maintaining skepticism about what the coaching can achieve? If the client is receiving coaching to remedy performance problems, does she agree that these are the problems that need to be solved? Does the client feel she is being treated fairly by the organization or singled out? Does the client suspect that there may be a hidden agenda within the organization, such as the coaching being a screen for a planned termination? Has the client had prior experiences with coaching that were unsatisfactory? If the client has previously participated in psychotherapy, does he understand the difference between that and coaching?

Focus

What will be the focus of the coaching (tasks or skills the client needs to learn or broader career, program, or even life matters)? Again, this may not be clear at the beginning, and the client's expectations may change as you go. Often coaching begins with a specific task focus and moves into other areas as the dialogue advances and coach and client discover more about the real issues and needs.

Meeting Frequency

When and how often should meetings occur? Does the client want programmatic or circumstantial coaching? How frequently? How regularly? There may be some real-world constraints on what is possible because of work schedules, conflicts, sudden crises, and so on. Our experience is that this changes, too, as the process evolves. Generally, clients need more time at the beginning of the coaching process and less time later.

Meeting Location

Where should the meetings occur? This seems like an innocuous question, but the answer has potentially large ramifications. Do the topics being discussed require privacy? Should others in the organization know that the client has a coach? Does the intended location offer the right resources? The right atmosphere? Does coaching via telephone or e-mail convey the appropriate level of gravity? Does it allow the coach to observe the client—to know the client sufficiently—and to interact at the necessary level of intensity?

Other People

Who else might be involved? Who else should the coach talk to or get information from? Besides the client, are there any key stakeholders in this process? People who should know about or participate in the coaching? People whose feedback is crucial? Are these sources of information acceptable to the client? Are the sources reliable?

Commitments

What commitments are both coach and client expected to keep? For example, are both committed to being on time? To completing the process? To doing the homework (if there is any)? To being forthright and candid with one another? To saying when something isn't working? To maintaining confidences? To being accountable to any third parties that are involved?

Confidentiality

To what extent is the coaching confidential? Should anyone other than the coach and client be privy to the coaching process and outcomes? These questions are not as simple as they may appear. In our coaching, we generally argue that the goals and outcomes of the coaching process, along with the personal development plan, should not be confidential because of the need for accountability and reporting back to the sponsoring organization. However, any personal information or discussions that arise must be kept in confidence. Furthermore, if we promise confidentiality to anyone, we keep it. Generally, we do confidential interviews with people the client works with, for instance. We promise confidentiality so that people will be candid with us, but this means we can't share what we learn from them except in an aggregate sense (summarizing what we learned from all of the confidential interviews).

Measurement and Accountability

How will you measure success? To what degree are the coach and client accountable for the outcomes? What are the organization's expectations? What does the client expect? To whom, ultimately, are coach and client accountable? The measurement part of the process is often neglected because it is difficult to measure progress—although it is easier in a coaching situation than it is in therapy. If 360-degree surveys, employee satisfaction or climate surveys, or other instruments are used, then pre- and post-testing can be an effective means of measuring progress. It is important to measure behavioral change (as observed by people the client works with) and achievement of the coaching objectives, as well. It is critical to determine the measures up front. Why? This helps establish accountability for results; it is a motivator (clients want to succeed); it sets a clear path forward, with clear change expectations; it provides a focus for both the client and the coach; and it helps the coach gauge progress.

Information Gathering

How will the coach gather information? With 360-degree assessments? Through psychological assessments? Using performance data? From interviews with people the client works with? By observing the client during performances? Through reviews of the client's work?

Information Sharing

What will the client agree to share with the coach (e.g., previous performance reviews, employee or customer satisfaction survey reports, 360-degree survey results)? Coaches typically have a preferred set of diagnostic tools like the ones mentioned that help them understand the client, diagnose the client's needs, assess the client's performance, and perform reality checks on the client's perceptions. Clearly, the client needs to understand what the coach would prefer to use, but this must also be negotiated. The client may be averse to certain types of assessment or may already have completed some of these assessments. Or the organization may prefer to use its own assessments and provide data rather than have the data gathered again. Part of the adaptive process is knowing what the client and the organization expect and then agreeing on tools that will give coaches what they need and will be acceptable to the client and the organization.

Client Preparation

What should the client do to prepare for coaching? What should the client bring to the sessions? The coach may have some ideas about what clients can or should do, such as reviewing their previous performance reviews, 360-degree surveys, or other assessment reports; thinking about what they want to get out of the coaching and writing their goals; preparing a personal vision statement; and so on. However, coaches should also ask their clients, "What would help you prepare for this coaching?" Some clients like to write out a list of questions for the coach.

Coach Preparation

What will the coach do to prepare, and what will the coach bring to the sessions? The coach should share what she normally does and how she prepares and should make sure that the client is comfortable with her methods.

Communication Outside the Coaching Relationship

Will the coach's role extend beyond the one-on-one relationship with the client? Sometimes coaches are able to uncover organizational problems that undermine the client's effectiveness. A coaching engagement may carry the expectation that the coach will convey these perceptions to the leadership group. Or, a coach may feel compelled to communicate a view of problems that are beyond the capacity of the client to address. These issues are not obvious at the outset, but if they crop up, the coach's actions should be carefully negotiated with the client so as not to jeopardize confidentiality, not to place the client at risk, and not to undermine trust.

Work Between Sessions

Will the client be expected to do anything between meetings with the coach? Typically, yes. Often the coach gives the client some "homework," such as keeping a log, writing a summary, developing a presentation, working with others in the organization to identify problem behaviors, trying out new behaviors, and so on. Good coaches have a repertoire of exercises and self-development tools that clients can use in the areas they need to work on. The expectation of doing homework between meetings should be established early. We have found that very few clients resist doing these kinds of exercises unless they seem juvenile, irrelevant, or pointless. The right self-discovery or skill-building exercises, some of which we will describe later in the book, are engaging to most people because they help them learn more about themselves.

Process Checks

How and when should you do process checks along the way? We will talk further about process checks, but we want to mention here that they are "time-outs" from the coaching *content* in order to reflect on the coaching *process.* You don't have to schedule process checks formally, but it's important to remind clients that they should be thinking about whether the process is working for them or not, and they have an obligation to tell the coach if the coach is doing something that is not working.

Ending the Coaching Relationship

When will the coaching relationship end? It's a good idea to consider how long the coaching relationship might last. You can always cut it short or extend it, depending on how the process is going, but it's good early on to think about how to wrap up the coaching and move on. For one thing, this gives clients an expectation of closure (this is not an open-ended process; I have goals to meet by a finite time in the future).

You may not be able to answer all the questions we've just raised in an opening discussion with clients, but they are all relevant and should be addressed at some point as early as possible in the coaching process. Clearly, it's okay to revisit decisions you have made as both of you learn more about each other and as the client's expectations evolve and his needs become clearer.

An Example of Negotiating Expectations

The coaching dialogue that follows allows you to see how the process of negotiating expectations works in practice. The dialogue includes some poor responses from the coach and explains in brackets why these responses are ineffective, followed by a better response. Also included are some annotations about the coaching dialogue that illustrate good coaching practices. In this example, the coach and the client work for the same company but do not work together. The coach is a midlevel manager in the engineering design group, and the client is a young engineer who works in the field with customers. The client has recently become a team leader and aspires to manage large projects but lacks management experience. The client is part of the company's high-potential program and has been encouraged to seek coaching as part of a broader development program.

COACH I understand you wanted some coaching on managing projects.

CLIENT No, well, I do, yeah, but I'm not a project manager yet. I've just been made a team leader in our implementations group, and I've never managed people or projects before. Or teams. I mean, a lot of it seems intuitively obvious, but in the spirit of "I don't know what I don't know," I wanted to get some help. It's important that I do this right, and I already see some problems I'm not sure how to handle.

Some wrong coach responses:

COACH   Well, here are my rules of thumb on management. First, . . .
         [Here, the coach is jumping in to solve the problem far too
         early. Besides, just listing best practices is one of the least
         effective ways to help people grow.]

COACH   What would you like to know about managing teams and
         projects? [A good question, but it comes too early in the
         process. There are still many basic expectations to set before
         delving into content.]

COACH   What problems are you seeing? [Same issue as above. It's too
         early to go this deep on the problems. Neither the coach nor
         the client knows enough yet to get into content discussions.
         The two of them need to figure out how they are going to
         work together first.]

A *right coach response:*

COACH   Okay. Well, before we talk about your new role and the prob-
         lems you're seeing, let's figure out how I can be most helpful
         to you. Have you had coaching before? [It's usually helpful to
         know if the client has had coaching and what his or her expe-
         riences were. What worked well? What didn't?]

CLIENT   Not formally. My manager's always been available to answer
         questions, and she's clear about what she expects and how
         she thinks you're doing, but I'm not sure whether that's
         coaching or just a normal part of management.

COACH   How about in previous jobs?

CLIENT   Yeah, actually, the first supervisor I had in the company was a
         good coach. He spent a lot of time showing me how things
         were done, and we talked a lot about what I wanted to do in
         my career, what kinds of challenges I should look for, that
         sort of thing.

COACH   And that was useful?

CLIENT   Yes.

COACH   How so?

CLIENT   Well, several ways. I appreciated learning what I needed to do to succeed. Having somebody who's been there lay it out for me was very helpful. I didn't always do things the way he suggested, but I appreciated his perspective. I also liked the fact that he was willing to help me out careerwise. We didn't just talk about how to get the immediate job done. We spent a lot of time talking about my options in the company, where I needed to work, who else I needed to work for, what other things I needed to do, you know.

COACH   So you like coaching that focuses on a broader range of issues, not just how to solve a particular technical problem.

CLIENT   Yeah.

COACH   And you'd like the benefit of a coach's experience in areas where you're developing.

CLIENT   That's right.

A misstep on the coach's part:

COACH   Okay, then let's get started. [Don't close this discussion too quickly. It's better to keep probing and ensure that you've touched all the bases.]

The right next step:

COACH   What else would be helpful to you?

CLIENT   I'd like you to give me feedback whenever you can.

COACH   I'd be happy to do that, but we don't work together, so the opportunities for me to observe you are likely to be limited. Would you be willing to share your performance reviews with me?

CLIENT   Sure.

COACH   And any other feedback you get?

CLIENT   Yeah, but, look, I also want to know what you think. One of the reasons I asked for you as a coach is because you're so good at what I need.

COACH   Fair enough, and I want to help you, but we need to be realistic about how much time I can devote to the coaching. Observing you leading your team is something I can do now and then but not regularly.

CLIENT   All right. That's fair.

COACH   Maybe I could also talk to your manager from time to time and get her perspective. Would that be all right?

CLIENT   Yeah. We'd just have to let her know what we're doing.

COACH   (nodding) I'll be happy to talk to her about it. Who else could give me some insights on how you're doing?

CLIENT   The people I'm managing, for sure. And the other team leaders.

COACH   What about customers?

CLIENT   Yeah, the ones I work with most of the time. They would have a good perspective, maybe not so much on team leadership but certainly on how we're serving them.

COACH   I'd like to be able to talk to all those people now and then and get their insights.

CLIENT   Sure.

COACH   Confidentially, of course. If what they tell me is in confidence, they are more likely to be completely candid, which is what we want, right?

CLIENT   Absolutely. But then how will I know how I'm doing and if I should be doing anything differently?

COACH   I'll summarize what I hear and offer suggestions, if that would be helpful.

CLIENT   Yeah, great.

COACH   As we get going, I would like you to notify anyone else I might talk to that I might call them to ask for their observations of you. You should tell them that it's okay to talk to me and that they should be candid.

CLIENT   Okay.

COACH   What else would be helpful? [Again, the "What else?" question is very powerful.]

CLIENT I guess I'd like your ideas on how to be an effective team leader.

COACH You sound a bit hesitant about that. [Listen carefully for subtleties in speech or nonverbal expressions indicating that the speaker means something other than what he or she is saying.]

CLIENT No, I *really* do want your ideas. It's just that I don't feel like I need to start at square one. You know, I've worked with some really good managers. I've seen what they do. I think, for the most part, I have a sense of what I should be doing.

COACH That's right. You said much of it seemed intuitively obvious.

CLIENT Right. I think it is, but I'd like to be able to ask for help when something happens that I'm not sure how to handle.

COACH Okay.

CLIENT And I'd like to do some periodic checkups, just talk about how things are going, what issues I'm seeing, how I'm handling them, that sort of thing.

COACH Okay. Like everybody else around here, my time is limited, but I could meet with you once a month or so. Would that work?

CLIENT That would be great. And if I have problems in the meantime, I could call you.

COACH Feel free to call anytime. Just leave a voicemail if I'm not in my office and I'll get back to you. So let's check calendars. Wednesdays or Fridays are probably best for me.

CLIENT How about Friday afternoons? They're usually lighter.

COACH I have a standing meeting at 2:00 every Friday, but I could meet with you at 3:30 or 4:00. How about the first Friday of every month at 4:00?

CLIENT I'll put it on my calendar.

COACH Why don't we meet in your office? That way, I can see your operation and get a better sense of your people and the things you're working on. [Nailing down the logistics is important because it makes the process more concrete and real.]

CLIENT   That sounds good.

COACH   There are a few more things we might want to touch on before we get started. I usually find it helpful to begin with the end in mind, so as we get our feet on the ground here, it would be useful to set some goals.

CLIENT   Makes sense.

COACH   Yeah, and it's good project management, by the way. So let's try to reach a point where we can agree on what you're trying to accomplish, and let's set a time frame for achieving those goals. Does that work for you? [The coach makes a small but important teaching point. Often, one of the best ways to teach is to model the principle and then explicitly point it out.]

CLIENT   Yeah. Do you have any idea what those goals should be?

COACH   [Option 1] Well, you said you wanted to be a better team leader. Clearly, that's your number one goal. [It's far too early to know this. The real issues may be quite different. Besides, the coach should not cite the goals. That's taking the monkey off the client's back. One key principle of effective coaching is to force the client to do most of the work.]

COACH   [Option 2] Not at this point. I suspect that we'll figure that out as we go. However, it would be useful for you to reflect on that. Maybe you could come to our next meeting with some initial thoughts on your goals for this coaching.

CLIENT   Okay. I have a few ideas already, but I'd like to give it more thought.

COACH   Great. You might also think about how we'll measure progress and success. What will it look and feel like when we've succeeded? What will that mean? And how will we measure it?

CLIENT   Makes sense.

COACH   Do you have any other questions or concerns at this point?

CLIENT   Will the work we do together be confidential, too, or do you have to let my manager know what we're doing?

COACH   You know, I think it would be best for *you* to share your development plan with her, once we've figured it out, and what the outcomes of the coaching will be when we're finished, but I'm under no obligation to report anything to anybody. So as far as I'm concerned, whatever we talk about is confidential. Does that work for you?

CLIENT   Yeah.

COACH   By the way, it's important to me that this coaching be useful for you, so I'll be asking you from time to time whether what I'm doing is helpful. If it's not, I'd rather know sooner than later so I can change what I'm doing. This coaching is for your benefit, so you should be vocal about what's working for you and what isn't.

CLIENT   Okay.

COACH   Great. Well, let me ask you to do one other thing before next time. Would you mind writing up what we talked about this morning and sending it to me in an e-mail?

CLIENT   No, not at all.

COACH   It would help ensure that we're on the same page. If I think you've left anything out or if I think of anything else, I'll add it and send the message back to you. Let's go back and forth until we both agree on how we want this process to work. That way we're likely to get started on the right foot.

CLIENT   I really appreciate it. Thanks for agreeing to help me out.

COACH   My pleasure. I'll see you in two weeks. In the meantime, call me if you have any questions.

In the rush to get to solutions, the initial phase of coaching often gets slighted. The client's perception that much of project management is "intuitively obvious" is an indication that the client wants to get on with solving his problem, and it is seductively easy for the coach to follow the client's wishes and jump too quickly to the heart of an ill-defined set of issues. This sample illustrates how, by putting on the brakes, the coach is able to help the client clarify his needs and expectations while the coach begins to learn how to work with this particular client. The sample also shows the collaborative nature of coaching, as coach and client construct a shared set of expectations ranging from high-level needs to logistics. The coach begins modeling a deliberative style of problem solving that pushes the client to break a big, amorphous problem into more tangible, well-defined specifics. It's unlikely that the client would walk away from this session feeling that he had wasted his time, even though almost none of the discussion focused on his opening request to get some coaching on project management.

As you negotiate expectations with clients, they may tell you what they think their issues are and what they need from the coaching—and they may be right. However, in our experience, clients' *real* needs are almost never apparent at the beginning of the coaching process. Uncovering their real needs requires some exploration, and the tool we use to help us learn what clients really need is the *needs compass,* which we describe in the next chapter.

3

The Needs Compass

Use all interactions to observe people and to think about ways to help them improve their skills and behavior.

Be more open-minded with the people you are coaching (and their ideas). Try to broaden the perspective, take a step back, and take time to reflect.

Ask your coachees more where they see improvement potential by themselves. Match their point of view with your observations and work out an individual development plan with defined tasks, milestones, and feedback loops together with the coachees.

SUGGESTIONS TO COACHES FROM THE "COACHING EFFECTIVENESS SURVEY,"
LORE INTERNATIONAL INSTITUTE, INC.

How do coaches know what their clients *really* need? Clients typically begin the coaching process with a sense of what they need from the coaching. They will often say, "Here's why I need coaching," or, "This is the problem I'm dealing with," or, "Here is where I need to be more skilled." However, in our experience, the presenting problem is rarely the real one. As insightful as people might be about themselves, they frequently don't understand what they need, can't acknowledge it to themselves, or can't verbalize it to the coach. Clients tend to present their problems in ways that give them a safe psychological distance. They may oversimplify the problem; they may objectify the problem; they may rationalize the problem; or they may avoid or deny the problem altogether. They may disguise the problem they present until they develop trust in the coaching relationship, or they may misunderstand the problem or even distance themselves from it psychologically.

While the client may not understand the problem, coaches cannot afford to be wrong about their clients' needs. If you work on the wrong problems, you can't help the client. Therefore, it's essential for coaches to identify accurately what is really going on. This chapter is the first of two devoted to this crucial issue. Here we introduce a model for a systematic exploration of information sources about the client—what we call the "needs compass." Chapter 4 shows how to use these sources of information in the coaching dialogue to discover the client's real needs.

THE NEEDS COMPASS

If you study maps of the Americas from the sixteenth through the eighteenth centuries, what you see is an effort to chart the discoveries of European explorers along with their inferences about what they hadn't yet explored. For about a hundred years, California appears as an island on many of the maps, apparently because the early explorers traveled up inside the Baja peninsula and assumed it continued all the way to the northern Pacific. Sometimes, mapmakers' superstitions and desires show up on the old maps. A 1655 map by French mapmaker Pierre Du Val shows the location of a fabled city of gold and locates Japan just northwest of California. The first widely disseminated map of the world, Abraham Ortelius' 1570 masterpiece, depicts various sea monsters in the Pacific. A 1750 map of what is now the northeastern United States has an elaborate cartouche that shows Native American people supplying raw materials to slaves, who ascend upward to deliver finished goods to the local gentry, who in turn offer the products to a royal figure seated on a throne. As exploration continued, the maps reflected an emerging awareness of how to match the map to the territory. South America, for example, changes from something that looks like a potato to something that represents its actual contours.

We developed our metaphor of the needs compass because we found that the process of discovering and mapping the client's psychological terrain is similar to the journey of exploration reflected in the old maps. Facts gradually replace inferences and assumptions, and the more varied the sources of information, the fuller and more accurate the picture becomes. Only the most naïve cartographer, however, would believe that the map is ever a fully accurate representation of the territory. Even today, there are places on the globe that are represented

Client's Perceptions

Coach's Observations

Others' Observations

Work Products and Performance Metrics

Figure 3 The Needs Compass

by best guesses on maps. The proportion of the known to the unknown, however, has dramatically increased, making the domain of inference relatively small and the inferences increasingly reliable. The needs compass offers a visual tool for helping coaches remember the four primary domains of information about clients' needs: the coach's observations, the client's perceptions, others' observations, and work products and performance metrics. These four sources of information are like the four poles on a compass, as shown in figure 3. To build a map of the client's needs, the coach must investigate all four poles of this compass.

THE WEST POLE:
THE COACH'S OBSERVATIONS

Your observations are your source of firsthand knowledge about the client. You need to see the client in action, and two sources of observation are available to you: observations of the client on the job and observations of the client during coaching sessions.

Observations on the Job

What to look for depends to some extent on the coaching content, but it's hard to imagine a coaching engagement that cannot be enriched by observing the client at work. You can observe clients to ascertain their needs or to monitor progress and behavioral change. People do tend to be on their best behavior when they're being observed, but you can still learn a lot by watching them perform. Note what your clients do that is effective or ineffective, that positively or negatively affects others, that demonstrates good or poor leadership or management, and so on. Note how they respond to challenges, stress, surprises, problems, and opportunities. Note how they influence others, how they use authority, and how they communicate. It's helpful to keep an observation log, noting specifics so you can remind clients of events or incidents later. You should be as unobtrusive as possible (or your presence will seriously skew what you are observing).

Observations During Coaching Sessions

Your relationship with a client is a microcosm of how the client builds relationships with other people, so it's often illuminating to observe how clients relate to you during all your encounters with them. Note how they behave toward you. Be curious about what your clients do and do not do, how they respond to you, how they attempt to control or influence the situation, how they position themselves, and how they present themselves. These are clues about clients' operating styles and interaction patterns with others. Every impression is meaningful. After your sessions, spend some time reflecting on the interaction you just had; write down your reflections in the observation log. Look for themes or patterns indicating what your client needs. Develop a format that allows you to distinguish your observations from the inferences, hypotheses, or judgments you draw from them.

Coaching from Observations

One powerful coaching technique is to make your in-session observations transparent. Clients are often unaware of their behaviors and the impact of those behaviors on others, so a primary coaching technique is to observe and discuss their behaviors during sessions. This can have a powerful effect on clients because most of the people they interact with will not point out their behaviors in real time. In the following example, the coach observes how the client is behaving during the dialogue with the coach.

COACH   Something I keep hearing as I talk to people who work with you is that you have a strong need for control.

CLIENT   I've heard that before. It used to be true, but I've worked on that a lot. I would say that I'm almost too much the other way now.

COACH   You feel like you've relinquished too much control?

CLIENT   Sometimes, yes. Look, I really don't think this is an issue, so why don't we move on.

COACH   Before we do, I have an observation. You're trying to control me right now.

CLIENT   No, I'm not. I just don't think this is important enough to waste time on it.

COACH   Well, it feels to me like you're being controlling. Maybe this is what the other people experience when they work with you, too. It has the feeling of "my way or the highway."

In addition to confronting clients for negative behaviors, you can observe and point out positive behaviors. In the following example, the client has historically had trouble recognizing and rewarding employees.

CLIENT   This has been very helpful. I appreciate the time you've taken to help me.

COACH   No problem. By the way, you just showed me some appreciation.

CLIENT   (a little surprised) I guess I did. It wasn't intentional.

COACH   (laughing) Maybe not, but it seemed effortless. Sometimes, all it takes is a little verbal pat on the back. Appreciation doesn't have to be expensive or time consuming.

CLIENT   You're right. I just don't think to do it.

COACH   But you did now. Why?

CLIENT   (reflecting) I don't know. You've been helpful to me. It just seemed like the right thing to say.

COACH   I think your instincts were good. Now let's apply that to the people in your department. When would a simple "thank you" be the right thing to say?

Beyond the coaching impact, observing clients during sessions enables you to better understand your clients' real needs. You observe with your eyes and your ears, and you look and listen for clues that indicate what the client's real needs are. For further information, beyond observation, see the text box "Transference and Countertransference" on pages 43–44.

THE NORTH POLE: THE CLIENT'S PERCEPTIONS

At the north pole of the needs compass are the client's perceptions. Early mapmakers conceived of four rivers flowing from the North Pole as a way to explain the existence of the oceans. Common sense dictated that the formation of the world flowed down from the top. They were wrong, of course, but the exercise in imagination was nevertheless revealing about what was on their minds. Similarly, the client's perceptions are important not so much for the truths they reveal, but for showing how clients think about themselves and how they present themselves to others: how they construct and communicate their self-image, where they are proud and where they are tentative, where they feel comfortable and where they don't, what they value, how they make and communicate decisions, what façade they've created and who they present it to.

The paradox is that these self-reports are rarely consistent with what others think about the client. Their value lies in helping coach and client develop a baseline for the changes to follow. Coaching is about managing human change, and the only person who can execute change is the client. It's essential, therefore, for coaches to know and clients to articulate their self-perceptions. As a coach, you note those self-perceptions and then return to them later—either to remind clients what they said and how they perceived themselves or to show how far they've come in their self-perceptions: "Sam, we've been working together now for eight months, and I just want to remind you what you said about your leadership skills when we began working together. . . ."

Gathering Baseline Data from the Client

Areas of concern for most coaching engagements are typically centered around four topics: leadership, management, interpersonal skills, and teaming. What follows are the kinds of questions coaches can ask to solicit a client's baseline perception of himself or herself. Note that you wouldn't use all of these questions in sequence. This is not intended as a

TRANSFERENCE AND COUNTERTRANSFERENCE

The coach's observations are obviously important, but they are only one source of information, and they are not fully objective. Thus, smart coaches do not rely on their own observations alone. Coaches have to beware of their need to shape the client in their own image, so to speak. Even the most detached observer still constructs a subjective view of the client. This perspective is influenced by many things: your worldview; your values; your gender, class, race, and cultural background; your experiences and personal history; your hopes and ambitions; and your unmet needs—all of which contribute inevitably to a psychological phenomenon called countertransference.

To understand countertransference, you have to start with transference. One of the most cogent explanations comes from a mystery novel, *Privileged Information*, by clinical psychologist Steven White (1999). In the following scene, White's main character, Alan Gregory, also a clinical psychologist, explains transference to his attorney, who is representing Gregory in a malpractice case.

> *Transference is a component of virtually all human relationships. It's the process of reacting to or responding to someone in a current relationship as if that person had important traits, motivations, behaviors, et cetera, of an important someone from the past. It's often based on purely unconscious motivations, or can be stimulated by traits that the current person may have in common with the important person from the past. The "as if" part is crucial. Transference is an "as if" experience; it's not real, but it feels real to the one experiencing it.* (p. 238)

Clients in therapy and in coaching relationships can transfer the feelings and perceptions that White describes to their therapist or coach. Conversely, therapists and coaches can, and often do, transfer their feelings, attitudes, and perceptions onto their clients through the process known as countertransference. For instance, a coach working with a much younger man or woman may come to think of the client as a son, daughter, niece, nephew, or other family member, and begin acting accordingly toward the client. These thoughts may be entirely unconscious, but they can affect the way the coach relates to, thinks about, and helps the client. Members of the various helping professions learn to cultivate a degree of therapeutic distance from their clients so they can discern these phenomena when they happen and mitigate their effects.

In therapy, it would not be unusual for clients to think of an older therapist as a parent and to start acting out parental fantasies with the therapist. The therapist, aware of the transference, uses it to help the client gain insights. But using transference is very tricky and requires a great deal of training. It's best for coaches to be aware of their own feelings of countertransference, if such feelings occur, and try to set them aside and remain objective. The chapters in Part 3 that focus on coaching women and minorities, coaching cross-culturally, and coaching cross-generationally are designed, among other things, to give coaches the insights they need into these special populations to lessen the possibility of transference or countertransference and to enable coaches to relate to these clients on their own terms.

Psychologist Rachel Harris told us that one of the major ethical challenges in coaching (besides knowing therapeutic limits) is not using clients to meet your own ego needs. According to Harris, "This is probably the biggest way countertransference gets acted out, and these two issues are related. I want to feel like I'm the greatest coach ever, so I'm going to help you resolve *all* your psychological issues. Or I'm going to make you think that you need me to succeed. Or I'm going to make you emotionally dependent upon me so I can be a hero and rescue you." To avoid confusing your own needs with the client's needs, you must be aware of the countertransference that inevitably occurs in a helping relationship and guard against its effects.

formula but rather as a list of possible questions. Some questions are redundant in order to suggest different wording. The ones you use will depend on the nature and purpose of the coaching.

FOCUSING ON LEADERSHIP

- ✓ How would you describe yourself as a leader? What kind of leader are you?

- ✓ What do you think you do well as a leader? What don't you do well? What would you see as your developmental needs at this point?

- ✓ If you were to list your strengths in one column and your weaknesses in another, what would you say? [This is a good exercise to ask clients to do during a first meeting.]

✓ [Here's another good exercise.] I'd like you to think of ten words that best describe you as a leader. Write them down and then rank them. Put the ones that are most descriptive and most relevant at the top.

✓ How would your direct reports describe you as a leader? What would they say you do well and not so well?

✓ What feedback have you received on your leadership? [Then ask, "What else?" when the client finishes. Keep asking "What else?" until the well is dry. This question is most useful for determining what the client remembers and what is most prominent in memory. We tend to remember longest the events and comments that had the greatest impact on us, so asking people to recall feedback is like asking, "What feedback had the greatest impact on you?" Note whether the first memories of feedback are positive or negative and whether they reflect strengths or weaknesses. If they are negative, then the client may have experienced an emotionally potent failure, been stung by some criticism, felt the criticism was especially accurate, or has heard the feedback more than once and is bothered by it.]

✓ How have you changed as a leader in the past two years? [This is an excellent question that helps uncover the client's perceptions of her growth and development. You should follow it up with: "How haven't you changed?"]

FOCUSING ON MANAGEMENT

✓ How would you describe yourself as a manager? What kind of manager are you?

✓ What are your strengths as a manager? What do you do exceptionally well? Have you ever been recognized for your management? If so, what was the recognition for?

✓ What are your weaknesses as a manager? What do you tend to neglect or not do well?

✓ What are the top three ways that you could improve your management skills?

✓ What would your direct reports say that you should do more of as a manager? What would they say you should do less of? [This type of question is particularly helpful in bridging the gap between the client's perceptions and the perceptions of others. Questions like this push the client into the mind-set of co-workers and are often surprisingly difficult for many clients to answer.]

FOCUSING ON INTERPERSONAL SKILLS

✓ How would you assess your interpersonal skills? What do you do well and what don't you do well?

✓ How comfortable are you in meetings where you do not know many of the attendees? How do you typically handle these situations?

✓ How comfortable are you in social situations where you don't know many people? How do you typically handle these situations?

✓ How skilled are you at handling conflict? When conflict occurs, what do you typically do?

✓ How influential are you in situations where you have no authority? How do you typically try to influence others? What works for you and what doesn't?

✓ Would you describe yourself as a people person? Why or why not? How well do you get along with people? Which kinds of people do you get along with best and least?

✓ How well do you communicate with others? What are your favorite forms of communication? Least favorite? In what ways do you communicate well? In what ways do you communicate poorly?

FOCUSING ON TEAMING

✓ How would you describe the management team that you are part of? In what ways does this team function well and in what ways poorly?

✓ What role do you play on this team? Formally or informally?

✓ How would you describe yourself as a management team member? How would others describe you?

✓ What overt or covert conflicts exist on this team? Where are the disagreements or tensions? What role do you play in perpetuating or resolving these conflicts?

✓ Regardless of how effective you are now, what are the top three things you could do differently to be a more effective management team member?

Collecting Client Observations Through a Performance Log

Finally, because you will have only limited opportunities to observe clients during performance events, a useful strategy is to ask them to "observe" themselves by being aware of how they are performing. A "performance log" enables the client to keep track of opportunities to enact new behaviors and to record what happened during those instances. The performance log is a useful tool for clients to record when they've done something well or poorly. For instance, you may have a client who is working on controlling anger. You would ask the client to record in the performance log every instance when she became angry: what triggered it, times when the triggering event was there but she was able to control her anger and how she was able to do that, how she felt about the new behavior, and what she could observe about its effects on others. Performance logs are best if used to help clients focus on very specific problems and the new behaviors they are trying to implement, such as becoming more comfortable making client calls, giving recognition, reprimanding employees constructively, or handling particularly difficult people. Performance logs are great tools for helping clients make self-observations on a continuous basis, but they have to be used with clients who need to increase their awareness of behavior or practice skills. Furthermore, you have to be sure your client has sufficient motivation to use the log faithfully. Often, very senior people have the best of intentions but are in actuality too busy for this kind of assignment.

THE EAST POLE: OTHERS' OBSERVATIONS

Conventional wisdom in coaching recognizes the value of information from those who work with the client, and it distinguishes two sources of information: data from 360-degree assessments and interview data. Although the case can be made for using one or the other source of

information, we argue that they need to be used together for the data to
be truly meaningful.

Data from 360-Degree Surveys

In the past decade, 360-degree feedback has become much more widespread and accepted. Assessment instruments have achieved impressive
levels of validity and reliability, and the use of standard instruments over
time helps an organization achieve a consistent picture of performance
norms among various groups of employees. However, 360-degree feedback is still not a commonly used tool in some cultures and in some companies and is sometimes viewed with suspicion. The business must have
a culture geared toward professional development in a feedback-rich environment, in which people are expected to be accountable for their performance, listen to their stakeholders, and learn from their successes as
well as their mistakes. Otherwise, individuals will not take the process seriously or will sugarcoat their responses because they do not believe that
their reports are anonymous or are convinced that the instrument is really being used for evaluative purposes. Some professional services firms,
such as McKinsey & Company, and some large, mature firms, such as GE,
have feedback-rich environments in which 360-degree assessments are
commonplace and accepted.

Where you can use it, 360-degree feedback offers a number of insights
for coaching. First, it enables you to compare clients' views of themselves
with others' views of them along a number of dimensions. The better survey instruments calibrate the differences in scores so you know which
ones are significantly different, which are meaningfully different, and
which are not statistically different. The better instruments also provide
narrative feedback, so you have qualitative as well as quantitative data.

Second, 360-degree instruments show the patterns revealed in the
highest- and lowest-rated skills or traits. Often, these groupings of high-
est- and lowest-rated skills yield broader insights into the client's needs.
Bill W. is an example. On his leadership evaluation, he was rated highest
on these behaviors:

- **Giving recognition:** recognizing others for their contributions and
  celebrating people's accomplishments

- **Acting with integrity:** telling the truth at all times and maintaining
  the highest ethical standards

- **Encouraging contribution:** actively soliciting others' ideas and using them appropriately to improve results

- **Showing respect toward others:** treating people with respect, regardless of their role or level in the organization

- **Setting high professional standards:** setting high quality and performance standards and helping others achieve them

Bill W. was rated lowest on the following behaviors:

- **Removing barriers:** removing the obstacles and barriers that prevent others from taking action or achieving better results

- **Taking risks:** being willing to take calculated risks and accepting responsibility for the outcomes

- **Being candid with others:** always being honest and straightforward with others, delivering bad news when necessary

- **Challenging others' thinking:** actively challenging assumptions, opinions, and traditions, and encouraging others to seek better solutions

These patterns of highs and lows revealed a person who works hard at being professional and building harmony but who lacks an entrepreneurial edge. His desire to create a harmonious, respectful working environ ment overcame his willingness to be hard-nosed and assertive when necessary and blunted his effectiveness as a leader. To help him see this, his coach gave him a simple metaphor to keep in mind. He said, "Bill, you're working so hard at being a 'good boy' that the 'bad boy' in you can never get out. The bad boy takes risks, removes obstacles, is candid with others, and challenges them to think outside the box. The good boy, careful and respectful, engages others and builds a following. You need both—but you also need to know when each side of yourself should dominate at which times."

Third, 360-degree feedback is most useful when it helps clients see significant disparities between their own view of themselves and how others view them. Self-ratings that are significantly *lower* than others' average ratings can signal self-confidence issues or limiting self-perceptions (e.g., when clients think they are not good at something, they don't try it). Conversely, self-ratings that are significantly *higher* than others' average ratings can reveal arrogance and egotism, on the one hand, or deceptively inflated views of one's skills, on the other. Clients who rate themselves too low relative to others may not act with enough boldness or take enough risks; clients who rate themselves too high may not know when to seek help from others and may not be sufficiently aware of their limitations or skill-building needs.

Interviews with Respondents

In our experience, 360-degree feedback is useful but not sufficient as a tool for understanding clients' needs. It provides a panoramic view. Its results are sometimes dramatic enough to grab a client's attention. It can point the coach in the right direction. But rarely is it sufficient to permit a complete and accurate diagnosis. Instead, such instruments yield hypotheses to be tested through your interviews with others, your own observations, and your dialogues with the client. The east pole of the needs compass is best understood as the combination of 360-degree feedback with observations from people with whom the client works. These observations represent the human environment. In many cases, co-workers have observed the client far more than the coach has, so they have the deepest and longest-lasting impressions. They are likely to have seen the client at her best and worst. They will know the norms of the client's behavior, as well as her extremes. Furthermore, they are likely to be around later in the coaching process and can offer feedback on progress (or lack thereof). They are the behavioral witnesses to the coaching's success or failure. This means that it is crucial to select the right "others" to talk to.

You need to talk to a number of people in different roles relative to the client, just as with a 360-degree survey. Talk to the client's direct reports (who know what this person is like as a boss), to his or her peers, to his or her boss or other senior people, and perhaps to his or her customers or clients. (Some coaches may even ask to speak to the client's family members, although there are potentially serious unintended consequences to doing that, so we avoid it unless the family is part of the issue and volunteers to provide a perspective.) The point is to see clients from a variety of perspectives. Why? Because many people behave differently toward different stakeholders in their lives. The view from those who work for them (direct reports) may differ from the view of those whose needs they serve (customers). Some leaders treat their bosses and peers well but are dismissive or patronizing toward their staff. Others are conscientious and caring team leaders who don't communicate well to their boss and aren't effective collaborators with peers. You can't really understand a client's needs until you see that person from multiple perspectives, because then you learn how he or she handles different people at different levels in different situations.

The interviews with others need to be confidential, which means that what the respondents tell you will remain with you. You will not repeat it or share it with the client. Respondents will be more inclined to be open and candid if they know that what they tell you will not go anywhere else. We tell the respondents we are interviewing that we are coaching this person and that he or she has given us permission to talk confidentially with people he or she works with. We say that it's important for us to learn where the client is strong and where he or she has developmental needs. If they have completed a 360-degree assessment on the client and we have a copy of their responses, we let them know that and say that we may ask them some questions based on their responses to the survey. We are especially interested in why they made the narrative comments they did and why they rated the client low on the lowest-rated skill areas and high on the highest-rated skill areas. We emphasize that the information they provide will not be repeated; however, it will be aggregated with all the other confidential interviews and in that form will be shared as a profile with the client. If people ask if they can see the aggregate profile, we decline because it is confidential between the coach and the client. We don't tell them who else is being interviewed, but at the end of each interview, we do ask them who else they think we should talk to.

The trickiest part of getting observations from others is assuring them that your intentions are honorable and that the information they give you will be used with integrity. It helps them to know that this is part of a developmental process, not an evaluative process, and that the client is being helped, not hurt, by the coaching. It helps them to know that the client is not "in trouble," "going to lose his job," or anything of the sort. It's helpful if the coaching is being done as part of normal executive, leadership, or management development or is otherwise part of a normal development program in the company. It helps, frankly, if the coach is from outside the company, because people may be less forthcoming when the interviewer is from inside the company or, heaven forbid, is the client's boss. In those instances, people are likely to "toe the line" and "play good."

One of the most important characteristics of coaches conducting confidential interviews with people who work with the client is curiosity. You have to continually push for more information, more examples, more detail. What is this person like? How does he make decisions? How does she prioritize? What are her strengths, and how does she use them? What are his weaknesses, and how do they affect him and others? What are the implications of the way this person operates? How has he grown in the past two years? Where will her skills need to be in the next two years? What does this person say he needs, and what does he really need? What would be most helpful to this person?

Curiosity drives a coach to drill deeper, learn more, ask more questions, and form a more complete picture of the client. The following list offers specific kinds of questions and responses that help elicit more information and help coaches assess the validity of what they are hearing.

✓ Can you give me an example of that?

✓ What else was going on when you saw that behavior?

✓ What else did you observe?

✓ Please explain.

✓ Tell me more.

✓ Have you seen that any other time?

✓ What was the effect on the team?

✓ How did you feel about that?

Even with the most systematic use of 360-degree feedback and carefully chosen interviewees, coaches must maintain a degree of skepticism about what they are hearing. You must be suspicious of information from sources that are too far outside the "norm" of everything else you are hearing from respondents. Reports that are too positive or too negative generally indicate that the respondent is not being candid, has a grudge, or feels protective of the client. Reports that are too general indicate that the respondent does not know the client as well as he needs to for the information to be of much use. In rare instances (although it does occur), the client may pressure respondents to give him or her a good report. If you sense that people are not really being forthcoming, you may need to talk to someone who no longer reports to or is no longer under the influence of the client.

Finally, as Lester Tobias (1996) says, "Because the problem is usually described as 'in' the person," these interviews usually provide "a good opportunity to point out the systemic nature of most individual problems or at least to emphasize that amelioration of the problem may necessarily involve the individual's manager or other relevant people in the organization" (p. 88). The others whose observations you get are people who are part of the system in which the client operates. Not only are they sources of information, but they may be part of the problem and part of the solution. So it's important to view their information in the context of an interconnected whole in which the client plays a part. The combination of 360-degree feedback with interview data is powerful. One final way to use these two sources of information together is to know how the person you are interviewing responded to the 360-degree feedback assessment. Obtaining the individual feedback report before the interview helps you structure the interview and cross-check what you are hearing. When you have these two data sources working together, you have successfully navigated the east pole of the needs compass.

THE SOUTH POLE: WORK PRODUCTS AND PERFORMANCE METRICS

Ultimately, the goal of executive coaching is improved work performance, so an important measure of success and indicator of need is how the client has been performing. The south pole of the needs compass covers the client's work products and performance metrics. Businesses usually have an abundance of performance data on their employees, but these are the guiding questions for using that data for coaching engagements:

✓ What are the organization's expectations of the client? What does he or she produce, create, or manage?

✓ How is the client's business performance measured? What metrics or standards indicate how well the client is performing?

✓ Looking as far back as relevant, what do these measures indicate about the client's need for improvement?

This last question is the key, of course. The client may not be producing work products quickly enough or with high enough quality, and that may indicate a coaching need. In some cases, the business metrics are simple enough but the needs may be more complex. Terry coached a business unit president, for instance, whose unit was the lowest performing of eight business units in a company. The unit's costs were too high for the revenue it produced, and it had been losing market share for several years. Market conditions contributed to some of the unit's problems, but as Terry and the client examined the situation in more depth, it became apparent that the client's leadership style was largely to blame for the unit's decline. He was not visible enough with his frontline employees and was not spending enough time with key customers. In this case, the outcomes of the coaching were readily measurable as the unit's fortunes improved.

Beyond metrics such as top-line revenue, bottom-line profit, market share growth, and so on, business metrics can also include the kind of data revealed in climate, employee, or pulse surveys, on the one hand, and in customer surveys, on the other. Internal surveys, which go by different names, reveal how employees feel about the organization and various aspects of their employment (morale, the work environment, compensation, fairness, challenge, and so on). These kinds of surveys are good indicators of the effectiveness of the organization's leadership. Customer surveys reveal how the organization and its people and products are being perceived in the marketplace. Whenever we coach for a company that has these kinds of surveys available, we jump at the chance to use them because they reveal a tremendous amount about how the company's leaders and managers are working, how employees or customers feel about the company, and where our coaching clients may have needs.

As our discussion in this chapter suggests, there are numerous sources of information for coaches about what a client needs. The needs compass we have described is a simple framework for remembering the four major sources of information. Experienced coaches invariably use all four sources, but we have seen many less-experienced coaches who rely too much on their own observations alone, or on the clients' perceptions as the principal source, or on quantitative tools without regard for the illuminating effects of others' observations of the client. In our experience, coaches need to consider all four sources of information. None is complete or accurate by itself. Even with information from all four sources, however, you may still not understand clients' real needs.

Dealing with surface behaviors is almost never effective. Imagine a client coming to you and saying, "I need coaching on how to be more of a people person. My staff says I'm too focused on tasks and not enough on people." If you accepted that and offered suggestions on how to be more of a people person, you might give the client a handful of tactics that would make him appear to be more of a people person, but his underlying operating style will not have changed. As time wears on, he will gradually forget or stop using the tactics you gave him, and it will become business as usual. We have seen this happen countless times. The only way to *really* help this kind of client is to understand the underlying reasons why he focuses more on tasks than on people. Your sources of information may repeatedly tell you that he is insensitive, occasionally abrasive, and fails to encourage or recognize people, but those are symptoms, not causes, and treating the symptoms will not solve the problem. To solve the problem, you have to uncover the client's real needs, and that is the subject of the next chapter.

4

The Real Issues

Listen to all the facts before jumping in with suggestions.

Release your own agenda and take a genuine interest (shown through questioning) in the person you're coaching. Listen carefully and build the discussion to his or her needs.

Don't use the same approach with everyone. Alter it based on what works best for that person.

SUGGESTIONS TO COACHES FROM THE "COACHING EFFECTIVENESS SURVEY,"
LORE INTERNATIONAL INSTITUTE, INC.

Jan-Olof opened the coaching session and began the process of discovery that would help him understand his client's needs. Terry was supervising him as part of his coach certification. His client was Manuela F., a thirty-one-year-old software engineer who was considered a high-potential professional in her firm. In her high-potential program, Manuela was receiving coaching to assist in her ongoing development as a leader. After the preliminaries in their discussion, Jan-Olof asked about some of the feedback she had received from members of her program team.

JAN-OLOF   As I spoke to members of your team, I heard the same thing several times—that you are a very hands-on leader.

MANUELA   I think that's fair.

JAN-OLOF   I did sense some frustration from people, however. They said you check every detail of their work and frequently stay well into the evening going over the work that was done that day.

MANUELA   It's been frustrating for me, too, but the project is heating up. You know, we're only three months from launch, so I hope they're ready for it. If anything, we'll have to work harder.

JAN-OLOF   Why?

MANUELA   Because we have to get it right. Too much is at stake.

JAN-OLOF   So as you look ahead, you see even more late nights.

MANUELA   I don't see any way around it. I'm responsible for the quality of this work, and it has to be done right.

JAN-OLOF   I'm getting the sense that you don't delegate very well. Could you delegate some of the oversight you're doing?

MANUELA   Maybe. But if I have others review the coding, then I will just have to review the reviewers, right? So maybe I should just eliminate the middleman.

JAN-OLOF   You wouldn't trust others to be as good at reviewing as you are?

MANUELA   I have some great people working with me, but I have to keep the whole project in my mind. If I lost sight of what the programmers are doing, then I couldn't be sure that everything will come together at the end.

JAN-OLOF   Okay, well, let's talk more about delegation.

TERRY   Jan-Olof, let me interrupt here. Do you think you know what the real issue is?

JAN-OLOF   Yes, I think so.

TERRY   What is it?

JAN-OLOF   Manuela is checking every detail of the team's work instead of delegating that to others. She is frustrating the team and working many late nights herself. It's an unsustainable situation.

TERRY   So the fundamental problem is her unwillingness to delegate.

JAN-OLOF   Yes, I think so.

TERRY   Manuela, does that feel right to you? Is this the real problem?

MANUELA   No.

EXPLORING THE PROBLEM SPACE

In our experience as supervisors and coaches of other coaches, we have found that Jan-Olof's experience is not unusual. Many coaches jump too quickly from preliminary problem identification to solution. In his desire to be helpful, Jan-Olof is like a problem-seeking missile. As soon as he detects a problem, he hones in on it and tries to solve it. In doing so, he is making a rookie coach's mistake: treating effects rather than causes. Consider what Jan-Olof defined as Manuela's problem: she's checking every detail of the team's work, she's not delegating the responsibility for reviewing, she is frustrating the team, and she's working many late nights herself. These are *consequences* or *outcomes* of some underlying problem; they are not the problem themselves. Until he understands the root causes, he cannot truly be helpful to her because, like physicians, coaches have to address the disease, not the symptoms.

It's useful to think of the problem solving we do in coaching as it is shown in figure 4. The left side of this figure is the *problem space;* the right side is the *solution space.* Before you can move to the solution space, you have to explore the problem thoroughly. Metaphorically, you need to *open up* the problem space until you have identified the core issues. Only then should you begin exploring the solution space. If you are impatient and leap to the solution space too quickly, as Jan-Olof did, you risk trying to solve the wrong problem or giving superficial advice for superficial issues, as Jan-Olof would have done had he said, "Here are some tips on delegating."

Clients' real needs emerge through a process of discovery. They are almost never evident from the *presenting problem,* which is what clients may say they need help with when they enter into a coaching relationship, or from the data coaches gather prior to coaching, although such data

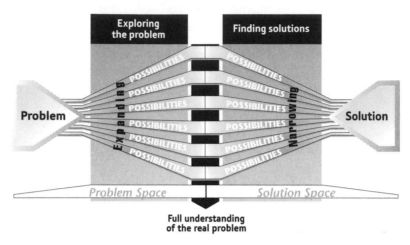

Figure 4   The Problem-Solution Sequence

may be very suggestive. The real need is the root of the problem; it is the core issue that must be resolved or addressed for clients to change their behavior. Coaches and clients generally co-discover the real need by forming hypotheses about what the real need might be and then testing those hypotheses by looking for confirming or disconfirming information.

Physicians view symptoms as likely indicators of the underlying malaise. Then they seek confirmation of their diagnosis by interviewing the patient, ordering lab tests, and observing the patient over time. Eventually, the additional information they receive helps them pinpoint the real problem. Coaches view clients' behaviors as likely indicators of the underlying problem, and they use the four poles of the needs compass to generate the additional data needed to confirm or disconfirm their hypotheses. Eventually, they arrive at the root cause that should be addressed. The difference between physicians and coaches is that physicians are experts and their patients generally are not, so physicians rely far more on their knowledge and expertise to discover the underlying illness. Coaching, on the other hand, is a process of co-discovery in which both parties are experts in various ways. Coaching and medicine are alike, however, in that the core issue is a *cause*, not an *effect*. In coaching, you have not discovered the real need until you have identified the reason why clients behave the way they do.

Throughout the rest of this chapter, we will explore how coaches identify the real needs. The cases we examine will illustrate various coaching techniques, but we should note that experienced coaches do not rely on techniques. They rely on instincts formed by years of coaching experience and a good understanding of people and organizations. For every technique we illustrate, there are dozens of variations that different experienced coaches favor. It may be helpful to think of these techniques as tools in a toolbox. The best coaches possess many tools and know when to use them.

MANUELA'S REAL ISSUE

Let's return to the case that opened this chapter and see how Jan-Olof might have continued to explore the problem space to uncover the real issue.

MANUELA   I have some great people working with me, but I have to keep the whole project in my mind. If I lost sight of what the programmers are doing, then I couldn't be sure that everything will come together at the end.

JAN-OLOF   And, clearly, that's important.

MANUELA   Absolutely.

JAN-OLOF   Help me understand something. Are you particularly concerned about *this* project? Or do you approach every project this way? [*Exploring context* is a useful coaching tool. You need to know whether this event or behavior is unusual and, if so, why is it?]

MANUELA   (reflecting) No, I think it pretty much describes how I normally work. I'm probably more finicky about the details than most people.

JAN-OLOF   That's interesting. Why do you think that is? [He could speculate about why she's more finicky, but it's best to go to the source and ask the client.]

MANUELA   I don't know. I just have to make sure that everything is all right. Sometimes I double and even triple check things to be sure that nothing has been overlooked. I'm compulsive like that.

JAN-OLOF   Are you like that in other areas of your life?

MANUELA   My husband seems to think so. I drive him crazy sometimes. So I guess that's a fair statement.

JAN-OLOF   Have you always been that way? [Note that the coach does
not ask more about her family life. Coaching is not therapy
and, unless there seems to be some bearing on the problem
at hand, the coach stays away from areas of the client's life
that would be inappropriate to explore.]

MANUELA   (pausing to reflect) No. I mean, it's hard to remember. I was
always the one who dotted the *i*'s and crossed the *t*'s. You
could count on me to get my homework done. You know,
I don't know if this has anything to do with it, but I was
really sick as a kid. I nearly died.

JAN-OLOF   I'm sorry to hear that. What happened?

MANUELA   I was riding in my aunt's car and we had an accident. Another car hit us broadside, and it broke my leg. I was in the
hospital for a week, and then when I got home I got an infection and wound up back in the hospital, this time for
almost a month. They said the infection almost killed me.
I don't remember much of it.

JAN-OLOF   Sounds like a terrible experience. How old were you?
[showing empathy]

MANUELA   Eight or nine. Eight, I think. (pause) I remember that it really scared me, not the almost dying part, which is hard
for a kid to understand, but just the suddenness of it, you
know. It was just so random. One day you're riding down
the street on your way to the grocery store, and then
something totally random happens and you nearly die in
a hospital.

JAN-OLOF   Sounds like a tough lesson for an eight-year-old to learn.
[showing empathy]

MANUELA   (nodding) I think it really shook me up. Afterward, I was always so careful. You know, always looking both ways before
crossing a street. And when I was riding in a car, always
checking the crossing streets ahead to see if a car was coming.

JAN-OLOF   Always dotting the *i*'s and crossing the *t*'s? [making the connection between her behavior following the accident and
her behavior later in school and at work]

MANUELA   Right.

JAN-OLOF   Is that what you're doing when you check every detail of your team's work?

MANUELA   Yes, I think I'm just being cautious.

JAN-OLOF   Because you never know what could happen.

MANUELA   Right. I'm doing everything I can to control the situation.

JAN-OLOF   Even if you have to work late every night.

MANUELA   Yeah.

JAN-OLOF   And even if you continually frustrate your team.

MANUELA   It's a heavy price to pay, but I just feel so vulnerable. If I don't control every aspect of the situation, I feel like it could all come crashing down around me.

JAN-OLOF   I think this is the key thing we need to work on. As long as you feel vulnerable, you're going to behave in ways that protect yourself, no matter what the cost.

MANUELA   I think you're right.

This case illustrates a number of fundamental techniques in coaching: empathizing, making connections between parts of the client's narrative (that the client may not see), holding up the mirror to clients, and exploring the context. Holding up the mirror to clients means helping them see themselves as others see them. When Jan-Olof says, "Even if you have to work late every night," he is holding up the mirror, showing his client the consequences of the unconscious choice she is making. In Manuela's case, her feelings of vulnerability are the core issue. Through the coach's skilled questioning, she arrived at that insight herself, and awareness is the first step toward change. When you explore the context, you ask these kinds of questions:

- ✓ Is X true in every part of your life? [If not, then what is different about this part of your life?]

- ✓ Do you do X in every case? Do you always respond this way? [If not, then what is different about this situation?]

- ✓ Has X always been true for you? [If not, when was it not true and what's different between then and now?]

This last question is especially powerful. Karen worked with Simon T., whose presenting problem was an incapacitating fear of public speaking.

As she explored this issue more deeply, Karen asked, "Is this true for you in every situation where you talk to large groups of people? Are there any circumstances in which this is not true?" As he thought about this, Simon realized that he was not fearful when he addressed his church and community groups. He taught Sunday school and periodically addressed the congregation. He was also a community advocate and frequently talked to various groups about civic and community issues. Karen then asked him what was different about those groups that made him less fearful. Simon realized in their further dialogue that he felt passionately about the issues he spoke about with his church and community groups—and that was not the case at work. One of the issues Simon and Karen later dealt with was why he felt no passion for his work. Had Karen merely given him tips on controlling stress and public speaking, she would have failed as a coach, because she would not have been addressing the real issue.

Nicola's Team Leadership

Sometimes you have to triangulate to discover the client's real needs. In ethnographic research, anthropologists refer to the process of cross-referencing at least three versions of the same story or experience as *triangulation*. By triangulating multiple points of view, you get closer to the truth of things because the anomalies can be identified and potentially eliminated. We are using the term in much the same way: to describe how coaches use the four poles of the needs compass to find patterns or themes that indicate what help clients need. Nicola R. is a case in point. She was a newly promoted senior executive in an insurance firm and received some executive coaching as part of her transition process. In her new role, she was responsible for the Asia-Pacific field sales force. In her previous roles, she had inherited intact teams that were already well functioning, but in her new role she had to build strong teams over a large geographic area with people who had not already gelled as teams. It was a challenge she had not faced before, and she told the coach that she thought that would be one of her biggest challenges. So team building was one of her presenting problems; however, team building is a broad skill area and her needs were still not clear.

Nicola's Leadership Assessment

To gather more information, the coach asked Nicola to complete two 360-degree assessments and the *Myers-Briggs Type Indicator®* (MBTI®) per-

LEADERSHIP DIMENSION	RESPONDENTS	LEADER (SELF)
Visionary/ Inspirational	94	94
Moral	103	112
Intellectual	115	103
Courageous	108	111
Collaborative	87	95

Table 1   Nicola's LLA Summary

sonality inventory. The 360-degree instruments would provide some baseline data from others who have worked with Nicola, and the MBTI instrument would help her and the coach understand her operating style. The first of the 360s was the *Lore Leadership Assessment* (LLA), which evaluates leaders' capabilities in five dimensions: visionary/inspirational, moral, intellectual, courageous, and collaborative leadership. Nicola's LLA results showed the overall pattern in table 1. The numbers are indexed scores; the mean for the database is 100, and 15 points above or below the mean represents one standard deviation.

These data told the coach that Nicola is an above-average leader on most dimensions. She is clearly an exceptional problem-solving leader who is willing to take risks, but she is not as inspirational as she might be, and she has a clear developmental need in collaborative leadership. The gap between her self-perception on collaborative leadership and the perceptions of others indicates that she is not fully aware of her weaknesses in this area. Next, the coach examined her lowest-rated collaborative leadership skills. These are shown in table 2.

The emerging picture is that of an extremely bright producer who has been promoted based on the quality of her individual contributions but who lacks some fundamental skills in fostering a collaborative work environment. Most striking is her apparent insensitivity to how other people feel. She seems to lack emotional connectedness, which may explain her apparent (this word is also used in the previous sentence) lack of skill in handling conflict. She may simply be unaware that conflict is occurring or that emotional issues are derailing or could derail the group's

LEADERSHIP DIMENSION	RESPONDENTS	LEADER (SELF)
Being aware of emotions. Is very perceptive about people's feelings and is responsive to the group's mood.	79	91
Handling conflict effectively. Intervenes quickly and effectively when conflict arises and is able to resolve interpersonal conflicts so people can work together well.	82	99
Coaching. Demonstrates his or her commitment to developing people by investing his or her time in their development and coaching or mentoring them regularly.	84	95
Building community. Fosters a strong sense of community in the group or organization; helps people feel that they belong.	85	102
Expressing curiosity. Is curious about how others think and feel; asks for their opinions and attends to their attitudes and perspectives.	87	105
Having a positive attitude. Creates positive attitudes in others and sets a positive tone for the quality of interpersonal relationships in the group or organization.	89	98

Table 2   Nicola's Low-Scoring Behaviors

effectiveness. This may not have mattered in her previous positions, or her skills in other areas may have convinced people to overlook her lack of skill with people. However, in her new position, she will need to be much more perceptive about people and much better at building effective teams. The narrative comments some respondents wrote in her LLA offer further clues:

- *Needs to learn to delegate and have some confidence in the people who work for her. In many cases, she has given me the impression that she feels she is the only person capable of doing something correctly.*

- *Needs to learn how to listen. She will ask for one's opinion about something, but if her mind has been made up at this point, it will not change. Why bother asking?*

- *More sensitive to feelings of subordinates . . . downright rude at times.*

- *Develop middle management into a more cohesive team.*

- *Less emphasis placed on control and more on teamwork.*

- *She seems aloof and distant sometimes. And meetings come to an abrupt end when she's gone through her agenda, even if there is more to talk about.*

- *Learn to trust her direct reports. We have excellent skills and could make her life easier.*

These comments from her previous direct reports suggest that teamwork was an issue for them as well. Some additional issues have surfaced (listening, delegating, projecting trust and confidence), and the underlying themes of disconnectedness and insensitivity to others are reinforced.

Nicola's Interpersonal Skills Assessment

The second 360-degree instrument Nicola completed was the Lore International Institute's (2000) *Survey of Influence Effectiveness* (SIE), an interpersonal skills survey that assesses how well people influence others. Nicola's SIE report revealed that she relies primarily on two tactics, logical persuasion and stating, to influence others. The influence tactics she uses far less frequently include appealing to values, socializing, alliance building, and consulting (asking others for their opinions). The skills portion of this survey yielded predictable results. She was rated highest on *asserting, persisting, behaving self-confidently, logical reasoning, finding creative alternatives,* and *negotiating;* she scored lowest on *showing genuine interest in others, building rapport and trust, having insight into what others value, being friendly and sociable with strangers,* and *sensitivity to others' feelings and needs.* Interestingly, in the "power sources" section, she rated herself significantly low on *attraction,* which is defined as "being open and approachable, available when others need you, and being able to make friends easily."

Nicola's profile suggested someone who is logical and driven but who lacks some basic social skills and sees herself as essentially isolated. A therapist might speculate about why that is the case, but her coach was principally interested in understanding what she really needed to function more effectively in her new role. The final pieces of the puzzle had not yet come together, but another interesting piece was her MBTI profile, which showed that her preferred operating style is INTJ (Introversion, Intuition, Thinking, and Judging). We won't explain the entire MBTI construct here, but we will note that INTJs are the most independent of all the sixteen types. They tend to be very analytical, to behave confidently and forcefully, to make independent judgments, and to live in a conceptual world. Very task focused, they can easily overlook others and may keep important ideas and decisions to themselves far too long.

Debriefing Nicola on Her Assessments

It goes without saying that the patterns revealed in these three assessment and survey tools are consistent. They show an accomplished, strong-willed executive and an independent thinker who has probably made significant intellectual contributions to her company but who lacks some key people skills. Given the demands of her new position, she is likely to hit a career-limiting wall unless she figures out how to be more sensitive to people and to work with them in a way that fulfills their needs. At least those were our coach's hypotheses after reviewing the data and meeting with Nicola. During that meeting, he added his own observations and got Nicola's perspective. Here is a part of the dialogue that occurred after the coach and Nicola had reviewed the findings from the survey instruments:

COACH   So what do you conclude from the feedback?

NICOLA   It's pretty consistent with what I've heard before. But there were a few surprises.

COACH   Like what?

NICOLA   Like the comment that I was rude.

COACH   You don't recall ever acting that way?

NICOLA   (shaking her head) I guess I don't know what that means. I do my job. I'm good at it. I don't mean to ruffle anyone's feathers while I'm doing it, but there's only so much time to observe the niceties.

COACH You seem like you're very task focused. [a synthesizing observation]

NICOLA I am.

COACH (pausing; observing; letting her think about it) [Sometimes the best coaching technique is silence; while clients are thinking, they are working, and it's best not to disturb them.]

NICOLA I keep hearing that so-and-so had a birthday, or Marcia got married last week and why didn't I congratulate her. Nobody tells me about these things, so it's hard to stay on top of all the social events.

COACH They probably don't think you're interested.

NICOLA Well, I am and I'm not. I've got a family. I care about these things, but work is work. When you come to work, you leave that stuff at home.

COACH Do you notice when someone at work isn't acting normally? [This is really the crucial question: Does she have any degree of social awareness?]

NICOLA What do you mean?

COACH Oh, when someone seems subdued or preoccupied? When someone who's normally a hard worker seems distracted? Or when two people are sharp with each other?

NICOLA Not normally. Oh, sometimes, sure. But . . .

COACH But what?

NICOLA I just ignore it. They need to get over whatever's bothering them and get on with their work.

COACH So I'm hearing that you do notice when people are out of sorts or moody, but you choose to ignore it. [reflecting back what he's heard as a way of reinforcing the conclusion she's reached]

NICOLA Usually, yes. Well, not usually. Most of the time. I just don't want to deal with it.

COACH	You know, some of the comments on your feedback describe you as being insensitive to others, and your lowest-rated score on the LLA was on "being aware of emotions." That's what you're demonstrating to me now. [sharing what he observes in the moment]
NICOLA	(frustrated) Okay, but how important is that, really?
COACH	It seems important to the people who responded to your assessment. (pause) Let me ask you this. We agree that in your new position it's going to be crucial for you to build effective, smoothly functioning teams, right? [responding to her question about how important this issue is]
NICOLA	(nodding)
COACH	Well, teams are about people. Are you going to be able to build effective teams by ignoring the people in them and focusing only on the tasks? [Implication questions like this one are powerful challenging tools.]
NICOLA	No, clearly not.
COACH	Then learning to become more sensitive to people is a critical issue for you.
NICOLA	(frustrated) So it would seem.
COACH	Well, let me put it this way. If you aren't able to improve your people skills and build high-performing teams, will you succeed in your new job? [a follow-up implication question]
NICOLA	No.
COACH	(pausing, noting her hesitation) What?
NICOLA	I just don't know how to do that. I've never been a "people person," whatever that means, and I'm too old to become someone I'm not.
COACH	I think in anyone's dictionary this would be called a dilemma, and you seem frustrated by it. [showing empathy] I don't know that you need to become a people person or that you should even try to be someone you're not. That would be inauthentic and is not sustainable or satisfying in

the long run. [challenging her assumption that she has to become someone she isn't]

NICOLA   Absolutely not.

COACH   Maybe you just need to exercise some muscles that have been dormant a long time.

NICOLA   What do you mean?

COACH   You said yourself that you notice when people are moody or out of sorts. You ignore it, so you aren't using what I'll call your "sensitivity muscle." But clearly you have this muscle or you wouldn't notice in the first place. Maybe being sensitive to others is more of a choice than a skill. Would it be useful to work on that?

NICOLA   Yes.

Nicola, it turned out, was virtually a poster child for the professional person with highly developed cognitive intelligence and relatively low emotional intelligence. In his book *Emotional Intelligence,* Daniel Goleman (1995) (whose book, by the way, along with his subsequent books on emotional intelligence, should be required reading for all coaches) describes a number of people like Nicola. Her need is not a seminar on team building, which would not address her real issues. Her real need is to build better people skills, which for her will mean developing greater awareness of others, becoming more politically aware, building bonds with others, learning how to foster cooperation and collaboration, and becoming more emotionally aware herself. In short, she needs to be more emotionally intelligent, and this is something she can learn, although it won't be easy for her.

What we have tried to illustrate with this case is how a coach triangulates from multiple sources of data to understand a client's real needs. Inexperienced coaches tend to focus on surface issues. In this case, an inexperienced coach might have concluded that Nicola needed instruction on team building (maybe by attending a class on it) and that she needed to become a better listener. One can imagine such coaches saying to Nicola, "Here are some tips on better listening." But these are surface issues and do not address the fundamental problem, which is that Nicola is choosing to be insensitive to people. A therapist might want to probe deeper into Nicola's psyche to understand what in her childhood led her to be so task driven and insensitive to others, but coaches should not follow that path unless they are therapists themselves and are trained to do so. Even then, the focus of coaching is different. A coach is less concerned about the subterranean roots of a problem than about how to help clients resolve the problem by reflecting on and changing their behavior. A coach, having surfaced the real problem, then says, "Okay, now what do we do about it?"

Nicola's case illustrates several important points about finding the real needs. First, having multiple data points is essential. As you triangulate from different perspectives, themes and patterns emerge. You hypothesize from these patterns and themes. Then you look at other data points to see if your hypothesis is confirmed or not. Throughout the process, you seek those crucial moments of insight that enable you to glimpse what the real problem might be. In Nicola's case, one such moment occurred when the coach read this respondent comment from the LLA: "And meetings come to an abrupt end when she's gone through her agenda, even if there is more to talk about." This comment told the coach that Nicola is highly task driven and that other people's needs are low on her radar screen. He hasn't asked her about this comment yet, but he will remember it and use it at the appropriate time to help her become more aware of other people's needs. Some of his coaching help may come down to advice, such as suggesting that before she ends meetings she ask if there are any other issues. However, Nicola is unlikely to achieve real growth until she learns to be more sensitive to others' feelings and needs—and more aware of her own.

JOHN W. NEEDS MORE BALANCE

John W.'s presenting problem was that he needed more balance in his life. He was working too many weekends and evenings, and it was starting to affect his family. He worked the long hours, he said, because he loved what he was doing. Now and then, he had tried to cut back on his work hours and stay home more, but inevitably a crisis occurred that kept him at the office, or a new project started that required his guiding hand, or an important customer would be in town, or whatever. He sought a coach to help him figure out how to achieve more work-life balance.

The feedback from a 360-degree survey showed that John was well respected by his boss, peers, and direct reports. He was known as a dependable, hard-working, high performer. Everyone—from his boss to his mother—had told him to slow down and spend more time at home. People worried about John burning out, but it never seemed to happen. He had heard all the advice and was aware of the potential consequences if he didn't slow down, but nothing had moved him to change. Knowing this, his coach's opening question conveyed some genuine puzzlement:

COACH Why are you coming to me now? [A great question to ask— What's different? Why now? What has made this coaching more urgent for you?]

JOHN I don't understand.

COACH Well, people have been telling you for years that you should slow down and spend more time at home, but you haven't done that. I doubt that you need to hear that advice again. Has something changed?

JOHN You mean, has my wife threatened to leave me, or something like that?

COACH (nodding) Something like that.

JOHN No. I just can't keep this up.

COACH All evidence to the contrary. You seem to have incredible energy and a real love for what you're doing. [Confronting clients like this is a valuable coaching technique, especially when they say something that seems self-deceiving or contrary to reality.]

JOHN I do, but I'm worried about sustaining this pace and realizing one day that I've missed out on a lot because I've been so focused on my work.

COACH You want to smell the roses before they're gone.

JOHN That's right.

COACH I'm curious about something. It sounds like a lot of people have advised you to slow down and find more work-life balance, but you haven't heeded their advice. Why not? [first why]

JOHN Well, I've tried to, but then something happens and I'm pulled back in.

COACH Why are you pulled back in? [second why]

JOHN	In a lot of cases, I'm the best person to handle the problem, and it's my area. I'm responsible.
COACH	Is someone else pulling you back in or are you doing it yourself?
JOHN	Usually it's me.
COACH	And you're pulling yourself back in because you are the best person to handle all of these problems? Are you the only person who can handle them?
JOHN	No, certainly not. We have a very capable group.
COACH	So you are choosing to handle them yourself even though you have other capable people who could do it. Why? [third why]
JOHN	That's the million-dollar question.
COACH	I don't have that much in my wallet, but I'd still like to know the answer.
JOHN	Why do I choose to do it myself? (reflecting) I guess because I want the outcome to be perfect.
COACH	Why? [fourth why]
JOHN	I have very high standards. I want everything leaving my unit to be top-notch.
COACH	And you can't trust the people in your unit to do top-notch work?
JOHN	No, that's not fair. They do a great job.
COACH	So you choose to do the work yourself, even though it takes you away from your home and family, not because only you can make it perfect, but for some other reason.
JOHN	Yes.
COACH	What? [fifth why, in a different form]
JOHN	(pausing to reflect) I don't know. I think it just boils down to the fact that I like the work. I never get tired of it. You know? I like the action.
COACH	Sounds really satisfying.

JOHN	It is.
COACH	Then what's the problem? [sixth why, another form of the question]
JOHN	I don't know. When I really think about it, I don't have a problem. I'm doing fine. Everyone else keeps telling me I have to slow down.
COACH	So it sounds like the real issue is figuring out how to help other people in your life understand and accept your choices.
JOHN	I think you're right.
COACH	Before we move on, let me just test one thing. You said earlier that you were worried about waking up one day and realizing that you had missed a lot. What are you afraid of missing?
JOHN	You know, at this point, I'm not sure.
COACH	Would it be worth thinking about as we work together?
JOHN	Yes, but at this point I'm clueless, frankly. I mean, yes, I'd like to spend more time with my wife and kids—not that I don't spend time with them now. My family isn't complaining. But I don't see every soccer game or go to every school event.
COACH	And that's okay?
JOHN	It's okay with me. My wife enjoys that stuff, but I can only handle so much of it. And my kids don't seem to care one way or another.
COACH	You have good relationships with them?
JOHN	Oh yeah. Great.
COACH	Okay, so what would be most helpful to you at this point? [This question is a great general question for coaches to ask. Use it often.]
JOHN	I'd like to spend more time talking through my priorities and then figure out how to help everybody be okay with that. Or what to do about it if they're not.

This work with John illustrates another coaching technique for surfacing the real needs—the technique of the *five why's*. Its origins are in the quality assurance movement, and we've heard it hails from Japan, but that may be apocryphal. The point of the technique is to keep asking why until you arrive at the root cause. Children, with their boundless curiosity, seem to use this technique naturally, as anyone with a two-year-old at home knows. *Why, mommy? Because. But why? Because I told you so. Why?* And so on, until mommy is forced to admit that she doesn't know why. Being as curious as a two-year-old about why clients behave as they do is one of a good coach's greatest gifts. Boundless curiosity helps both coaches and clients drill down until they reach bedrock. Table 3 summarizes the techniques we have discussed in this chapter that help coaches surface their clients' real needs.

THE TEN RED FLAGS

Now and then coaches encounter the kinds of needs that cannot and should not be dealt with through coaching. When the behavioral problems are serious enough, only trained therapists or psychologists should be involved. But this begs the question: How can coaches who are not trained psychologists recognize when serious psychological problems are present? They may not know it when they see it. The answer, we believe, is that coaches should learn how to recognize problem behaviors so they know when to refer clients to a therapist. The worst case, as Steven Berglas (2002) rightly argues in "The Very Real Dangers of Executive Coaching," is for unqualified coaches to either ignore serious psychological problems or try to handle them without having the proper training. To help coaches recognize referable behaviors, we suggest they look for the following ten behavioral red flags. Our red flags are based on our experiences as coaches but also on the American Psychiatric Association's (1994) *Diagnostic and Statistical Manual of Mental Disorders*, 4th edition [DSM-IV], the bible for clinical diagnosis of psychological problems.

1. The client has low affect (i.e., does not demonstrate emotional highs or lows); the person's expressive range is very narrow; he seems to be chronically depressed, is profoundly unhappy, or has a sense of hopelessness. (indicates depression)

TECHNIQUE	QUESTIONS OR STATEMENTS
Exploring Context	Is this true in every part of your life? If not, what's different? Has this always been true? If not, why not?
Questioning	Why do you think that is?
Empathizing	That sounds frustrating. You seem troubled by that. You look pleased.
Making Connections and Synthesizing	You are always dotting the *i*'s and crossing the *t*'s.
The Five Why's	Why? Why? Why? Why? Why?
Trusting Silence	After asking a great question, wait at least 15 seconds for the client to respond before speaking again.
Reflecting; Paraphrasing	You said yourself that you notice when people are moody or out of sorts.
Identifying Contradictions	All evidence to the contrary. You seem to have incredible energy and a real love for what you are doing.
Returning Later to Issues	Earlier, you mentioned [topic]. Tell me more about that.

Table 3   Coaching Techniques for Discovering Clients' Real Needs

2. The client is excessively dependent on others, is incapacitated without the constant approval of others, fears being rejected by others, fears being abandoned, and has low self-regard. (dependent personality)

3. The client's life is very chaotic; she cannot seem to get it under control. Or the client has extreme emotional highs and lows, is moody and unpredictable. (manic depression)

4. The client has a pattern of unstable relationships with others; behaves impulsively; and alternates unpredictably between feelings of boredom, anxiety, anger, and depression. (borderline personality)

5. The client's beliefs are not consistent with reality, such as hearing voices or seeing things that aren't there. (may indicate schizophrenia)

6. The client does not trust others, is reluctant to confide because the information could be used against him, or is unreasonably suspicious of others' motives or actions. (paranoia)

7. The client is persistently angry or aggressive and shows no concern for the welfare of others. (antisocial personality)

8. The client expresses thoughts about suicide or has other self-destructive impulses or behaviors. (suicidal tendencies)

9. The client is very egocentric and seems to care about no one but herself, displaying grandiose self-importance. In addition, this person may be clever, articulate, and extremely manipulative. (narcissism/psychopathic personality)

10. The client says to you something like, "You are the only person who cares about me." There are similar or other inappropriate expressions of love toward or interest in you. Or there are frequent comparisons of you with someone else in the client's life toward whom he has a strong positive or negative reaction. (transference)

These kinds of behaviors indicate the potential for serious psychological problems and are not within the purview of coaching. Only certified mental health professionals and physicians should handle them. Having said that, we should add that in our many years of coaching, we have not experienced these kinds of problems with any regularity except for depression and narcissism, the latter of which can cause a client to be uncoachable, as we describe in the coachability chart later in this chapter.

COACHABILITY

As we are assessing clients' real needs, we should also assess how coachable they are. The plain fact is that not everyone can be coached, and both the coach and the client should know that up front. A number of factors affect a client's coachability, including the following.

- The client's ego strength (sense of self, pride, humility versus arrogance)

- The client's feelings of vulnerability—the more vulnerable the person feels, the greater the ego defenses are likely to become and the less coachable he or she may be

- Openness to feedback (the client's willingness to hear and accept messages that disconfirm his or her self-image)

- The client's self-assessment of need, along with a sense of urgency; also, extrinsic indicators of the need for change—such as poor performance numbers, the results of 360-degree feedback, observations from others

- The client's perception of the value of the process and the likely outcomes

- The client's trust in the coach

- The client's experience with coaching (favorable, neutral, or unfavorable)

- The client's awareness of the need for change

- The client's fear of consequences if he or she does not seek and accept help; the executive's excitement about the positive outcomes if he or she does change; in short, risk versus reward

- The client's responsiveness to extrinsic pressure (from boss, peers or subordinates, the environment)

- Finally, the presence or absence of serious psychological problems

These factors combine in complex ways to determine how willingly a client enters into a coaching relationship and how motivated the client is to change. Helping clients change is the principal purpose of coaching, so it's important to know at the outset of coaching how coachable a client is. To help coaches assess coachability, we have developed a framework that includes seven levels of coachability—from C0 to C6. Our scale reflects the degree of difficulty in coaching a particular client. The lower the number, the less coachable the client is likely to be. Table 4 describes each of these coachability levels, the behaviors normally observed, and the requirements for change (which can help coaches determine the right approach to the client).

Coaches should make a coachability determination early in the coaching process. Clients who seek coaching are generally more coachable

COACHABILITY LEVEL	BEHAVIORAL DESCRIPTORS	OBSERVED BEHAVIORS	REQUIREMENTS FOR CHANGE
C0 (not coachable at present)	Identified psychological or medical problem, such as depression, border-line personality disorder, obsessive-compulsive disorder, chronic substance abuse, and schizophrenia. Dysfunctional behavior resists typical coaching. Normal functioning is impaired beyond the scope of a coaching intervention.	Stressful life events have recently occurred. Is inattentive or easily distracted. Anger is poorly managed or inappropriately expressed. Appointments are missed or canceled. Decisions are avoided or made too quickly. Typical activity level is lowered or inconsistent. Has very little affect (emotional range is narrow). Direct reports express a high level of dissatisfaction with behavior and leadership.	Needs help from a trained clinician; coaching is not the appropriate relationship for the change needed. Coaching may need to be revisited at a later time or when more normal functioning is restored.
C1 (extremely low coachability)	Narcissistic personality. Is strongly independent; may have an arrogant/over-bearing manner; sees no need to change; will not admit to serious weak-nesses or areas for improvement; feels invulnerable. May be antagonistic or hostile toward the coaching process and the coach; may lobby against the coaching program, labeling it wasteful and unnecessary.	Exhibits impatience; is easily frustrated. Works alone. Doesn't invite feedback or participation. Doesn't listen or respond empathically to others. Shows up late for appointments. Closed to new learning and shows no interest in change or new experiences. Interrupts during conversations. Expresses a strong need to be right. Direct reports express detachment, complacency, hopelessness, or low expectation of change. Turnover may be higher than expected.	Is often unresponsive, even to the strongest threats or potential consequences; may leave the organization and blame others rather than "submit" to change; may change only in response to a significant, dislocating life or work event (divorce, death of a loved one, loss of a job, failure to be promoted, etc.). May need more time and effort to engage in coaching than most organizations are willing to give. May accept consultation from an "expert."

Table 4 Coachability

COACHABILITY LEVEL	BEHAVIORAL DESCRIPTORS	OBSERVED BEHAVIORS	REQUIREMENTS FOR CHANGE
C2 (very low coachability)	Resists or deflects feedback; uses defenses to deal with reported "flaws," weaknesses, or development needs; for example, explains away issues or offers rationale for negative perceptions. May behave indifferently toward the coaching process, but puts no effort into creating or executing an action plan. Tends to be negative toward the coaching process, saying that it is not helpful.	Demonstrates a lack of self-knowledge in interactions with others. Uses a variety of defenses to avoid change. May behave as though feedback is criticism. May act in an indirect way rather than confront an issue openly. Reports express fearfulness and lack of two-way communication. During coaching, may try to dominate the discussion or otherwise seek to deflect the focus away from feedback and coaching needs.	Needs strong extrinsic motivation (rewards or threats), typically not from the coach. Must be faced with the consequences of inaction or lack of commitment. The coach must be extremely candid; must have development plan closely linked to performance measures, and progress should be tracked by coach *and* boss, with frequent periodic reviews.
C3 (fair coachability)	Is complacent and unmotivated to change; feels that personal performance and business results are fine. Considers this coaching process another fad (it will pass). May pay lip service to change but is not really committed to it and will make only token efforts to execute the action plan.	Behavior is geared toward maintaining the status quo. Comfortable behaviors are repeated. Unable to identify any needed areas of change. Behavior is consistent, but low risk. Reports express lack of challenge or creativity. May acknowledge some change needs but has no sense of urgency. May accept coach's suggestions but show no real commitment to change.	Typically, must be shocked out of complacency through the implications of not changing; best motivator is an alteration of the conditions that led to complacency; may respond to authority. Can be deceptive with coach by appearing to agree to change but with no real commitment; individual feedback comments are often more powerful than feedback scores.

Table 4 Coachability (continued)

COACHABILITY LEVEL	BEHAVIORAL DESCRIPTORS	OBSERVED BEHAVIORS	REQUIREMENTS FOR CHANGE
C4 (good coachability)	Prior to the assessment, saw no need for change. Accepts some feedback; did not initially see the value of the 360° process but acknowledges that it gave an accurate picture; may not be certain how to proceed to learn effectively. Demonstrates some resistance to the coaching process, but has a growing awareness of the need for change; urgency depends on the implications of not changing.	Demonstrates adequate performance. Behavior is consistent, but there is more potential. Demonstrates adequate to good problem-solving and interpersonal skills. Responds to logical and factual presentations, but behavior may lack consideration of emotional input.	Will respond to strong feedback and an assertive but helpful coach; walk carefully through the 360° results and build buttoned-up development plan; tie coaching process concretely to performance metrics and monitor closely. Needs to see concrete benefits of change and is likely to support the process and stick with it if early results demonstrate those benefits.
C5 (very good coachability)	Accepts feedback and shows an earnest desire to improve; sees the value of the 360° process; is busy but feels that self-development is important and will find a way; initially may not be enthusiastic about coaching but becomes committed to it as the benefits become clear.	Demonstrates talent. May lack work-life balance in behavior. Demonstrates competitive behavior. Work skills are solid, with specific needs for improvement evident. May have behaviors that promote a sense of unavailability. Reports express satisfaction, but may have more potential than is demonstrated currently.	Will be intrinsically motivated once the picture is clear; coach should primarily use questions to help discover acceptable trade-offs. Change may be inadvertently derailed by day-to-day business, so monitor and provide continuous feedback and reinforcement.

Table 4 Coachability (continued)

COACHABILITY LEVEL	BEHAVIORAL DESCRIPTORS	OBSERVED BEHAVIORS	REQUIREMENTS FOR CHANGE
C6 (excellent coachability)	Has an intrinsic need to grow; has been a lifelong learner; personal history shows evidence of self-directed learning; strong achievement motivation. Sees 360° feedback as intrinsically valuable and seeks it beyond the coaching program; is widely read and can cite favorite books on leadership, development, and related areas. Is often modest and has a realistic sense of self.	Demonstrates high potential in behavior. Demonstrated skills are above average with many strengths. Expresses need for new challenges and learning. Places a high value on performance and growth. Challenges others and holds high expectations for achievement. Keeps schedules and commitments. May not readily exhibit the effects of stress. May have difficulty understanding and motivating those who are different in style. Reports express respect for leadership, feel challenged and want even more.	Is likely to be self-directed, so monitor loosely, act as a sounding board, provide resources and ideas; ask client to share other feedback he/she is receiving; inquire about client's next steps and ongoing development plans. May respond best to facilitative approach.

Table 4 Coachability (continued)

because they are more motivated to seek help and feel a more urgent need to change. When clients have not sought coaching, however, a low degree of coachability can hamstring the process to the point of making it worthless. So coachability is no trivial matter. We also advocate that coaches share their coachability determination with their clients (except for C0), especially if the coachability is C1, C2, or C3. If you don't think a client is coachable, it is best to be transparent about that and discuss it with the client. If the client disagrees with your assessment, then you have a fruitful area for dialogue. If the client agrees, then you may both want to consider whether the likely outcomes of coaching are worth the investment of time and energy. We have known coaches who view low coachability as a challenge, but we've also noted how frustrated they are by the lack of progress. Coaching is about helping people change, and if they don't want to change, don't like the message, or don't believe they need to change, then trying to force them to endure coaching is a bit like trying to push cooked spaghetti across a table—and keep each piece in a straight line. You are unlikely to succeed, and the process and the result are likely to be messy.

5

Adapting to Clients' Preferences

To be more effective as a coach, realize that each person has specific skill sets and tailor the coaching to each person's needs.

Know your audience. People are at different places in their lives. You should determine where they are and not use a cookie-cutter approach to coaching. For some people, the "rah-rah" approach is best, but others need personal reflection.

If appropriate, hold back your advice and focus on helping coachees find their own options and make their own plans.

SUGGESTIONS TO COACHES FROM THE "COACHING EFFECTIVENESS SURVEY,"
LORE INTERNATIONAL INSTITUTE, INC.

Megan Jones is a department manager for a large insurance company. She manages a group of two hundred people and has nine direct reports. Megan is fifty-seven and has been working in this industry for more than thirty years. She is considered one of the most knowledgeable people in the company in her functional area. When she coaches her direct reports, she usually observes them, gives them feedback on the specific things she's noticed, and offers advice based on her many years of experience. She feels that their careers and personal lives are their own business, so she confines her coaching to matters related to their performance. Megan is capable of coaching differently, but this is the approach she prefers. We would call her coaching style *directive, circumstantial,* and *specific.* She coaches the way a typical manager coaches subordinates.

In contrast, Rolf Petersen prefers a *nondirective* style. Like Megan, he is a department manager and is very experienced and knowledgeable in his industry. But when he coaches people, he prefers to ask how they feel about their performance, what they conclude from the outcomes, and what they would like to do differently. He is considered a mentor by a number of younger people, and he coaches them regularly, about once every other month. He prefers to meet them for lunch or to talk casually after work, and he tries to help them think through a broad range of issues—from what assignments to seek and what training courses to take to how to think about their careers and, in some cases, how to resolve personal problems. Rolf believes that building their job skills won't be enough for them to succeed; they also need to mature as professionals, understand themselves better, and become leaders in their own right. Because he coaches people regularly and focuses on the whole person, not just the person's job skills, we would call his coaching style *nondirective, programmatic,* and *holistic.* He acts more like a counselor than a manager.

Both Megan's and Rolf's approaches to coaching are appropriate for some clients and inappropriate for others—and indeed this is one of the major themes of this book. In coaching, one size does not fit all. Some clients want a wise elder to advise them; others want a more collegial coach who will listen to them and ask the right questions. Some want to benefit from other people's guidance; other clients want to bounce their ideas off someone who is a stimulating thought partner. Though at first glance these distinctions may appear superficial, they have profound implications for how coaches provide help, and if coaches are to be equally helpful to all their clients, they must be adaptive in their approach.

In the first chapter we introduced our coaching styles taxonomy, which has three dimensions: directive versus nondirective, programmatic versus circumstantial, and specific versus holistic. The first dimension—directive/nondirective—reflects **how** coaches prefer to give help. The second dimension reflects **when** coaches prefer to help—during regularly scheduled meetings that constitute a coaching program or circumstantially as needs arise. The third dimension reflects **what** coaches focus on during coaching—specific tasks, skills, or behaviors on the one hand, or the client's overall life and development on the other. Although most coaches are capable of operating on either side of these three dimensions, depending on the circumstances, we have found that coaches usually prefer to use one style of coaching. We have also found that the people being coached have their preferences. Naturally, they are most satisfied with the coaching they receive when they are coached the way they wish to be coached. These three dimensions of coaching form eight distinct coaching styles, on which we will elaborate in this chapter.

How You Prefer to Give Help: Directive Versus Nondirective

Fundamentally, the difference between directive and nondirective coaching, from the coach's perspective, is the difference between telling and asking. This difference reflects a perspective on helping that has to do as much with the coach's assumptions about how people learn as with the client's self-concept and individual needs. Directive coaches believe that they help best by teaching and advising; by sharing their knowledge, experience, and perspective; and by observing others perform and giving feedback and corrective suggestions on what they've observed. In this mode of helping, impetus for change begins with the coach, and the coach's perspective drives the interactions. Nondirective coaches believe that they help best by asking insightful questions and listening; by stimulating their clients to think, reflect, and explore; and by helping clients observe themselves and learn from their own experiences. In the nondirective mode of helping, the impetus for change remains centered in the client, and the client's perspective drives the interactions.

Most coaching involves some combination of both approaches, but coaches generally prefer one approach to the other. Coaches who prefer the directive style have probably internalized this style from their childhood experiences and have learned that this is the right way to help. Coaches who have difficulty engaging in anything but directive coaching usually have a need to impart their knowledge and experience to others as a way of attaining or exercising their expertise. Such coaches are confident in their perspective, believe they are accurate observers of others, and have the authority (moral or positional) to advise others. The underlying assumption about learning is that people need to be guided, motivated, or instructed via sources external to themselves and need to be protected from failure by having the right answer from the start. Directive coaches may also be exercising their authority as managers or may believe that the management function requires or expects managers to coach directively.

Directive Coaching

Directive coaching is seductive. Our memories are filled with larger-than-life figures, often from the sports arena, like Vince Lombardi, Don Shula, or Phil Jackson, who help people perform at their peak or lead their teams to victory. In the popular imagination, anyway, these gruff but wise masters of motivation enable us to do better than we ever thought we were capable of doing. They always seem to know what we need. They see things about us that we can't see. Their confidence inspires us. Their criticism may sting, but it also motivates us to get back on our feet and try even harder. When we grow up, we want to be like them. Their power and their wisdom draw us to them as our idealized models. Beyond its validation by popular culture and mass media, directive coaching may be preferred by many coaches because it satisfies a deep human need to be respected, to be valued for one's knowledge, to be seen as someone whose opinion counts. In short, directive coaching is a form of self-validation and a source of validation by others.

Directive coaches coach from their perspective. They have a viewpoint about us and our performance, and they tell us what that viewpoint is. They observe us performing and tell us what they think, good or bad, about how we're doing and what we could be doing differently. At best, they really are experts in their field. They know more than we do, and we benefit when they share their insights. Some directive coaches are managers or supervisors whose roles dictate that they give direction to those who work for them, and this is how they think they should coach, whether or not they always know what they're talking about. Thus, the fundamental characteristic of directive coaching is that it springs from within the coach. The coach's perspective drives the dialogue with the client. The "arrow of influence" goes essentially one way, from the coach to the client. The directive coach is sharing his knowledge, his perspective, his opinions, his observations. These are conveyed to the client in order to be helpful, but in a purely directive mode; the coach does not solicit the client's views or ask the client to reflect on her own. The flow of knowledge is one way. The coach is the source, and the client is the vessel for receiving the coach's perspective. Directive coaches may ask insightful questions and be good listeners, but their fundamental *modus operandi* is to *direct* us toward the path they think we need to take. If they are right, and we submit to their will, then we may perform better and profit from the experience.

This may sound one-sided—and it is—but we should remember that this is what some clients want. Directive coaching is a perfectly legitimate and appropriate way to coach in some circumstances, as we note below. Clearly, directive coaching can be powerful, and it has a place in human development. It is the most appropriate form of coaching when the coach is much more of an expert in the topic than the client is. You wouldn't want an expert coach to be teaching you how to operate a piece of heavy equipment and say, "How do you think this equipment works?" When the coach is more knowledgeable, the most efficient way to be helpful is to share the knowledge. Likewise, when the situation is hazardous or requires special handling of materials, directive coaching is more appropriate. No one wants novices experimenting in situations in which safety is an issue. Similarly, if there is one and only one way to do something, then directive coaching makes the most sense. Finally, when there is little time for coaching, then directive coaching may be the most efficient way for a coach to provide help.

As these situations suggest, directive coaching is sometimes the most appropriate way to coach, regardless of the coach's or the client's preferences. Telling people how to do something is simply less time consuming than leading them through a process in which they discover the answers for themselves. Directive coaching is appropriate when you are imparting knowledge, explaining how to do something, and showing a client how something works, or when you don't have time to do anything more than very quickly tell the client to do something. Obviously, directive coaching is also the right approach when clients ask for advice and when it is what clients want.

Nondirective Coaching

Coaches who prefer to work nondirectively have often had a significant experience in their childhood or young adulthood with a nondirective coach whose approach had a profound effect on them. As a consequence, they hold a more egalitarian view of themselves as members of society in which they have no special right or privilege to advise others. Or, they may resist telling others based in a belief that they can never fully understand the nuances of another person's situation and thus can never really provide trustworthy advice or instruction. At most, they can advance highly qualified suggestions or alternatives that the client must weigh independently to reach his or her decisions. This style of coaching can sometimes look as if the coach lacks the confidence to advise someone else, but the reality is usually quite the opposite: nondirective coaches must exercise considerable self-restraint against telling their clients what to do (particularly when they are reasonably sure they know), and they exercise great patience born of confidence in the other person that he or she will find the right path with the proper support and subtle guidance to evaluate alternatives for themselves. Thus, nondirective coaches have learned to help others by helping them to help themselves. Such coaches view themselves as managers or leaders more in the servant leadership mode.

Nondirective coaches don't have the glamour associated with directive coaches; in fact, by design they choose to work with subtlety and near invisibility as their influence fades into the choices they help their clients make. As a result we have fewer models of nondirective coaching embedded in our collective psyche. Nondirective coaches prefer to act as counselors and guides. If you prefer to be nondirective, you tend to *ask* rather than *tell*, and you facilitate coaching sessions by soliciting the client's perceptions and ideas, asking probing questions, listening, and counseling by helping clients to explore issues and generate their own solutions. Your fundamental orientation is bilateral. You try to ensure that clients accept ownership for the discovery, problem-solving, and skill-building processes.

Here's one example. When Karen was a freshman in college, she had one of those life-changing encounters with a teacher that characterizes the best in nondirective coaching. She was taking the requisite freshman English course and learned from the student grapevine even before the term began that her teacher was notorious for failing most of her students. So when Mrs. Mackie called her up after class on the second day to discuss the diagnostic essay the class had written the day before, she was sure that her college career was about to end before it even began. Instead, Mrs. Mackie told her that the essay revealed a level of preparation in writing far beyond that of anyone else in the class. What she wanted, Mrs. Mackie said, was for Karen to decide for herself whether each writing assignment was sufficiently challenging, or whether she wanted to do something that would challenge her further.

Karen came up with her own assignments for the rest of the term. Far from giving her a free ride, though, Mrs. Mackie was as tough, if not tougher, in her feedback (and her grades) as she was on the other students in the class. The lessons Karen learned, however, went way beyond becoming a better writer.

What Mrs. Mackie had done was issue an invitation to Karen to re-construct school on her own terms: to set higher standards for herself than were the norm, to do work that was intrinsically interesting to her rather than take the easy way out just to get high grades, to define problems in her own way and to solve them in her own way, to develop the courage to work in the unknown. Although not obvious to Karen at the time, Mrs. Mackie's invitation reflected a philosophy of teaching and a set of values about human development grounded in notions about individual freedom and self-actualization that ran counter to prevailing educational notions anchored in the behaviorism of grading and authority. Equally important, she touched Karen's life at what educators would call a "teachable moment"—a moment when Karen was willing to accept the challenge and to work without a net. Mrs. Mackie was both resource and critic, the knowledgeable guide who helped along the way but didn't map out the journey beforehand.

The two primary skills of nondirective coaching are asking and listening; the basic orientation is one of holding back. The best nondirective coaches have an elegant repertoire of questions and know how to ask the right questions at the right time to evoke insight in the client. This is the real key to success in nondirective coaching. Questions that merely elicit facts are not particularly insightful. Insightful questions are those that provoke the client into questioning why something is the case or what the implications are of various courses of action, or that capture the imagination by getting the client to think of possibilities.

The best nondirective coaches are masters of nuance. They know how to listen with the heart as well as the head, with the eyes as well as the ears. They become so deeply engrossed in the client's narrative that they sense and explore the subtleties that less skilled coaches would miss, and this is where the real power of nondirective coaching comes into play. We can imagine that the client's narrative is like a city street. Coaches who stay on the surface may see some interesting shops along the way, but unless they go underground, to the subway system, they will not understand how things really work. Otherwise, the problem is this: clients already know what is on the street level. If the coach stays there, nothing insightful is likely to happen. Only by exploring the subterranean structure do you provoke greater insight, because clients generally don't go there themselves (although they know it exists).

Another aspect of nondirective coaching that is key is people's desire to be self-sufficient. Clients want to be fully functioning, effective people and they want to be treated that way. All of us want to be capable. For the most part, we want to discover things for ourselves. Our need for self-actualization demands that we exercise our intelligence and achieve on our own merit (rather than being pulled along by some "wiser" person). We think this is why 87 percent of clients we surveyed said they prefer coaches who ask questions rather than "being told what to do." Nondirective coaching appeals to most people's need for self-sufficiency and self-directed growth.

Clients' Perspectives on Directive and Nondirective Coaching

We have been exploring the philosophical and psychological underpinnings of directive and nondirective coaching from the coach's point of view. The client's perspective on these dimensions of coaching is equally revealing. In our research on coaching style preference, we asked clients what their coaches should do to be more effective. Some clients indicated a strong preference for directive coaching:

- *Be more to the point and sometimes more directive.*
- *Be more specific and outspoken about what you want people to do.*
- *Take a more assertive and active role in the coaching process, looking for long-term coachee growth and development.*
- *Assume more leadership and make coaching more explicit.*
- *Give more positive feedback and provide direction.*
- *Be more forceful.*
- *Share experiences that have worked in helping the coach be more successful in his career to help encourage new ideas.*
- *Tell more experiences based on examples while coaching.*

Overall, 39 percent of the thousands of clients we surveyed said that they preferred directive coaching. However, 83 percent of these clients said, "I prefer the coach to ask questions and help me explore the issues myself," while only 17 percent said, "I prefer the coach to tell me what he or she thinks I should do." This suggests that while some clients want an advisor or an expert coach to show them how to do things, most clients nonetheless still prefer that their coach use questions to stimulate them to think about the issues themselves. Indeed, the vast majority of the comments we received in our research indicated a preference for nondirective coaching methods:

- *Ask for self-observation first. Then give your feedback.*

- *Empower the person with a procedural question to find the answer, assisting them, if needed, in finding it.*

- *Ask more open questions and make people think themselves first.*

- *Take time to sit down with people, probe for the understanding of their behavior in a specific situation, and help them see different ways to act in that situation.*

- *Work on becoming more of a probing coach by becoming a "master of the question."*

- *Probe deeper into the individual to better understand how to help.*

- *Solicit the other person's perspective before offering opinions.*

- *Allow me to search and discover the best way to do things, instead of telling me what to do.*

- *Dominate less in discussions.*

- *Ask open and insightful questions that encourage me to explore my ideas further.*

- *Minimize lecture. Not many people are good at just listening.*

- *Allow the people being coached to make the final decision for what they need to do and take responsibility for their decisions.*

The irony is that most coaches prefer to coach directively, but most clients prefer to receive help nondirectively. For coaches to move beyond their more "natural" preferences to be directive, they need to come to terms with the philosophical and psychological assumptions beneath the two approaches and try on those that undergird the nondirective approach. Directive and nondirective coaching are not merely different sets of techniques. They reflect very different paradigms about human agency and change, and they demand that coaches approach the task from very different places regarding themselves and others.

WHEN YOU PREFER TO GIVE HELP: PROGRAMMATIC VERSUS CIRCUMSTANTIAL

The second dimension of coaching style involves the frequency and regularity with which you prefer to coach. If you prefer the programmatic approach, you view coaching as an ongoing developmental activity with the people you coach. Programmatic coaches typically see themselves as mentors or long-term counselors. They want to take clients under their wing, so to speak, and guide them over a long period, much as a parent helps a child develop or a master guides the development of an apprentice. Programmatic coaching relationships can extend for months or years. Coach and client meet regularly, and there is a sense that the coach is strongly invested in the client's welfare, growth, and development over the long term. The coach takes the long view and creates a program for helping the client develop continuously. For programmatic coaching to work, both the coach and the client must make a long-term commitment to the process. In contrast, in circumstantial coaching, the coach provides help on the spot, often immediately after the coach observes the client doing something or when the client shows the coach one of her work products and says, "What do you think?" Circumstantial coaches are typically more spontaneous in their coaching. They coach when it occurs to them to coach, when an opportunity presents itself, or when someone asks for coaching or feedback. Circumstantial coaching tends to be much more short term and task focused and is consequently more tactical than strategic.

We've known many coaches like this. Ben James is one. A senior consultant for a major accounting firm, Ben frequently travels with younger consultants and uses travel time in airplanes and rental cars to coach them. His coaching isn't regular, but he rarely misses a chance to give younger consultants advice, give them feedback on something he saw them doing, or inquire about their interests and counsel them on their opportunities with the firm.

Like the differences between directive and nondirective coaching, those between programmatic and circumstantial coaching are more profound than they seem at first. Programmatic coaches commit to the long-term development of the person, so they tend to think long term—where the client needs to be in a year or two and how she is going to get there, how the person learns best, what kind of progress the person is making (or not), and so on. For clients to prefer this style, they must likewise have

a long-term development perspective, which implies that they see themselves as developing continuously. They have a sense of their evolving
possibility, and they want to be more than they are today. They also recognize that getting where they want to go will take time and a commitment to continuing evolution. They don't expect to get there overnight;
in fact they may realize intuitively what developmental psychologists have
discovered over time: that you can't skip stages to get to the end of the line
fast, that in fact there is no end of the line. Development unfolds along a
series of plateaus, with mastery at the next level possible only as a result
of mastery at the previous level. Clients who prefer programmatic coaching expect to make a continuing investment in their own development—
and they may be doing so outside of the coaching as well—with
continuing education classes, self-directed study, and so on.

Clients asking for circumstantial coaching generally know what they
want. For client and coach alike, there is a sense of short-term gratifica-
tion working in circumstantial coaching. The goals are easily specified,
often in concrete, behavioral terms, and the payoffs are generally crisper,
cleaner, and more easily achievable. Circumstantial coaches are adept at
reading the situation quickly, helping the client identify the needed behaviors, and providing the needed support and feedback as the client tries
out new skills. Such coaching takes place as the need arises.

What makes programmatic coaching different is the presence of a
program and, in the coach's mind, a model of development that informs
that program. The coach, for instance, may subscribe to any of a number
of models of adult development: stage models, holistic or incremental
models, cognitive development models, moral or character development
models, leadership models, or behavioral models. (For an extended discussion of the various models of adult development and their implications for executive development, see Karen Spear's [2001] "Understanding
Executive Development.") But effective programmatic coaches maintain
a coherent theoretical perspective that informs the developmental plan
that drives the coaching, and they usually articulate that plan to engage
the client's informed participation. Clients may not know precisely what
they want when they ask for programmatic coaching. The payoffs may
not be well defined or even understood at the beginning of the process.
Developmental models help to establish a framework that makes sense to
the client but also allows the coaching to unfold and the emphasis to
change. With this kind of defining framework, programmatic coaching
tends to be scheduled regularly over a sustained period of time, with even

the busiest clients making a commitment to the discipline of regular meetings.

In our research on coaching style preference, we asked coaching clients to answer the question, "What should your coach do to be a more effective coach?" A number of the suggestions we heard indicated a clear preference for more programmatic coaching.

- *Ensure that coaching is part of an ongoing process of professional development.*

- *Set regularly scheduled meetings with the individual team members, and then hold them sacred!*

- *Establish a set schedule for coaching sessions.*

- *Set aside more specific time for coaching with the people he needs to coach.*

- *In my opinion it is important to view coaching more as a part of a long-term development process, instead of a way to solve specific performance problems.*

- *Do it in a more structured, intentional way—not just as needed for specific projects.*

- *Take a more assertive and active role in the coaching process, looking for long-term coachee growth and development.*

- *Focus more on long-term issues.*

- *Given exceptionally difficult time constraints for coach and myself traveling frequently, a monthly formal coaching meeting could be arranged.*

- *More strategic, less tactical.*

- *More long-term/structural approach to coaching.*

- *Chart out long-term coaching goals and benefits.*

- *I would love for the coaching to be constant and not necessarily when I have a problem. His advice has been so valuable and helpful that the more I get, the more confident I feel.*

- *Develop a professional development plan for all the team members and revisit the plan periodically to make sure the coach and team members are on the right track.*

▣ *Do coaching more regularly. Raise the bar for yourself and for others. Be more aware of your coaching role.*

▣ *Be more proactive in coaching. Coach on a regular basis, without being explicitly asked, and not only on technical skills.*

▣ *Create a long-term plan of action that goes through the following process:*

  ✓ *Highlight areas of improvement.*

  ✓ *Highlight long-term goals—both personal and professional.*

  ✓ *Create a specific plan of action to address the weaknesses and move toward the goals.*

  ✓ *Create a structured mechanism to review the above.*

▣ *Take a more strategic view of long-term growth needs of your team members.*

▣ *Review each team member's goals for development and develop a game plan to get there. We've had discussions, but neither party committed to a real plan.*

▣ *Agree to a coaching approach and schedule with the people to be coached by you. Try to stick to these commitments even in busy times.*

Some coaching clients also expressed a preference for circumstantial coaching. Here are a few of their suggestions to their coaches.

▣ *I would like short talks between the regular sessions. Half a year is too long for feedback linked to specific observations.*

▣ *I would appreciate it if he can increase* unrequested *coaching/ support for my job. I suppose that this can increase the level of professionalism in our daily work.*

▣ *He could concentrate the coaching more at moments when it is needed the most instead of at moments when there is sufficient time.*

▣ *Provide more frequent coaching such as casual, impromptu sessions to let the coachees know when they are doing a good job or also when they have made mistakes.*

Only 22 percent of clients we surveyed prefer circumstantial coaching. They may feel that they don't need much coaching, just a little now and then and at the right moments. They may not have a good programmatic coaching relationship or may not feel the need for programmatic help. However, 78 percent of clients enjoy the sustained attention from a coach and would prefer to receive regular coaching from someone they trust. The research on coaching styles shows that an overwhelming majority of clients would rather be coached programmatically. The problem with circumstantial coaching, they say, is that it can be too infrequent, and it sometimes comes too late to be helpful.

WHAT YOU FOCUS ON WHEN COACHING: SPECIFIC VERSUS HOLISTIC

The last of the three dimensions of coaching style preference concerns what coaches focus on when they coach: specific tasks, skills, or issues (specific) or the whole person (holistic). Specific coaches tend to coach on one behavior or issue at a time and make it the only focus of their coaching. If this is your perspective, you tend to give specific feedback and coach only on the skills related to that feedback. You tend to be short-term focused, and your interest is to improve one skill or issue at a time.

Gordon Fulbright is such a coach. He's a district manager for a nationwide printing company, and he coaches sixteen people on an ongoing basis. He thinks one of his primary roles as a manager is to help people build their skills, so he regularly gives people new assignments and then works closely with them to ensure that they have the skills to succeed. When he thinks they need skill development, he takes the time to work with them, pairs them with more highly skilled people for a period, or sends them to skill-based training programs. He focuses on very specific developmental needs. Like most managers, he sometimes becomes aware of personal problems someone is having, and if those problems impact the person's work, he will get involved. Otherwise, he prefers to keep work and life separate and does not feel he has the right to "impose" himself on people. Nor is it his responsibility to solve their life problems. People sense that he is reluctant to get involved in people's personal lives, so they don't ask him for advice or help in these areas unless it is to request time off for a doctor's appointment or some other urgent life need.

In contrast is Liddy McKay, who takes a more holistic approach to helping people. Holistic coaches like Liddy prefer to coach on broader issues of professional development. People who view coaching holistically believe that coaching serves the larger goal of total personal and professional growth, so they are more likely to focus on the long term and to view the whole person as their coaching domain. Liddy is a branch manager for a brand name merchandiser. She regularly coaches about twenty-five people in her territory, and she views her role as helping them in every way, so when one of her department heads needs help dealing with a family problem, Liddy offers her counsel; and when another of her people wants career counseling, Liddy provides it. Liddy doesn't impose herself on her direct reports or get involved where she hasn't been invited, but everyone knows that she is available to help them work through any issue.

Specific coaching tends to be more behavioral and, as the profile of Gordon Fulbright indicates, it remains bounded by the demands of the job. Specific coaching is more skill based and more tactical. Holistic coaching blurs the line between life at work and life outside work. The two are linked, in the coach's perspective, and they influence each other. As in programmatic coaching, the coach must have an espoused theory about professional life as an integrated part of the client's overall lifestyle. And the client must understand and accept the coach's philosophical position as something that has a ring of truth about it.

The danger of holistic coaching is that it can foster dependence on the coach and even manipulation. Philosophical positions taken in holistic coaching are not value neutral; they come with a certain set of expectations or assumptions about how life "ought" to be lived. Really good coaches are aware of these potential traps. They articulate their values and help clients consider those values self-consciously and take personal responsibility for making their own value decisions.

Despite these dangers, our research on coaching style preferences indicates that the overwhelming majority of clients (85 percent) prefer to receive holistic coaching. Only 15 percent prefer specific, skill-focused coaching. Most of the people who receive coaching want a coach to take a more holistic approach, yet in our research only 51 percent of clients said that their coach "takes a more strategic view of my long-term growth needs" and "focuses on all aspects of my development." Some of the clients who said they wanted more holistic coaching offered these suggestions to their coaches:

▪ *Try to coach more on a general level than on individual technical skills.*

- *I would appreciate more attention to career options and guidance regarding the skills needed to remain competitive as the organization evolves.*

- *Don't just coach on business stuff. It is okay to coach personal stuff, such as family, stress, and attitude.*

- *Look at the total objective—not just the specific issue: How can the coaching improve my overall performance?*

- *Support career development and personal goals.*

- *Focus feedback not only on specific problems but also on overall effectiveness.*

- *Offer more comprehensive overview of performance development versus coaching on a specific area that needs improvement.*

- *Attempt to look at the broader picture.*

- *Don't separate personal topics.*

- *I would like to have more feedback, not only regarding the project but also regarding social skills and competencies.*

- *Coach not only on specific expertise areas but also in overall development.*

- *Try to develop the attitude and skills to coach people on their overall development. In my opinion you tend to focus on the here and now. You miss the opportunity to help people in a broader way with their development.*

Of course, some clients do prefer more focused coaching on specific skills or issues, and these were some of their comments to their coaches.

- *Help to overcome one or two specific weaknesses.*

- *Make coaching more explicit by discussing short-term goals and actions.*

- *Have more frequent dialogue on what's working and what is not working.*

- *Schedule coaching on a regular basis, as a group, on various skills to be developed, such as computer review, selling skills, negotiations, and so on.*

- *Coach on more specific items or tasks.*

- *Occasionally focus more on specific coaching needs than the more general needs.*

- *Offer more time to discuss specific areas where improvement or change is needed to help obtain consideration for special projects.*

- *Keep coaching on a more direct point or points.*

The lesson we draw from our research and the suggestions clients made to their coaches is that while different people prefer either end of the spectrum, specific or holistic, there is a similar mismatch between what coaches do and what clients want. At least half the time, clients want a more holistic coaching experience, while their coaches are providing specific, highly focused coaching. The obvious lesson is that coaches should be more aware of their clients' preferences and should adapt their coaching style and approach accordingly. However, coaches may very well be operating not just in their personal comfort zone but in their professional comfort zone by sticking to more specific coaching. Less obvious, though perhaps more difficult to resolve, is the implication that coaches need considerable education, training, skill, supervision, and certification to be able to offer the kind of holistic coaching that clients so often want.

THE COACHING STYLES TAXONOMY

These three dimensions of coaching style preference form the taxonomy of coaching styles shown in table 5. To help distinguish the eight coaching styles, we have given each of them a label indicating the kind of coaching being provided or received. Following the table of coaching styles are suggestions for coaching the people who prefer each style.

Teacher (DPS)

For clients who prefer teacher coaches, do the following.

- Use the directive process.

- Based on your skills and knowledge of the subject matter area, create a long-term skill development plan for the clients. Be able to show them a sequence of stepwise improvements in performance and be able to demonstrate each skill along the way. Your credibility as a coach depends on your mastery of the skills.

DIRECTIVE

SPECIFIC	HOLISTIC

	SPECIFIC	HOLISTIC
PROGRAMMATIC	**① Teacher** Teacher coaches are experts in their field who coach by instructing, giving feedback, and demonstrating skills. Working from their knowledge and experience, they focus on specific skill-based issues, such as performance skills. They coach on an ongoing basis over an extended period—and their goal is to build a broad but tactical set of skills or knowledge. These coaches often create development programs that lead coachees through a sequence of learning steps over time.	**② Parent** Parent coaches are committed to the long-term development of their coachees. They take a directive approach because of their hierarchical position or superior knowledge base. They may, in fact, know better than their coachees, but their goal is to help coachees achieve equal status and effectiveness. They are prone to giving career advice and take a strong interest in their coachees' growth along many dimensions. They typically coach over an extended period and see their coachees evolve significantly.
CIRCUMSTANTIAL	**③ Manager** Manager coaches are typically busy, coach only in response to a specific need, and focus on the isolated skill or task they think needs improvement. Because they generally have a hierarchical relationship with the people they coach, they favor a directive approach. Their experience and expertise often make them more knowledgeable than coachees, so they tend to make performance observations, give feedback, and set expectations. These coaches expect to see short-term performance improvements.	**④ Philosopher** Philosopher coaches interact with coachees only occasionally, and when they do, they are mainly concerned with the development of the whole person. Their guidance tends to come from a position of superior knowledge, expertise, or moral certitude—though their advice is not necessarily spiritual in nature. They often coach by telling stories or relating experiences from their own lives and hold themselves up as examples to follow. "Words of wisdom" typically come from this type of coach.

Table 5   Coaching Styles Taxonomy

NONDIRECTIVE

	SPECIFIC	HOLISTIC
PROGRAMMATIC	**⑤ Facilitator** Facilitator coaches have a long-term interest in helping coachees develop, and they focus on specific skill-based growth needs. They are often more highly skilled at tasks than coachees are, but they prefer that coachees work through the issues themselves. They see their goal as helping others help themselves, and they tend to refrain from giving advice or exercising authority. Oftentimes, they are team members or peers and may have a mutual coaching relationship with the coachee.	**⑥ Counselor** Counselor coaches take a broad view of their coaching responsibility and strive, through a series of regular interventions, to help coachees develop the full spectrum of their capabilities. They believe in self-development, so they are supportive and encouraging but generally refrain from telling coachees what they should do. They are often not subject matter experts, and they may not be highly skilled in areas where coachees want help. Their role is to guide others in self-discovery.
CIRCUMSTANTIAL	**⑦ Colleague** As the name implies, colleague coaches often have a peer relationship with the coachee, and their preferred mode is to act as a thought partner or sounding board for their coachees. They generally coach only when asked for coaching, and they focus entirely on specific skill-based needs. They may tell coachees how they have done something previously, but they mainly coach by asking questions, listening, and thoughtfully responding to questions in order to help coachees solve the problems themselves.	**⑧ Mentor** Mentor coaches serve as wise advisors. They are generally older and far more experienced than their coaches, and they act as shepherds—gently guiding in the right direction, posing questions that help coachees discover the path for themselves. They are often exemplars—models of the way to live one's life or assume particular responsibilities. They coach infrequently, but because of their stature, their interventions are likely to have great impact.

Table 5   Coaching Styles Taxonomy (continued)

- As these clients are looking for expert guidance and direction, be willing to tell them what to do, but confine your advice to the skills they need to improve.

- Model the skills and explain what you're doing as you do it.

- Give specific, concrete feedback after observing them trying to use a skill. If they've done well, then recognize their success and reinforce the things they did right. If they haven't, offer constructive suggestions and, once again, show them what skilled performance looks like.

- When they have mastered the skills, recognize them in public for their successes.

Parent (DPH)

For clients who prefer parent coaches, do the following.

- Use the directive process.

- Based on your knowledge and experience, create a long-term development program for the clients. Your credibility as a coach depends on their view of you as a wise counselor and guide, so you must be a good role model in every respect. It won't be enough for you to be highly skilled in the areas in which they need development; you must show them the way in every aspect of professional life—from how to do a particular job to how to choose the right opportunities, from how to behave like a professional to how to lead and motivate others.

- These clients are looking for wise counsel, and they may view you as a mentor. Give them direction, but also find ways for them to grow independently and encourage them to find their own way. It probably won't be the path you took, so they must be encouraged to develop their own sense of direction.

- Give honest feedback but try to be encouraging always. And applaud every little success along the way.

Facilitator (NPS)

For clients who prefer facilitator coaches, do the following.

- Use the nondirective process.

- Be sure to devote enough time to the contracting phase. Help them define what coaching they want, when they want it, and how they want to be coached. You may have ideas, but they must always feel in control of the process.

- Ask clients to articulate their long-term growth needs and the specific skills they want to improve. Offer suggestions but let them drive the process.

- Resist the temptation to give advice; instead, ask questions that will help clients identify their skill gaps and discover the right way (for them) to close those gaps.

- Prompt them to set a schedule for the coaching. They will probably want to be coached at intervals over a long period, so ask them to set a schedule that is comfortable for them and acceptable to you.

- Remember that you are, in essence, facilitating a process of self-discovery. So begin meetings by asking what progress they've made and end by asking what they want to achieve by the next meeting. Ask, ask, ask, ask—don't tell.

Counselor (NPH)

For clients who prefer counselor coaches, do the following.

- Use the nondirective process.

- Take a broad view of your coaching responsibilities. Clients who want counselor coaches are seeking self-improvement on many levels, so be prepared to deal not only with job-related problems but also with life and career concerns.

- Be totally supportive and encouraging, forgiving when clients err and enthusiastic when they succeed. You should have an attitude of unconditional positive regard toward clients, and they must always feel that you're on their side.

- Be a resource to clients—help them find the teachers, models, and experts they need. You don't have to be a role model and expert in the field or a master of the skills they are learning.

- Use feedback and observations of their performance to help them learn how they appear to others, and don't be afraid to confront them on tough issues.

Manager (DCS)

For clients who prefer manager coaches, do the following.

- Use the directive process.

- Take a strong lead in shaping the coaching agenda. Clients who prefer manager coaches expect a lot of direction. You should not be overbearing or too controlling, but you should lay out the plan and state the development goals as you see them.

- Find specific events when you can observe clients' performances. Tell them what you will be looking for and give constructive feedback immediately after the event. To help them calibrate their progress, tell them how much better they did than last time you observed them (or say that you don't see any progress) and make concrete suggestions for improving performance from there.

- Tie clients' performances to the performance of the business, unit, section, or other group. Be sure they know how their performance impacts the whole.

- Do progress checks with clients periodically to ensure that they are receiving what they need. Modify your approach if they aren't.

Philosopher (DCH)

For clients who prefer philosopher coaches, do the following.

- Use the directive process.

- Be willing to share your view of what's right and what's wrong. Clients who prefer philosopher coaches are looking for overall guidance and direction. They want a guru who can impart words of wisdom on a variety of subjects.

- Take a holistic view of the clients. Consider not only their job performance but every part of their lives. If you confine your coaching to narrow job concerns, you will not be satisfying their needs.

- Ask questions to stimulate their own thinking and to help them develop their own insights, but they will not be fully nourished unless you also tell them what you think. Use stories and anecdotes to illuminate your ideas and find pithy ways to summarize your points. Clients will want to know "the moral of the story." That's why they came to you.

Colleague (NCS)

For clients who prefer colleague coaches, do the following.

- Use the nondirective process.

- Act like a peer. Clients who prefer colleague coaches don't want a higher authority (even if you are one). They want a peer-like coach who can act as a thought partner or sounding board. They are not looking for wisdom; they want to talk to someone who shares their experiences and can see the problems from their perspective.

- Be sure that your contract with them is clear and not too ambitious. You should be available when they need you, but don't set a regular schedule or have a long-term plan.

- Show a lot of empathy. You must put yourself in their place as you are asking questions and helping them explore the issues. Show that you feel or have felt the same thing they are feeling.

- If appropriate, ask clients for help, too. Mutual coaching is often an excellent way for peers to help themselves develop their skills.

Mentor (NCH)

For clients who prefer mentor coaches, do the following.

- Use the nondirective process.

- Be interested in the people you are coaching and be dedicated to helping them grow as working professionals and human beings. Clients who prefer mentor coaches expect someone who is committed to them as individuals and to their long-term career development, and they are looking for guidance along many dimensions.

- Recognize that each person has to create his or her own path. Guide clients through questions, suggestions, and modeling of the self-discovery processes that you went through in your growth as a professional, but expect them to make their own way.

- Be a resource to your clients. Help them meet the right people and build their networks. Help them uncover the right opportunities for them, learn to exploit their strengths, and mitigate their weaknesses. When you spot something that would be helpful to them, be sure they know about it. Give advice now and then, but guide mainly by helping them see what's necessary and right for them.

In our research on coaching style preferences, we surveyed more than two hundred coaches and several thousand coaching clients. The results indicate interesting disparities between how coaches view themselves (see table 6), how clients view their coaches (see table 7), and how clients prefer to be coached (see table 8).

As table 6 shows, two-thirds of coaches view themselves as either parent coaches (36 percent) or counselors (31 percent). An overwhelming majority of coaches say they prefer to be programmatic (87 percent) and holistic (71 percent) in their approach, while 59 percent believe they use directive coaching. The composite profile, then, of the average coach is that of the parent—directing the coaching, taking a programmatic view of clients' development, and focusing on the whole person. This profile is consistent with the composite view of coaches by clients themselves, although clients tend to see their coaches as slightly more directive (62 percent) and considerably less programmatic (64 percent) and holistic (61 percent).

Most clients want to be coached programmatically and holistically. In fact, according to table 8, nearly 80 percent of clients prefer programmatic coaching, and nearly 90 percent prefer holistic coaching. However, the most dramatic finding in this table is that two-thirds of clients prefer nondirective coaching. They want coaches who are thought partners and counselors rather than advisors and teachers. Most clients don't want to be told what to do; they want to figure it out for themselves through a coach's skillful questioning and listening. Remarkably, 49 percent of the thousands of clients we surveyed told us that they prefer counselor coaching: nondirective, programmatic, and holistic. However, only 22 percent of clients say their coaches coach this way. Clearly, there are some significant mismatches between how coaches prefer to coach and how clients prefer to be coached.

Of course, coaching is really not a numbers game. You can't coach by percentages. No matter what the aggregate numbers look like, coaching is always a personal and individual relationship—one coach and one client at a time. So we present these statistics to demonstrate that there are important differences between how coaches prefer to coach and how clients prefer to be coached. However, the key to effective coaching is to adapt your approach to each client's preferences.

	DIRECTIVE		NONDIRECTIVE	
	SPECIFIC	**HOLISTIC**	**SPECIFIC**	**HOLISTIC**
PROGRAMMATIC	*Teacher* (DPS) 13.60%	*Parent* (DPH) 36.40%	*Facilitator* (NPS) 6.58%	*Counselor* (NPH) 30.70%
CIRCUMSTANTIAL	*Manager* (DCS) 6.14%	*Philosopher* (DCH) 2.63%	*Colleague* (NCS) 2.19%	*Mentor* (NCH) 1.75%

Directive	58.8%	Nondirective	41.2%
Programmatic	87.3%	Circumstantial	12.7%
Specific	28.5%	Holistic	71.5%

Table 6 How Coaches View Themselves

	DIRECTIVE		NONDIRECTIVE	
	SPECIFIC	HOLISTIC	SPECIFIC	HOLISTIC
PROGRAMMATIC	*Teacher* (DPS) 10.25%	*Parent* (DPH) 27.60%	*Facilitator* (NPS) 4.69%	*Counselor* (NPH) 21.97%
CIRCUMSTANTIAL	*Manager* (DCS) 16.01%	*Philosopher* (DCH) 7.84%	*Colleague* (NCS) 7.90%	*Mentor* (NCH) 3.75%

Directive	61.7%	Nondirective	38.3%
Programmatic	64.5%	Circumstantial	35.5%
Specific	38.8%	Holistic	61.2%

Table 7 How Clients View Their Coaches

	DIRECTIVE		NONDIRECTIVE	
	SPECIFIC	HOLISTIC	SPECIFIC	HOLISTIC
PROGRAMMATIC	*Teacher* (DPS) 1.81%	*Parent* (DPH) 24.15%	*Facilitator* (NPS) 2.54%	*Counselor* (NPH) 49.38%
CIRCUMSTANTIAL	*Manager* (DCS) 4.71%	*Philosopher* (DCH) 3.92%	*Colleague* (NCS) 4.50%	*Mentor* (NCH) 8.99%

Directive	34.6%	Nondirective	65.4%
Programmatic	77.9%	Circumstantial	22.1%
Specific	13.6%	Holistic	86.4%

Table 8 How Clients Prefer to Be Coached

Adapting to Clients' Preferences

Although any coaching can be helpful, people benefit most from coaching when they get the type of coaching they prefer. If you are a directive coach, for example, but one of your clients responds best to a nondirective approach, then that's what you should use, regardless of your preference. A good time to discover what type of help a client prefers, obviously, is during the context-setting part of beginning a coaching relationship. At this point, you are explicitly asking what the client wants, and you should explore whether he wants to take a "tell" approach (directive) or an "ask" approach (nondirective); whether he would benefit from a series of scheduled coaching sessions (programmatic) or from occasional, on-the-spot coaching (circumstantial); and whether he wants to focus on particular job skills (specific) or broader career, personal, and professional topics (holistic).

As you work with someone over time, you will discover his preferences in any case. It will become clear to you and your client, for instance, that the two of you need to get together more or less frequently or that you need to focus on a particular key skill or that he responds best and learns more when you ask him questions that help him discover the answers for himself. Coaches who are not paying attention to these factors, however, are usually less effective in the long run because they aren't providing what the client really needs. It probably does not occur to many coaches that they should adapt their style. We've known some who had the attitude that "I am who I am" and if people want help, then "what they see is what they get." Like the guru in the cave at the top of the mountain, these coaches want supplicants to come to them for wisdom. They might benefit some people, but they don't have the kind of helpful attitude that is characteristic of the very best coaches.

The best coaches are like Carol Blum, a data management supervisor for the exploration group of a major oil company. Her preferred style of coaching is facilitator (nondirective-programmatic-specific). However, only a handful of the twenty people she coaches want that approach. Quite a few, like Julia Cortez, prefer directive coaching, so Carol meets with a group of them regularly and teaches them new skills, answers their questions about operational problems, and leads them through brainstorming and problem-solving sessions intended to help them learn more about data management.

Another group of employees, including Mike Girardi, prefers Carol to coach them in the mentor style. Mike likes her nondirective style, but he doesn't approach life programmatically himself, and he couldn't imagine having regularly scheduled meetings. So Carol meets with him whenever he asks for coaching or whenever she's reviewed one of his work products and has some suggestions. When they talk, she always asks how he's doing, how his plans are shaping up, and where he'd like to be in five years. Mike is self-directed on skill building, so that's not what he needs, but he appreciates Carol's willingness to talk to him about more holistic life issues. In her group of twenty, Carol has people with a wide range of coaching preferences. Some prefer a manager coach or a parent coach; others prefer a colleague coach or a counselor coach. What makes Carol so effective is that, as a coach, she is willing to be whatever kind of coach her clients need her to be.

A Self-Test on Coaching Style Preferences

How do you prefer to coach? To conclude this chapter, we include the following simple self-test to help you diagnose your preferred coaching style.

COACHING STYLE PREFERENCES SELF-ASSESSMENT

This is a forced-choice questionnaire. For each pair of statements, indicate which statement best describes how you prefer to coach by circling the corresponding letter in the right-hand column. Though some statements may seem close, force yourself to choose one or the other.

1	I prefer to observe the people I'm coaching, determine what help they need, and then offer suggestions, advice, and feedback.	D
	I prefer to act as a sounding board for the people I'm coaching, asking questions to help them think through their issues and needs and letting them discover the right answers for themselves.	N
2	I prefer to help my coaching clients build specific skills or deal with specific issues.	S
	I prefer to coach people more broadly on their overall development, including career choices and non-work-related issues.	H
3	I prefer to coach people on an ongoing basis—weekly, monthly, or quarterly—and to schedule coaching sessions regularly.	P
	I prefer to coach people only during periodic performance reviews or when the need arises.	C

COACHING STYLE PREFERENCES SELF-ASSESSMENT (CONTINUED)	
4	I prefer to coach by sharing my knowledge, experience, and perspectives with the people I'm coaching and telling them what I think they need to know. In my coaching, I am most like a teacher. **D**
	I prefer to coach by being a good listener and responding thoughtfully to what I hear. In my coaching, I am most like a counselor. **N**
5	I prefer to coach people on every aspect of their personal and professional lives. I am comfortable discussing people's career plans and enjoy helping them think through their options. **S**
	I prefer to coach people on particular performance problems or short-term skill development needs. I am less comfortable discussing people's career plans and don't see myself as a career counselor. **H**
6	I prefer to coach only when something happens that indicates I need to do some coaching. **P**
	I prefer to coach people regularly, as part of a comprehensive program for building their skills and improving their performance. **C**
7	I usually give people feedback on their performance and tell them how I think they are doing, making suggestions as appropriate. **D**
	I usually ask people how they think they are doing and use questions to help them explore their perceptions before I tell them what I think. **N**
8	I am very comfortable discussing people's personal problems and offering my suggestions, where appropriate. **H**
	I am not comfortable discussing people's personal problems and offering my suggestions. **S**
9	I prefer to coach people only when they think they need help, which depends on the circumstances. **C**
	I would rather meet with the people I'm coaching routinely so we can work together continuously on their development plan. **P**
10	I think that as a coach I should refrain from giving people advice. Instead, I should guide them through a process of self-discovery where they learn to solve their own problems and help themselves. **N**
	I think that as a coach I should set the agenda for coaching sessions and give people the kind of help I think they need. That's what they expect from a coach. **D**

COACHING STYLE PREFERENCES SELF-ASSESSMENT (CONTINUED)

11	As a coach, I am most interested in how people develop over time. I try to help them think through where they want to be in a year or two and what it will take for them to get there.	P
	As a coach, I am most interested in helping people solve their immediate problems and learn what they need to learn to be more effective now. I think the long term takes care of itself.	C
12	As I coach, I am most intrigued by someone's overall development as a person, and that may include his or her spiritual and personal growth. I enjoy coaching on a wide range of issues that help the whole person.	H
	As I coach, I am most interested in helping people build their work skills and become more capable in areas directly related to their job.	S
13	I don't have, or would prefer not to have, a personal development plan that defines my developmental needs and indicates how I am going to get there.	C
	I have, or would prefer to have, a personal development plan.	P
14	I don't like it when people won't just speak up and tell me what they think I should do.	D
	I don't like people to give me advice.	N
15	I most admire coaches who are masters of particular tasks, skills, or disciplines.	S
	I most admire coaches whose whole approach to life and work is worth modeling.	H

COACHING STYLE PREFERENCES SELF-ASSESSMENT SCORING

To determine your coaching style preferences, enter the number of times you circled each letter in the spaces below. The letter in each pair that you circled most often indicates your preference in the three dimensions of coaching style.

D (Directive)   _____
N (Nondirective)   _____   Your preference   _____

P (Programmatic) _____
C (Circumstantial) _____   Your preference   _____

S (Specific)   _____
H (Holistic)   _____   Your preference   _____

2

PRACTICING ADAPTIVE COACHING

This part of the book focuses on the skills required to practice adaptive coaching. The six chapters here offer a number of annotated sample dialogues between coaches and clients, as well as questions coaches might ask to further the dialogue and help clients develop insight.

We begin in chapter 6 with a discussion of how coaches can best initiate coaching relationships and open each coaching session. Openings are obviously important because they create first impressions, can build (or destroy) trust, and establish the environment in which the coach and client will work together. Equally important are closings, which we discuss in chapter 11. We believe that effective coaching follows a clear pattern of opening, middle, and closing. To achieve satisfying results throughout a coaching relationship, coaches must manage their openings and closings skillfully.

Coaching of all kinds is done largely through discussions between the coach and the client. We refer to these discussions as the *coaching dialogue,* and in chapter 7 we describe how effective coaches manage the dialogue. The dialogue is a journey of discovery, and the context we spoke about in the first part of the book is the territory in which that journey takes place. Knowing how to manage the dialogue and use it to provoke insight is one of a coach's most important skills. Because the dialogue is a process of discovery, it can lead to areas a coach is not prepared to address, such as serious psychological problems. When this happens, coaches must know how to stop the dialogue and refer clients to professionals who are competent to handle such problems. Responsible coaches know the ethical limits of their work with clients and do not violate those limits.

Chapters 8, 9, and 10 describe the core dialogue skills, including listening and asking questions; sharing your observations with clients, which includes giving feedback, reframing, and reflecting; and pushing clients (advising, teaching, and confronting), as well as pulling them (encouraging and doing process checks). We have used the push/pull metaphor to illuminate the dynamic nature of the coaching dialogue. Mastering the skills described in these chapters is crucial. Without them, coaches cannot sustain an effective dialogue with clients.

6

Initiating
Coaching Sessions

Start coaching at the beginning of the process, not in the middle.

Get to know the person very well, i.e., personal goal setting, how the person becomes motivated best, in order to provide an adequate coaching method.

Keep a clear record of what has been discussed during previous meetings or coaching sessions to chart progress and to revisit specific issues from previous sessions.

SUGGESTIONS TO COACHES FROM THE "COACHING EFFECTIVENESS SURVEY,"
LORE INTERNATIONAL INSTITUTE, INC.

In our research on coaching, we asked coaching clients how effective their coaches were at negotiating expectations up front. Forty-one percent of them agreed with the statement, "My coach is less effective at clarifying my expectations about coaching and making the coaching process explicit." Consequently, a number of clients don't know what to expect, and the coaches don't always know what their clients want and need from coaching. Clearly, it's difficult to meet someone's needs if you don't know what they are, so this step is an important element of the first meeting.

Aristotle's notion that "well begun is halfway done" applies very much to coaching. The coaching relationship, begun at the first meeting of the coach and the client, must start well if real trust is to develop. Because of the fragile nature of trust, rarely are there opportunities to overcome a bad start. In this chapter, we are going to explore what it means to start well: how to initiate a coaching relationship, what you can do prior to the first session with a new client, how to conduct the first session, and how to open subsequent coaching sessions. Our experience as coaches suggests that everything you do in the early stages of coaching is critical to developing a successful coaching relationship.

INITIATING A COACHING RELATIONSHIP

Coaching can be initiated in a variety of ways. Sometimes, clients seek out a coach and ask for coaching. Generally, when they do so they have already thought about who would make the best coach for them, and they approach someone who, they believe, can help them. Other times, coaches are appointed for clients, perhaps by clients' managers or a human resources manager. Sometimes a coaching relationship evolves because one person has been helpful to another and the latter asks for coaching. Coaches can sometimes initiate a coaching relationship when the client has not explicitly asked for it. Although it's possible to simply ask someone if she wants coaching, sometimes it's better not to use the "C" word. Instead of saying, "Would you like coaching?" you might say:

✓ Would you like to spend a moment talking about how else you might have done that?

✓ Would it be helpful to think through your alternatives?

✓ I would be happy to spend some time talking through this issue if you would find that useful.

✓ Would you like some suggestions on how you might deal with this?

Some people don't like to think they are being coached but will welcome the help and respond favorably to these kinds of statements and questions. This works even with very senior executives if they find the potential coach credible. Oftentimes, coaching relationships evolve over time. You do some impromptu coaching for someone and she finds it helpful and later asks if you would be willing to provide more coaching. Such coaching relationships can evolve from nothing to a formal coaching program in a matter of weeks or months.

In some cases, a coaching relationship is assumed, generally in hierarchical organizations. The boss is presumed to be a coach for her subordinates. The team leader is expected to coach the members of his team. In assumptive coaching relationships like these, an authority relationship already exists that can predispose the coach to take a directive approach and predispose the coaching "clients" to accept coaching even if they have a negative or neutral relationship with the coach and don't find that person trustworthy, credible, or compatible. In our view, these are not true coaching relationships but are merely extensions of the supervisory relationship that exists, and the "coaching" is more likely to be direction setting from an authority figure. Managers and supervisors who truly want to act as coaches need to establish coaching relationships that are parallel to the authority relationships they already have. In other words, they may need to step outside their roles as managers to act as coaches. In our experience, some managers are capable of this but many aren't. Further, some clients cannot suspend the reality that their "coach" is still the person who evaluates, promotes, and rewards them in the other role as boss or manager.

Whatever the case may be, for a coaching relationship to form and be sustained, the client must believe that the coach is trustworthy, credible, and compatible—and that there are tangible outcomes to the coaching being provided or a reasonable expectation of such outcomes. Coaching is an intimate relationship between one person who seeks help and another who agrees to provide it. Figure 5 illustrates that without trust, credibility, and compatibility (or chemistry), it's unlikely that clients will agree to be coached or will derive anything from it if the coaching is forced upon them.

Trust and credibility are bedrock fundamentals, but even credible and trustworthy coaches can sometimes strike out with particular clients because of a lack of chemistry. Chemistry is one of those concepts that is difficult to define, although most people know what it means. We like some people and don't like others, often for reasons that are mysterious but may revolve around how much commonality we feel with them and how compatible their values, attitudes, and behaviors are with ours. As people are considering a coaching relationship with us, they invariably subject us to a "chemistry test" by asking themselves the kinds of questions shown in the text box "Checking for the Components of a Good Coaching Relationship" on pages 123–124.

The "fit" question applies to coaches as well. You may be asked to coach someone and decide, for whatever reason, that this is not someone

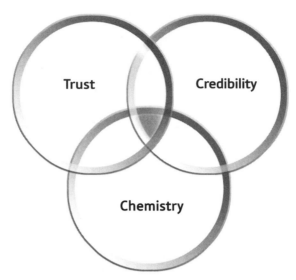

Figure 5   The Components of a Good Coaching Relationship

you *can* coach or, frankly, want to coach. The chemistry may not be right for you. When this occurs, it is best to refer the client to someone else whose style and approach are better suited to that person. Compatibility works both ways.

However a coaching relationship is initiated, there will be a moment or a period in which both coach and client reflect on whether this is a relationship they want to enter into. Either may feel compelled to do so because of existing relationships or a sense of obligation, but the most fruitful coaching relationships are generally those in which both parties consent to participate and in which trust, credibility, and chemistry are mutually felt.

Preparation for Coaching

One could argue that coaching begins even before the first meeting of coach and client as the coach prepares for that meeting. This is especially true of external coaches who may be serving a new organization or a new person within an organization, but to some extent it's true of any coaching relationship. The context setting we discussed in chapter 1 begins *before* the first meeting with the client and entails learning about the organization and how it works, identifying the stakeholders of the coaching

CHECKING FOR THE COMPONENTS OF
A GOOD COACHING RELATIONSHIP

TRUST

✓ Are you honest and worthy of trust? Will you always tell me the truth?

✓ Do you keep your promises and commitments? Will you do what you say you will do and deliver what you promise?

✓ Will you be candid with me, even if it means giving me bad news?

✓ Will you treat me fairly?

✓ Will you look out for my interests? Will you do what's right for me?

✓ Will you avoid surprising me with problems or costs I hadn't counted on?

✓ Will you keep any secrets I tell you? Will you be discreet?

✓ Will you be there when I need you?

CREDIBILITY

✓ Are you a reputable coach? Have you helped other people successfully?

✓ Do you have the education, experience, and background I need?

✓ Do you know what you're talking about?

✓ Do you understand my needs, and have you helped others with similar needs?

✓ Do you speak confidently?

✓ Do your answers to my questions reveal deep knowledge of the subject?

✓ Do you ask knowledgeable and insightful questions of me?

✓ Have you worked in my industry or company before?

CHEMISTRY

✓ Do we have any commonalities? Do we share the same values, perspectives, or attitudes?

✓ Are you interested in my industry? Are we curious about the same things? Do we have insights to share with each other?

✓ Do you understand my operating style and preferences, and are you willing to adapt? Will you work with me the way I want? Will you communicate with me the way I like to communicate?

✓ Do you know what's important to me, what my priorities are?

✓ Do I enjoy working with you, not just because you're a nice person and we have some common personal interests, but because you add value to me?

✓ Do I like you? Would I enjoy being in your company?

process and what they expect from the coaching, and understanding the climate for coaching and development in the organization. Finally, before the first meeting with the client, a coach may initiate data gathering through 360-degree surveys, psychometric assessments, and confidential interviewing of people who work with the client.

Prior to coaching, it's important for coaches, especially external coaches, to develop an understanding of the organization. How is the company organized? Who are the key people surrounding the coaching client? How does the organization work? What are its values and culture? In chapter 1, we argued that coaching does not occur in a vacuum. It's imperative for coaches to understand the environment in which the client operates and the values, perspectives, and expectations at work in the organization. We've worked in organizations, for instance, that are highly competitive, where individual accomplishment is most highly rewarded, where feedback is threatening, and where coaching tends to be a top-down activity associated with annual performance appraisals. We've worked in other organizations that are highly collaborative, where teamwork and co-operation are most highly rewarded; where feedback is encouraged and shared openly; and where coaching is valued, flows in all directions, and occurs almost spontaneously at many points throughout the year.

We have found, not surprisingly, that clients' receptivity to coaching depends to a large extent on the organization's climate and culture. We have also found that many organizations do not have a culture that is conducive to coaching. In our research on coaching, for instance, 37 percent of the respondents said that managers or team leaders in their organization are not expected to coach others regularly. Fifty-two percent of respondents reported that in their organization coaching is not used as a systematic tool to help people develop professionally. Seventy-two percent said that coaches in their organization are not recognized and rewarded for doing coaching. Finally, only 21 percent of respondents said that they receive coaching in conjunction with regular, formal evaluations of their performance. Although these numbers may not be surprising, it is nonetheless difficult to believe that more organizations do not take advantage of coaching as a primary tool for developing their people. In any case, it's important to know, before coaching in an organization, how coaching is perceived in that organization and how open clients are likely to be toward it.

Beyond understanding the organization, it's important to identify and negotiate expectations with the relevant stakeholders. The stakeholders include not only the person being coached but potentially a range of people including the client's direct reports, peers, and boss or other people higher in the organization. They could also include the relevant human resources manager and others responsible for talent development in the organization. An important reason for identifying and talking to these stakeholders is that they form the "ecosystem" within which the client operates. Not only can they be helpful in assessing the client's strengths and weaknesses (they are the "east" pole of the needs compass we discussed in chapter 3), they are a source of ongoing feedback and information during the coaching process. They can help reinforce behavioral changes the client is trying to make, and they can help evaluate progress. Where it is feasible to do so, involving these members of the client's ecosystem in the coaching process makes the client's development a more open and collaborative endeavor.

In most of the coaching we do, we interview the key members of the client's ecosystem during our initial information gathering and diagnosis of the client's real needs. We also suggest to clients that they be transparent with these people about what they are working on and what they are trying to accomplish. If they are willing to share their development goals and measures of success—which, together, constitute a large part of clients' personal development plans—then these people can participate in the development process by reinforcing positive changes, telling clients when they have backslid, and keeping the coach informed on progress. People in clients' ecosystems become part of their broader support network, and having such a network is obviously beneficial in human change programs (it's one of the fundamentals of group therapy, for instance). Even if clients are not willing to be transparent about their coaching program with the people they work with, it's still important for coaches to know who those people are and to interview them confidentially prior to coaching.

CONDUCTING THE FIRST COACHING SESSION

The first meeting between a coach and a client is obviously very important. It can set the tone for everything that follows. For that matter, it may determine whether *anything* follows. In our view, the initial meeting should be an ambitious one. In the professional coaching we provide, that meeting can last from two to four hours, and the coach can achieve the following.

- Building rapport and trust

- Exploring the context of the coaching by learning more about the organization and the client's role (see chapter 1)

- Negotiating the expectations for the coaching relationship (see chapter 2)

- Discovering the client's self-perceptions and sense of needs

- Sharing feedback and observations gleaned from confidential interviews

- Exploring the client's real needs

- Agreeing on initial steps in the client's development plan

This approach to the first meeting may appear to be most appropriate if you are doing programmatic coaching. However, coaches using the circumstantial approach should also begin the process with a lengthy first meeting that accomplishes many of the same things.

Building Rapport and Trust

If you don't know the client well, you need to spend time becoming acquainted. It's best not to rush into the coaching until both people are comfortable with each other, and this requires a slow and sensitive approach in most cases. Typically, you would introduce yourself, ask the client to introduce herself, give some background information on yourself, and ask if the client has any questions about you.

Exploring Context and Negotiating Expectations

Generally, after getting acquainted, it's important to explain how the process will work, especially if the client has never had coaching before, if this coaching process will be different from what the client is accustomed to, or if you are coming in from outside the organization and the client has never worked with you before. In most cases, the client's chief concern is the degree of confidentiality of the process. In most of the coaching we do, the process is entirely confidential except that we prefer for the client's development plan to be shared with key stakeholders, so this is the expectation we express. Whatever the particular ground rules are, it's important to make them clear in the first meeting and ensure that the client understands and agrees with them. In chapter 2, we referred to this as negotiating expectations, or contracting. Essentially, you are trying to become aligned on the ground rules you both will follow during this coaching relationship.

Some coaches prefer to explore the contexts of coaching (see chapter 1) before they talk about how the process will work. It probably doesn't matter which comes first as long as the client is comfortable. In any case, when you explore the contexts, you are trying to understand both the client's organization and her role in it. Generally, context setting and contracting takes the form of casual conversation in which the coach asks a lot of questions and solicits questions from the client. Some of the questions you might ask include these:

✓ Who are you? Tell me about yourself and your organization.

✓ What would you like to know about me?

✓ Why do you want coaching?

✓ Why now?

✓ How important is this coaching?

✓ What do you expect from the coaching?

✓ What would be the best outcome of this coaching for you?

✓ How do you want to work together? What works best for you?

✓ Have you had coaching before? How did that turn out?

Discovering the Client's Self-Perceptions

If the client has completed 360-degree assessments or psychometric surveys, or if the coach has observed the client beforehand or conducted confidential interviews with people who work with the client, then there is a temptation to share this feedback early in the first meeting. Clients will obviously know if they have completed an assessment and are often aware of the coach's other data-gathering activities. They will be curious about what the coach found. However, to avoid biasing their perceptions, it's best to defer sharing feedback and observations until after you have explored how they perceive themselves and what they think they need.

In chapter 3 we suggested the kinds of questions you might use to ask clients about their leadership, management, or interpersonal skills. Even before asking these questions, you might open by asking clients what they believe are their strengths and what are their weaknesses. We often ask some variation of these questions:

✓ What do you think you do well? What don't you do well?

✓ How would you describe yourself as an [executive assistant, engineer, designer, team leader, etc.]?

✓ What do you think are your developmental needs?

✓ What would you like to focus on?

The purpose of these questions is to get clients' high-level views of themselves, to force them to synthesize from their perceptions of themselves and the feedback they've gotten from others. It's often insightful to compare their own view of themselves with the views you glean from 360-degree surveys, psychometric assessments (such as the *Myers-Briggs Type Indicator®* inventory, the *FIRO-B®* assessment, and the *California Psychological Inventory™* assessment), and confidential interviews.

Sharing Feedback and Observations

If you have gathered information on the client prior to the first meeting, then you need to share that information in some form. If the client has completed some assessments, then you should give her the feedback reports (if she doesn't have them already) and walk through them with her. It's important that you have read the reports already and developed a perspective on what you've discovered there. Clients can read it for themselves, but they are usually curious about what conclusions you have drawn from their reports. However, refrain from saying, "Here are your reports and here's what they mean." Instead, you might first ask what the client got from her report, what surprised her, what confirmed what she already knew, and so on. Note any significant findings, positive or negative, and inquire about them.

✓ Did you expect to be so highly rated in these areas?

✓ Were you surprised to receive lower scores in these areas?

✓ Why do you think people rated you high (or low) in this area?

✓ What does this profile suggest to you?

If the client has completed a 360-degree survey that includes narrative comments from respondents, then it is especially important to discuss all narrative comments. Look for patterns among the narrative comments that suggest key strengths or weaknesses.

✓ This is an interesting comment. What do you think it means?

✓ Why do you think someone would make this suggestion?

✓ When you read these comments, do you see any patterns? What about these three comments? They seem to suggest the same thing, don't they?

✓ Now that you've read all the comments, how would you summarize your feedback? What do people say are your strengths, and where do you have developmental needs?

Generally, it's best to ask clients to interpret the data and draw their own conclusions, although you should have your own perspective and share it with clients, especially if your interpretation of the reports differs from theirs. If you have done confidential interviews, you obviously cannot share the confidential information, but you should synthesize it and give clients an overview of the impressions you received. You might also ask clients how they are performing in their jobs and what their performance measurements indicate. Are they meeting or exceeding expectations or do they have a gap to close? Essentially, you are trying to close the loop on the four poles of the needs compass that we described in chapter 3, taking in all relevant information to help understand where the client is now and where she needs to be.

Exploring the Client's Real Needs

In the dialogue that follows the discussion of feedback, you synthesize initial impressions and begin to explore the client's real needs, as we discussed in chapter 4. In our experience, the real needs emerge over time and through a number of conversations. It's unlikely that clarity on the client's real needs will come during the initial meeting, although you will probably make *some* progress and perhaps *substantial* progress. Generally, identifying the real needs is like peeling an onion. You may peel some layers during the first meeting, but there will probably be more layers to go. To peel the remaining layers, you need to build more trust and stimulate more insight through the continuing dialogue and your ongoing observations of the client.

We have found it useful near the end of the first meeting to ask clients to summarize. We keep a running summary ourselves, so we can compare the client's views with our own. We ask clients to summarize the feedback, noting where people thought they were strong or weak, and to identify the two or three key things they need to work on. These are their developmental needs, and if clients list more than a handful of needs, we suggest they prioritize. People may want to improve in dozens of areas (we've seen this), but they won't be able to focus on more than two or three things at a time. Prioritizing forces them to decide what areas of development would have the greatest immediate impact on their work or their lives and results in the greatest degree of improvement. When clients list more than two or three developmental goals, we suggest that they take a phased approach and focus on less important areas only after mastering the more important ones.

Creating a Personal Development Plan

In the programmatic approach to coaching, this discussion of needs and goals leads naturally to the creation of a personal development plan. (In circumstantial coaching, you may simply agree on what to look out for as you observe the client performing.) One of the primary tools in programmatic coaching is a development plan, so creating one is an important outcome of the first meeting. If you don't know enough to complete the plan by the end of this meeting, then you should at least discuss how you will get it done. When clients prefer programmatic coaching—and 78 percent of them do—they expect you to help them develop through a systematic process.

However, 41 percent of the coaching clients we surveyed said that they do not have a plan for their professional development. They aren't sure what skills or knowledge they need to build and do not have a clear set of developmental goals. Moreover, 56 percent of clients report that the coaching they receive is often not focused on the right things and does not help them learn exactly what they should do differently to be more effective. These statistics indicate that a significant number of coaches are not helping their clients identify what they need to change and are not helping them find systematic ways to accomplish their goals.

Personal development plans can take many forms, but most identify three things: clients' goals based on their needs, the steps they have agreed to take to reach those goals, and how they will measure success. The steps they agree to take generally involve behavioral changes and are very concrete. In the epilogue we discuss a human change process model that helps coaches lead clients through the difficult process of change, and we will defer further discussion of action steps until that chapter. The key, during this first meeting, is to end with some formal or informal sense of the path forward. If you are doing programmatic coaching, then that path should be articulated in a personal development plan that the client agrees to undertake.

Opening Subsequent Coaching Sessions

In subsequent meetings, the opening is important but less crucial than in the first meeting. If all has gone well, trust will continue from the first meeting and will build steadily as the coach is being helpful. Nonetheless, the opening is a "warming up" period in which the coach reestablishes and builds upon the context, learns what's been happening, and continues to show (by asking questions) that the client's world, interests, and needs are the focus of this process. As you open subsequent sessions with clients, you can reestablish the dialogue by asking these kinds of questions:

✓ How are you?

✓ How are things at work? (at home, if relevant)

✓ What's happened since our last meeting?

✓ What progress have you made? (or failed to make?) Why?

✓ How did you feel about our last meeting?

✓ Should we do anything differently this time?

✓ Is there anything we need to talk about today?

✓ What would you like to accomplish today?

✓ Where should we start?

Of course, you might want to do a number of other things early in subsequent meetings: discuss any "homework" you might have asked the client to do, share your observations of the client's performance, look at particular work products, and so on. However, opening the meeting with the kinds of questions listed above accomplishes several important coaching goals. First, it reminds the client that this change and development process is essentially his, not yours. You are a helper, but he is driving the changes. Second, it emphasizes that your perspective is less important than his perspective and that you are primarily interested in knowing about him. Third, opening this way lets you know what's on the client's mind and can help guide the dialogue in the right direction.

Initiating the coaching process can seem mundane if you perceive that the initial session serves primarily social purposes: introducing oneself, getting acquainted, asking context-setting questions, and so on. However, just as on the first day of school or the first day in a new job, openings create indelible impressions, and our research on coaching suggests that many coaches squander the best chance they have to create powerful coaching relationships. It doesn't have to be that way.

7

Managing the Dialogue

Ask probing or leading questions, exhibit patience, and voice disagreements so that discussion can help facilitate the coaching process further. Make certain you voice the thoughts you wish to express (don't assume others are reading your mind).

Listen and let the client explain the problem/situation before offering a solution prematurely.

Avoid a lot of miscommunication by asking the right questions at the right time.

SUGGESTIONS TO COACHES FROM THE "COACHING EFFECTIVENESS SURVEY,"
LORE INTERNATIONAL INSTITUTE, INC.

The work of coaching is done largely through conversation. In fact, over the period of time a coach works with a client, there will be many conversations. Together, these conversations constitute the *dialogue* between the coach and the client. Coaches typically begin the process knowing very little about their clients; clients begin knowing a lot but may be unable to articulate their experience in insightful ways and may be blind to some aspects of themselves and their operating style that influence where they have been and where they are going. *Dialogue is a process of discovery.* It is intended to chart uncharted territory, to map what clients have done well and poorly, to explore what challenges they've faced and how they have responded to them, to find and remove roadblocks, to uncover possibilities, and to scout the territory ahead. Dialogue is an act of exploration to help clients determine what they must do to navigate the rest of their journey safely and successfully. What can make coaching so powerful is that clients don't have to take this journey alone. Their coach is a guide, a helper, a friendly ear and voice, an experienced navigator who can help handle the rough spots, identify dangers, and point out the important sights along the way. Coaches, then, are co-creators of their clients' journeys, and the primary tool they use is dialogue.

DAVID BOHM'S CONCEPT OF DIALOGUE

One commonly thinks of dialogue either as a conversation between two or more people or as the words spoken by characters in a work of fiction. The term acquired a more specialized meaning in the early 1990s when British physicist and philosopher David Bohm used it to describe a multifaceted process that helps groups of people explore their perceptions and assumptions and deepen communication and understanding. Bohm felt that many of the world's problems occurred because people talk at cross-purposes, don't examine their assumptions, are unaware of how their perceptions influence their thought processes, and try to prevail in conversations by imposing their "truth" on others. The result is a thoughtless form of communication that leads to misunderstanding and conflict.

In 1991, Bohm outlined his ideas on dialogue in a paper entitled "Dialogue: A Proposal" (coauthored by Donald Factor and Peter Garrett). First, the authors explain their use of the term and their purpose for proposing this new form of communication:

> *Dialogue, as we are choosing to use the word, is a way of exploring the roots of the many crises that face humanity today. It enables inquiry into, and understanding of, the sorts of processes that fragment and interfere with real communication between individuals, nations and even different parts of the same organization.* (Bohm, Factor, and Garrett 1991; see http://world.std.com/~lo/bohm/0000.html)

According to the authors, "In dialogue, a group of people can explore the individual and collective presuppositions, ideas, beliefs, and feelings that subtly control their interactions" (ibid.). This enables them to communicate more clearly and explore ideas in an unbiased atmosphere that allows for more reflection—and therefore more insight. As Bohm explains:

Dialogue is a way of observing, collectively, how hidden values and intentions can control our behavior, and how unnoticed cultural differences can clash without our realizing what is occurring. It can therefore be seen as an arena in which collective learning takes place and out of which a sense of increased harmony, fellowship and creativity can arise. (ibid.)

The key to having a fruitful dialogue is removing the element of competition among the people conversing. As Bohm says, "In dialogue . . . nobody is trying to win" (1996, p. 7). Author Deborah Flick elaborates on this concept by distinguishing between the "Conventional Discussion Process," which she says is an artifact of the "debate culture" that exists today, and the process of dialogue, which she refers to as the "Understanding Process." In her book *From Debate to Dialogue*, Flick (1998) observes, "The framework of the debate culture is built with a host of interlocking, invisible assumptions about the way to discover 'the truth' and what is right, good, and of value, or not. These assumptions encourage and reinforce beliefs and behaviors that place a premium on being right, persuading others, winning, and finding 'The' answer" (pp. 3–4). What makes dialogue so difficult for most people is that we are trained from an early age to be right. In virtually all of our educational experiences, being right is rewarded and being wrong is punished. We are encouraged less to explore, listen, and be open to other perspectives than we are to have our own point of view or to discover the "truth." Consequently, we learn the mind set, habits, and interactional patterns of the debate culture—attitudes and behaviors that remain with us as we later try to coach others.

What makes dialogue difficult for most people is that it feels like you're giving something up. You have to suppress the urge to be right (and prove others wrong). You have to listen without reloading. You have to be willing to examine your assumptions and beliefs publicly and with an eye toward uncovering where they came from—no matter where that might lead or what it might expose. It can be a frightening experience, not one you can undertake with a steady hand and a calm heart if your ego depends on being right and you fear being vulnerable. However, if dialogue is not about being right, it's also not about being wrong. Rather, it's about suspending judgment and exploring ideas in an atmosphere in which exploration itself is both the journey and the outcome. Once people make the leap from a debate mind-set to a dialogue mind-set, they find that dialogue is liberating and mind expanding, not threatening. As Flick explains,

The Understanding Process invites us to surrender our assumptions, the building blocks of our opinions and perspectives. In a dialogue atmosphere that is accepting rather than faultfinding, ideas flow more easily and our willingness to explore them deeply and nondefensively is heightened. We are inspired to ask insightful, illuminating questions as our understanding deepens. (p. 17)

Dialogue does not demand that we give up our own ideas while we listen to someone else we might disagree with. It merely asks that we suspend our judgment and explore those contrary ideas with an open mind. Flick adds, "A key to practicing the Understanding Process is the knowledge that understanding someone from their point of view does not necessarily mean agreeing with them. Nor does deeply understanding another perspective require we surrender our own beliefs and values" (p. 7).

One of the principal benefits of dialogue is that it fosters more open communication by removing the element of judgment. If I am participating in a dialogue, as Bohm defines it, I should be able to say what's on my mind without fearing that others are judging me, finding fault with my ideas, or forming adverse opinions about me. Of course, I have to trust that what I say will not be used against me later, so dialogue requires a degree of trust among the participants. Interestingly, trust is both a prerequisite and an outcome of dialogue. In his 1991 proposal, David Bohm describes how trust builds through the experience of dialogue.

As sensitivity and experience increase, a perception of shared meaning emerges in which people find that they are neither opposing one another, nor are they simply interacting. Increasing trust between members of the group—and trust in the process itself—leads to the expression of the sorts of thoughts and feelings that are usually kept hidden. There is no imposed consensus, nor is there any attempt to avoid conflict. (http://world.std.com/~lo/bohm/0000.html)

Bohm's concept of dialogue applies to coaching in numerous ways. To show the parallels, here are the precepts and practices of dialogue:

- The purpose is to facilitate open communication.

- A key method is to examine perceptions and assumptions, to try to understand the basis for long-held beliefs and behaviors.

- The participants should be unbiased and open to exploration.

- One key goal is not about debate, where there are winners and losers.

In dialogue, everyone wins.

- Another goal is to understand how "hidden" values and intentions control behavior.

- There is no single right answer. There may be multiple "truths" from multiple perspectives.

- Two of the primary skills are asking and listening.

- Participants must learn to suspend judgment. Fault finding is anathema to the process.

- Participants do not necessarily have to agree with one another. The goal is not to reach consensus, though that may be an outcome.

- As trust grows, so does the participants' willingness to disclose thoughts and feelings that are usually hidden, which results in greater insight.

- A successful outcome is the emergence of shared meaning.

It should be apparent that these are also the precepts and best practices of coaching. Coaching is not about imposing one's will, perspectives, or ideas on another person. It's about helping clients explore, understand, develop insight, and change their attitudes and behaviors so they become better leaders, managers, colleagues, and contributors to the enterprise.

Dialogue is particularly relevant in coaching executives because, with rare exception, the coach will not have performed the client's job and cannot give direct, experience-based advice on how to handle the situations and challenges the client is facing. Sure, it would be great if every CEO could have Jack Welch as a coach (notwithstanding Welch's personal choices after retiring from GE), but the reality is that most of the people coaching CEOs have not been a CEO themselves. Furthermore, even if they have, they are unlikely to have been a CEO in their client's industry, in a business the size of the client's business, or in a business with the same challenges and problems their client is facing. Most executive coaches do have a background in business and a good understanding of general business issues, but they will have only a proximate understanding of the issues, challenges, problems, and opportunities each of their clients is facing. Besides, coaching is not about offering specific problem-related advice to struggling executives. It is about helping those executives grow and develop in their own ways. That's why the dialogue is a journey

THE BENEFITS OF DIALOGUE

■ Dialogue engages clients much more than a one-way monologue does. It engages the other person's mind and makes him part of the solution building. The alternative, advice giving, is generally not as helpful, partly because it has a parent-child feel to it and partly because advice is frequently off target or irrelevant.

■ Because dialogue is more engaging, clients tend to be more committed to the results. People are generally more committed to solutions they helped create.

■ It is collaborative, so the outcomes are usually better. As the cliché says, "Two heads are better than one."

■ It helps coaches avoid making damaging assumptions. More often than you might think, coaches make assumptions that are simply incorrect. They assume that they understand the problem, that they know what's best for clients, that there is one right way to solve the problem, and so on. Because it's collaborative, coaches don't have to shoulder all the burden of being right. In dialogue, what's "right" is co-discovered, so the responsibility is shared.

■ It enriches the problem-solving process by expanding the possibilities. Dialogue generally opens up more avenues because people view problems from different perspectives. So dialogue helps expand the solution space.

■ It teaches clients how to think about their problems and challenges. Dialogue has the benefit of educating clients on what kinds of questions to ask themselves. In observing their coach guiding the dialogue, clients learn how to do it and become better able to help themselves—and others.

of discovery for both the coach and the client. The text box "The Benefits of Dialogue" above further describes the value of dialogue.

Coaching can be powerful—indeed, life changing—if the journey is interesting, the discoveries unexpected, and the insights actionable. Or the journey can be dull, uninspiring, and empty. The two primary factors that determine the difference between these two outcomes are the client's openness and willingness to explore and the coach's skillfulness in guiding the dialogue.

If dialogue is a journey, then context is the territory in which the journey takes place. It affects how the dialogue is shaped and what is possible. Good coaches remain acutely aware of the context all the time. They take care to understand the departure point and establish the right context at the beginning of the coaching process. They try to understand how the context affects the client's openness and willingness to explore. They also use the context to help shape the dialogue as coaching continues. So one of the ways to assess a coach is to observe how well he or she understands the context and uses it effectively. Even bad coaches are aware of the context, but they are often incapable of managing it or using it to their and the client's advantage. Instead, the context can become an impediment ("The culture doesn't support the kinds of changes he needs to make") or an excuse for lackluster results ("She wasn't willing to listen to feedback").

Beyond knowing and using the context effectively, coaches must be skilled at guiding and shaping the dialogue. As we said earlier, the two primary factors that determine whether coaching will be effective are the client's openness and willingness to explore and the coach's skillfulness in guiding the dialogue.

DIALOGUE SKILLS FOR COACHES

It would be difficult to argue with the proposition that the two most fundamental coaching skills are asking and listening. Being attentive to the client, *really* hearing what's being said, and being facile at asking insightful questions take coaches a long way. These fundamental skills, by themselves, would probably suffice in many coaching situations. However, to create a rich and insightful dialogue, coaches must also express empathy, give feedback, reflect on what they've heard, make generalizations, and advise or confront, among other things. Asking and listening are the foundation skills; the additional skills discussed below add depth, nuance, and character to the interaction between coach and client. A full set of dialogue skills includes the following.

Opening	Encouraging	Specifying
Listening	Giving feedback	Advising
Empathizing	Reflecting	Confronting
Questioning	Process checking	Reframing
Collaborating	Generalizing	Closing

In chapters 8 through 11, we will elaborate on these skills, noting in particular how they further the dialogue and how the most artful coaches use them.

MANAGING THE EBB AND FLOW OF THE DIALOGUE

In his *Journals* (1835–1862), Ralph Waldo Emerson said, "The art of conversation, or the qualification for a good companion, is a certain self-control, which now holds the subject, now lets it go, with a respect for the emergencies of the moment." He might have been talking about how you manage the ebb and flow of a coaching dialogue. The art in coaching is knowing when to "hold the subject" and when to let it go, when to push and when to pull, when to listen and when to disagree, when to continue exploring the problem space and when to move to the solution space. Coaches who manage the ebb and flow of the dialogue artfully produce insight as well as a satisfying sense of pace throughout the conversation; those who cannot manage the dialogue artfully draw out parts of the conversation too long, cut other parts too short, and produce frustration rather than insight.

When you are coaching, you have to maintain a meta-level of awareness about the process, focusing not only on what the client is saying—engaging in the moment-by-moment flow of the dialogue—but on the larger journey being taken, knowing which paths the client feels comfortable going down, which ones are being avoided, and which ones the client doesn't see. To illustrate the art of the dialogue, we are going to follow part of a coaching session with Joe W., who became president of one of the divisions of a large manufacturing company last year. Joe is a strong operational manager with a record of successfully turning around financially troubled business units. In his current role, he has been able to cut costs and improve operations, but he has not been as effective at mobilizing people around a vision or motivating the people in his division. When he arrived, he replaced twelve of fourteen current executives with people he had worked with before. It's not clear that he knows how to build a unit from within. At the same time, he has not been as customer focused as people expected he would be. He is effective with customers when he meets with them, but he spends most of his time working on operational problems in the division and relatively little time in the field with customers.

As the coach began working with Joe, he asked Joe to take the *Myers-Briggs Type Indicator®* personality inventory and discovered that Joe is an ESTJ (Extraversion, Sensing, Thinking, Judging). According to Sandra Krebs Hirsh and Jean M. Kummerow (1998), "ESTJs are logical, analytical, decisive, and tough-minded, using concrete facts in systematic ways. They enjoy working with others well in advance to organize the details and operations to get the job done" (p. 13). Because they are so decisive and tough-minded, ESTJs like Joe are prone to make decisions quickly, perhaps without considering all the facts—or everyone's opinion—and pushing people to act before they are ready to. Indeed, as the coach interviewed people who worked with Joe, he heard a common refrain: that Joe is a "ready, fire, aim" type of manager. He asked Joe about this during one of their meetings.

COACH	Have you had a chance to read the MBTI® booklet I gave you?
JOE	Yes, I leafed through it last week. Interesting.
COACH	Did the description of ESTJs seem to fit you?
JOE	Yes. I was surprised, to tell you the truth. I've never put much stock in those things, but they nailed me. I guess I'm just not sure what to do with it. Okay. That's the way I am. So what?
COACH	Well, let's reflect on the implications of your style. One of the things I heard about you from some of the people I interviewed is that you're a "ready, fire, aim" type of leader. What does that imply? [Rather than deal head on with Joe's indifference to his MBTI profile, the coach adds another piece of data and asks the client to reflect on the implications. By doing so, the coach is an ally, not an adversary.]
JOE	That I make decisions too quickly. Without considering all the facts. But, you know, in our business you have to act quickly. You have to get to the core of a problem as quickly as possible and then solve the damn thing. You can't study things to death.
COACH	Help me understand that. [Here the coach is using the "Columbo" method, after television's Lt. Columbo, played by Peter Falk. The Columbo method means asking for clarification or asking a simple question, as though you didn't understand.]

JOE	What?
COACH	You said, "in our business." Which business? Manufacturing? Is this always true of manufacturing?
JOE	It is if you want an efficient operation, which is critical to making your margin.
COACH	Granted. So speed is of the essence in operational management?
JOE	Right.
COACH	And you said you need to solve problems quickly. That makes sense. How important is gathering the facts? [Using a question to challenge the client's interpretation of the "ready, fire, aim" description. Is it really about making decisions without having sufficient facts?]
JOE	Obviously, you can't make sound decisions without the facts. It's critical to have the right information before you make a decision.
COACH	So what do people mean, then, when they say that you are a "ready, fire, aim" type of leader?
JOE	I'm not sure.
COACH	How do you make decisions? [This question represents a fundamental shift in the dialogue. The client is not progressing in his understanding, so the coach asks him to reflect on how he makes decisions. The point is to ground him in his experiences of decision making. Note, below, that he hasn't been self-conscious about this process previously. One of Joe's issues is that he acts unself-consciously and may be unaware of his impact on others.]
JOE	I don't know. I haven't thought about it. (reflecting) I take in the information I need, you know, look at the numbers, listen to what people have to say, and so forth, and then make a decision.
COACH	Right on the spot? Just like that? [confirming what he's hearing]
JOE	Yes. The moment I know what needs to be done, I make the decision.
COACH	And you announce it to others?

JOE	Right.
COACH	And stop taking in more information? Stop listening?
JOE	Yes, I guess so.
COACH	So, bear with me here. I'm trying to imagine what it's like to work with you. I come to you with information, and you're listening to me. Suddenly, you make your decision, tell me what it is, and further discussion is cut off. *I'm* cut off, even if I have more to say or feel that other facts, which I haven't given yet, are relevant. If I worked for you, is that how it would feel to me? [This is an important element in Joe's education. He is not naturally empathetic, so the coach forces him to see what the experience looks like to others.]
JOE	I hadn't thought about it, but, yes, I suppose so.
COACH	What does it feel like for you when you make a decision? [This question helps the client be more self-aware. It's a kind of introspection he may not have done before.]
JOE	I don't know. I am considering the facts, sort of reformulating the problem or issue in my head as I'm taking in information, and then I suddenly see the solution. Like snapping your fingers. It's just suddenly there.
COACH	Then what?
JOE	Then I'm ready to move on. No, I see this now. I think I just literally stop listening at that point. I'm eager to move on, get this problem resolved, and deal with the next one.
COACH	(silent; listening) [This seems like an insightful moment for the client, so the coach remains silent. When the client is working, don't interfere.]
JOE	It's like a door slams shut. That's the only way to describe it.
COACH	How do you think the people working for you experience it? [Again, a question that calls for empathetic understanding of others—not Joe's strong suit.]
JOE	Like a door slamming shut. (pause) It must be frustrating as hell to work for me sometimes. [This bit of expressed empathy is a major victory in this dialogue.]

COACH	Do you ever go back and revisit a decision you've made? When more information becomes available?
JOE	Sure. All the time. You can't be right about everything. You have to understand. I'm not stubborn like that. I'm not afraid to admit when I'm wrong. If we need to revisit a decision, we do so.
COACH	That's good.
JOE	So I guess the "ready, fire, aim" comment is about being too impulsive in the first place. [Another major victory: Joe is labeling his own behavior, and naming it is an important step in changing the behavior.]
COACH	I'd say so.
JOE	All right. Good point. So I need to think more before making a decision. [The client has just articulated a change goal, which is a critical step in the dialogue, but the coach knows better than to leave it at that. The hard work is still ahead.]
COACH	Well, if the goal were to be less impulsive in your decision making, then reflecting more before making a decision is one way to do it. Would it be useful to explore more options?
JOE	Sure. Because as I think about it, I don't know how to slow down my decision making, honestly. When the door slams shut, it slams shut. How do you change the way you think?
COACH	Maybe you don't. Let's assume that door keeps slamming shut. Until now, what follows the door slamming shut is that you announce your decision and stop listening. Is that right?
JOE	More or less. (pause) Yes, that's about it.
COACH	So let's focus on that moment. What else could you do? [Exploring options is a useful device in dialogue. We've moved from the problem space to the solution space, but only temporarily, as we will see.]
JOE	I guess I could just keep it to myself.
COACH	(incredulous) Make the decision but then not tell anyone?
JOE	(shaking his head) That doesn't sound right.

COACH	Sounds really frustrating for you. [demonstrating empathy] What if you were to consider the decision a hypothesis about what should be done and put it out there for people to react to? [This is a straw man option, offered as a way to further the exploration.]
JOE	So just say, "Here's what we could do," instead of, "Here's what we're going to do."
COACH	Something like that. How would that feel to you?
JOE	I could do that. But I don't want to get into consensus decision making. In our business, that would kill you.
COACH	Joe, I want to make an observation. I hear you making connections and then drawing conclusions very quickly. You just did that when you went from "Here's what we could do" to the assumption that that would mean consensus decision making. Are those two things necessarily connected? [This is a key moment in the dialogue. The client has just demonstrated the behavior others criticize him for, so the moment is ripe for the coach to point that out. The observation is much more powerful when it is linked to immediate behavior.]
JOE	(reflecting) No, you're right. They're not.
COACH	(silent; listening) [Another moment of insight for the client, so the coach remains silent.]
JOE	I think I probably do that a lot.
COACH	What?
JOE	Make these intuitive leaps. You know, assuming that one thing follows something else, and maybe it doesn't.
COACH	Can you think of other times when you've done that?
JOE	Yes. I'd have to think about it, but it seems pretty characteristic of how I operate. [An important self-revelation for the client. Now the coach will try to help the client understand why he operates that way. This helps put his behavior in context.]
COACH	You've had to make decisions quickly in your previous roles. Isn't that right?

JOE	(nodding) I've always been a good turnaround artist. You know, come into a failing situation, diagnose the problems, make some quick decisions about what to change, cut costs, make the operations more efficient, and get on with it.
COACH	And you've been pretty successful at that?
JOE	Damn right.
COACH	So is that the situation you're in now? In this division? [The coach knows it isn't, but he uses a question to prompt the client to do the reflecting.]
JOE	It was when I became president last year. I've pretty much turned things around now.
COACH	So how would you describe your challenges at this point?
JOE	We have a stable situation now. The challenge is to meet the growth targets, which are aggressive but doable.
COACH	What will it take to accomplish that?
JOE	What will it take? Hmm. I need to build my management team, get the resources and skills in place throughout the division, and spend more time focused on customers. Those are probably the top three challenges for me at this point.
COACH	That sounds different from turnaround management. [This is the point. What the client is doing now is different from what he's done in the past. His leadership style may have been appropriate in his previous roles but not in his current role. Clients often cling to successful previous strategies, even when they no longer work in those circumstances.]
JOE	In some ways it is, yes. (pause) You know, it's interesting because in my past four or five positions I've done the turnaround and then left. This time I'm not leaving.
COACH	What are the implications of that? [A good question to ask when clients tell you that something is different.]
JOE	I guess the main one is that I need to have a team that can manage the division longer term. (pause) I can't make all the decisions, or I'll be the bottleneck. And, you know, I may not have the right management team. Some of the people who've been with me from one place to another may not be right in a growth-oriented environment.

COACH   What about you? [This question is meant to be challenging. It plays off the client's observation about his management team, but it also applies to him. Delivering this kind of question requires the right tone. It should prompt the client to think but should not sound aggressive or cynical.]

JOE   Am I right for this environment? I'd like to think so, but honestly I don't know. It means going from a shoot-from-the-hip style to something else, more inspirational, I guess, more charismatic, less authoritarian.

COACH   (silent; listening) [Wow. A powerful realization on the client's part. Don't say a word.]

JOE   I think I can do it, but it's clear that I have to change how I'm making decisions. (pause) For one thing, I need the team to make most of the decisions. Otherwise, they'll keep expecting me to do it, or waiting for me to do it, or thinking I'll override them. Right?

COACH   (nodding)

JOE   So the key to this whole thing is for me to be less impulsive about making decisions. How the hell do I do that? [Notice that the dialogue has come full circle—back to the question of what he should be doing differently. Now, however, he's clearer about the problem and the need for change. Now the options will be less speculative and more operational.]

COACH   We had one idea on the table: offering potential decisions as hypotheses. What else could you do?

As this example illustrates, the art of the dialogue is in managing clients' journeys so they develop insights about themselves along the way. You do that by providing just the right amount of information to prompt exploration; by using questions to provoke thought, examine causes and effects, challenge assumptions, and surface options; by confronting the client's perspective at the right moments; and by reframing what's been said so the client sees things in a new light. Effective dialogue is a combination of questioning, stating, observing, giving feedback, and remaining silent. In this example, the coach asked forty questions, made twenty statements, offered five observations, and remained silent four times. There is no secret formula for how these elements of dialogue should be combined, but in nondirective coaching in particular there should be more questions than statements.

WHY SOME COACHES
ARE NOT ARTFUL AT DIALOGUE

A number of coaches we have observed are simply not very skilled at dialogue, and it severely hinders their effectiveness. We suspect that many are talkers and advice givers by nature. They have a strong need to assert their knowledge or be in control of the situation. Highly opinionated people and those with narcissistic personalities often do not make good coaches because they cannot set aside their ego for the duration of the dialogue. Other coaches who are otherwise well intentioned are not good listeners. Some lack finesse in asking questions and asserting appropriately. Finally, a number of coaches we've observed seem unable to hold that meta-level of process awareness in their head. They become so immersed in the conversation that they forget to keep one eye on what's going on while it is happening. You won't be able to coach effectively unless you can, in a sense, step away from the flow of the dialogue and be thinking about pacing, disclosure, and the give-and-take of information as clients progress toward insights. Ultimately, this is what dialogue is about: helping clients gain insights about themselves that they would not have had without the dialogue. Without these moments of insight, clients are unlikely to change and grow. If what happens in coaching conversations is business as usual, then clients will have no reason to behave differently.

THE ETHICAL LIMITS OF DIALOGUE

We have argued throughout this book that coaching is not therapy; however, it *is* a thoughtful exploration of the client's behavior, choices, assumptions, and skills. Occasionally, the dialogue will lead coach and client into terrain the coach is not equipped to handle (and should not attempt to handle because it violates the ethical limits on coaching). Coaches who are behaving ethically know their limits and do not go beyond them. Even when coaches are licensed psychologists, we would argue that the coaching relationship is fundamentally different than the therapeutic relationship, and those coaches should not engage in therapy while coaching. The proper course of action is to refer clients to therapists if issues arise that should be handled by therapy. In chapter 4, we discussed the "ten red flags"—client behaviors indicating that the problems are outside the domain of coaching. When these or other problematic behaviors occur, the right answer for coaches is to stop the dialogue and find the right resources to help the client. You risk doing harm (and potentially being liable) if you trespass into areas you are not equipped to handle. Here are our suggestions for ensuring that you remain within the ethical bounds of coaching:

- Don't venture into areas where you're not qualified. If psychological issues arise, refer the client to someone qualified to address those issues.

- Don't offer advice unless you have sufficient expertise (don't fake it or make it up). Don't let your ego guide your decisions.

- Don't suggest or support courses of action that would be harmful to the client or to others.

- Don't divulge confidences or betray the client's trust in any other way.

- Remain objective but helpful. Avoid involvement with the client beyond the professional level. Coaching comes from a position of trust, and you must not betray that.

- Be transparent about what you know and what you don't. Be forthright about your ability to be helpful. Always be candid and honest.

We will close this chapter with a sample dialogue showing how one coach handled a situation that was outside the domain of coaching.

COACH   Tom, you've been telling me about your difficulties with the transition. I think if I were you, I would have been angry about being passed over.

TOM   Whatever.

COACH   It didn't matter to you?

TOM   Not any more than anything else. What the hell. Bad things happen to good people, right? It's the way my whole life has been going, so it wasn't a bigger deal than anything else has been.

COACH   I don't understand.

TOM   (shrugging)

COACH   (silent; listening)

TOM   You probably heard that my wife left me. That happened a month ago. Now my son isn't talking to me. Won't return my calls. Hell, it just seems like everything is crashing at once. You know, you just reach a point where it doesn't matter anymore.

COACH   (pause) Have you talked to anyone about this?

TOM   No.

COACH   I think you should.

TOM   Isn't that what you're here for?

COACH   No, it isn't, Tom. I'm here to coach you, but this situation sounds more serious than coaching. I have to be candid with you. I can't help you with the personal problems you're having. That's not what coaching is about, but I'm convinced you need help. Look, if I were having the problems you're having, I would want help from someone who could really help me deal with the situation.

TOM   So what do you suggest?

COACH   Let me make a few calls and get the names of some people you might want to talk to. Would you be willing to do that?

TOM   I don't know.

COACH   Well, think about it.

TOM   Why don't you just tell me what you think I should do?

COACH   Because you'd be hearing from a well-intentioned amateur, and that's not what you need. You need to talk to a professional, somebody trained to help with these kinds of problems.

TOM   All right.

COACH   I'll make some calls and get to you tomorrow morning. Will you be all right tonight?

TOM   Yeah.

Such situations are always tricky. The key is not to give in to the impulse to offer advice or to accept responsibility for the client's problems beyond the commitment you should make—which is to seek competent professional help. Incidentally, if in this example Tom had said he wasn't sure if he'd be all right tonight, then the coach would need to seek competent help immediately. It's the responsible and decent thing to do.

8

Listening and Questioning

Ask more open-ended questions to obtain more input.

Probe more and spend less time relating your personal experiences.

Give people your undivided attention.

SUGGESTIONS TO COACHES FROM THE "COACHING EFFECTIVENESS SURVEY,"
LORE INTERNATIONAL INSTITUTE, INC.

Thirty-four percent of the coaching clients we studied said that their coach is not very skilled at asking insightful questions that encourage them to explore their issues and needs further. Thirty-eight percent said that their coach is not adept at probing both for their ideas and feelings, and 26 percent said that their coach does not listen well and does not build upon their ideas throughout their discussions. Although *most* coaches seem to be skilled in these areas, these findings are nonetheless disturbing because they show that a significant number of people coaching in the business world lack the most basic skills of coaching: listening and questioning. Much of the art of coaching derives from these critical skills. In this chapter, we explore how coaches can use these two fundamental communication skills to manage the dialogue.

LISTENING

Much has been written about the art of listening. We are most fond of Stella Terill Mann's comment that "listening is a form of accepting." In conversation, the greatest show of acceptance is *patient* listening. This skill is so fundamental that without it a coaching dialogue is not possible. Even coaches who *are* listening can sometimes convey the impression that they're not. These are the kinds of signals an impatient coach sends:

- Fidgeting, writing notes, or failing to maintain eye contact while the client is speaking

- Speaking as soon as the client stops talking; "clipping" the ends of a client's sentences

- Interrupting

- Failing to respond to what the client last said (indicating that the coach was thinking about something else while the client was talking)

- Missing important verbal or nonverbal cues in the client's speech or behavior

Professional coaches and counselors are trained to be patient listeners, but most managers are not, and when they act as coaches they often fail to listen as carefully and thoughtfully as they should. Even trained coaches can sometimes lose themselves in the moment and forget to listen patiently. If the client trusts the coach, then a momentary lapse in listening is usually forgiven, but chronic lapses diminish trust and can cause clients to lose faith not only in the coach but in the coaching process itself. Listening is a skill requiring constant practice—and vigilance during the dialogue.

Beyond listening *patiently,* good coaches listen *attentively*—with their eyes as well as their ears. When coaches listen with their eyes, they are observing their clients' nonverbal signals: shrugs, gestures, eye movements, body posture, and so on. When they listen with their ears, coaches pick up on the tone of the voice, pauses, or unusual word emphasis. The full story being told comes as much or more from a client's nonverbal cues as it does from the verbal dimension. For this reason, coaching by telephone is considerably less effective than coaching face to face. Nonverbal communications are an important part of the dialogue—for both parties. Coaches' nonverbal signals are also observed and interpreted by their clients. So it's critical for coaches to understand—and manage—the non-verbal signals they send.

The core of the dialogue is the client's story, and this is fundamentally what coaches listen for. All people interpret their experiences in ways that reflect their worldview and reinforce their self-image. When people talk about themselves, they are revealing elements of their story as they have constructed it. Understanding how clients have built their own stories helps coaches understand why clients behave as they do—and, hence, what their problems and blind spots might be, as well as how they might best be helped. Virtually everything clients say about themselves is part of their story, whether or not they begin with "once upon a time." Even when clients are talking—not about themselves but about their companies, divisions, or projects—they are presenting their construct of reality, their interpretation of events and situations as they see them. That's an important part of their story. As you listen to a client's stories, you should be asking yourself these questions:

- How is this person interpreting his experience?

- How does he assign importance to situations, events, or outcomes?

- How does he define himself?

- How does he view himself as a participant in events?

- How does he view the importance of these events? And his own importance?

- How does he think about his skills? His ability to influence people, events, and outcomes?

- How does he draw conclusions about what has happened and why?

- What did he learn from these events?

- What did he conclude about how to behave in the future?

- What does this tale say about the teller?

The art in listening well is for coaches to hear what their clients are saying without projecting their own experiences onto the story. The danger is in coaches hearing what they want to hear, interpreting the clients' words from their own experience, and then constructing the clients' stories based on how they would construct them. These are the coaches who give advice that's right for them, regardless of whether it's right for their clients, and then fail to see the difference. Coaching is an art, and listening *patiently, attentively,* and *objectively* is the core skill. Coaches who do it well can develop enormous insight into the people they are coaching and can use this insight to create a meaningful dialogue with their clients.

So, how do you listen well? The skills include being there, going through the open doors, following the client's agenda, following the bread crumb trail, trusting silence, using minimal encouragers, pointing out the elephants in the room, synthesizing now and then, listening with your eyes as well as your ears, and listening with your heart as well as your head.

Being There

Being there means simply to be present and accounted for while coaching is taking place. Coaching is not a multitasking activity. It can't be done on a shop floor in the middle of a production run. It can't occur while the coach is taking phone calls or responding to e-mails or reading the ticker on the big board. When you coach, it's important to concentrate fully on the client, so you need to eliminate external and internal distractions. In a busy world, this is sometimes difficult, so it's best to think of coaching as "sanctuary time," a stepping away from the chaos and noise of the world outside so you can focus on the client.

Some pundits have observed that in contemporary life—with a degree of connectedness that would have astounded, and perhaps terrified, our parents—*everyone* is beginning to suffer from attention deficit disorder. When you're being pinged every ten seconds by one gadget or another, it's difficult to concentrate, and we are becoming more accustomed to juggling fifteen things at once. But in coaching this simply will not do. It's not possible, with a distracted mind, to engage in a thoughtful dialogue. It's also disrespectful to the person you're coaching. A number of the clients we surveyed in our coaching research reported that their coaches did not fully attend to them during coaching sessions. When asked what their coaches could do to improve their coaching, three of them made the following comments.

- *Listen to what is said all the way through before going on to something else. It's okay to be busy, but I would like to feel that I have your undivided attention for a few minutes.*

- *Better handling of interruptions when a coaching session is taking place. When meetings are held in your office, constant interruptions and taking phone calls reduced the effectiveness of the meetings. Off-site meetings seem to work better.*

▨ *Just a bit more relaxing and listening. I don't want to feel there are six-*
teen people outside the door waiting for us to finish, even if there are.
I don't need a quantity of coaching time. I am more concerned with
quality of coaching time since this is my biggest area of opportunity.
Not much is completed between the two of us when we have one eye on
each other and one eye on the door.

Going Through the Open Doors

When clients avoid a subject or seem unwilling to talk about it, you have
two options. You can continue to pursue the subject or you can move on
to something the client is more willing to talk about. If you do the former,
you are knocking on a closed door; if you do the latter, you are going
through an open door. In coaching, it is generally better to go through the
open doors. When the doors are open, clients are more engaged, more
likely to feel comfortable, and more likely to tell you how they feel. Yet we
have seen many coaches, like the one in the following dialogue, who are
determined to knock down those closed doors, no matter what.

CLIENT   So, anyway, I completed my report and followed all the
          guidelines they gave me, and Jim still sent it back to be
          redone. I couldn't believe it. *And* he sent it to Legal to get
          their opinion *after* I told him that I'd already had Legal
          review it. His basic problem is that he doesn't trust what
          you tell him.

COACH   You had problems with your previous supervisor, too, as I
          recall. Is there a pattern here?

CLIENT   You're missing the point. Jim doesn't just nitpick me to
          death. He does it to everybody in the department.

COACH   Maybe so, but you seem to have a pattern of problems with
          your supervisors. It's not just Jim.

CLIENT   Whatever. Jim is the guy I have to deal with right now, and
          I'd like to figure out what I need to do to get him off my
          back. I'm really frustrated that I can't seem to make any
          headway with him.

COACH   We'll get back to Jim in a moment, okay? Tell me more
          about your last supervisor.

This client is no doubt becoming frustrated with the coach, too. In
this example, the coach has probably made an insightful observation, but

the client is not ready to hear it. That door is closed. Rather than bang on that closed door, the coach should go through the open door (what to do about Jim) and come back to the broader issue later. At this point, the client is emotionally entangled in his immediate problem with Jim, and this is what the coach should follow. Go through the open doors. Return to the closed doors later.

Following the Client's Agenda

Related to going through the open doors is following the client's agenda, which means setting aside your own thoughts about subject matter and sequence and going where the client wants to go. Clearly, this "letting go" is fundamentally what nondirective coaching is about. In fact, it's virtually the definition of nondirective coaching. However, even directive coaches should periodically release their agenda and go where the client leads them. Coaching that is totally directive can make a client feel like a puppet in someone else's puppet show. Even in directive coaching, the dialogue is about the client's story, not the coach's, so the client's agenda must prevail.

To follow the client's agenda, you have to release your own, and this is especially difficult for coaches who need to feel in control or for those who are highly logical and structured. Releasing your agenda can mean feeling lost sometimes, which is an uncomfortable feeling for many of us. It can mean feeling that the dialogue is going nowhere or that you're not adding value. Coaches whose MBTI® preferences include T (Thinking) and J (Judging) can find it maddening to go where clients lead them, especially if the flow does not seem logical. But if you insist on being in control and guiding the conversation constantly, then you are likely to be a poor listener (because part of your mind will be planning the next few steps instead of following what the client is saying) and you are likely to miss some important, but perhaps subtle, clues in the dark folds of the client's story.

Following the Bread Crumb Trail

When clients talk, they leave clues, like bread crumbs left to mark a trail. Good listeners follow the bread crumb trail by picking up on clients' key words, thoughts, transitions, and other *dialogue markers* that signify an important piece of information.

CLIENT   I'm becoming increasingly impatient with Marcia and her team.

COACH   Say more.

CLIENT	Two days ago, we held an "all hands" meeting to discuss consolidating the Franklin and Wabash operations, and they spent the entire meeting complaining about one thing or another.
COACH	What did they complain about?
CLIENT	You name it: we're moving too soon, we're not moving fast enough, they want to be more involved in the transition, they don't want the space we've allocated for them. It frustrated the hell out of me.
COACH	You sound frustrated.
CLIENT	You know, I think I've done everything humanly possible to accommodate them. I've even invited Marcia or another member of her team to come to our planning meetings, although they aren't part of the transition team.
COACH	They're not on the transition team?
CLIENT	No, no, they're not. But . . .
COACH	But what?
CLIENT	I was trying to keep the transition team small. I thought if we had too many people on it we'd never get anything done. But I can see how Marcia felt about that.
COACH	How do you think she felt?

As this dialogue illustrates, the client is really solving the problem. By "connecting the dots," the coach reflects important thoughts from one moment to the next and furthers the client's thinking: *complaining—complained, frustrated—frustrated, not part of the team—not part of the team, but—but, and Marcia felt—she felt.* When you follow the bread crumb trail, you reinforce the flow of the client's thoughts and use the dialogue as a device for discovery. Note that at the end of this short dialogue, the client has begun to put himself in Marcia's shoes and is discovering the source of her team's frustrations. By listening carefully, the coach is able to guide the client's self-discovery, which is a more powerful way for the client to learn than being told why Marcia's team may be complaining so much.

Trusting Silence

Mark Twain is said to have observed, "The right word may be effective, but no word was ever as effective as a rightly timed pause." Silence is one of the great, underused tools in coaching. We observed hundreds of coaches who seem uncomfortable with silence. They ask their clients great questions and then, while the client is thinking, destroy the moment by talking again. It often looks like this:

COACH   As you've said, your style is really not aligned with the style of this organization. If you aren't able to align yourself with the executive team here, what is likely to happen?

CLIENT   Hmm.

COACH   It's unreasonable to expect all of them to change for you, don't you think?

CLIENT   (pause; thinking)

COACH   I mean, look, their team has been together for a long time, right? They are comfortable working the way they work. As the relative newcomer, isn't it up to you to adapt?

We have to remember that coaching is about change, and people don't change through a harangue. They change because they work through the mental processes themselves and decide to behave differently. We have much more to say about this in the epilogue. Suffice it to say here that the point of coaching is to help clients think. When they are thinking, they are working, and if you interrupt their work, you risk frustrating them and stalling the process. When clients are thinking, let them think! So when you ask a provocative question, remain silent while the client thinks about it. Silence may be uncomfortable for you, but it's also uncomfortable for clients, and they will eventually break the silence with their next thought or question. The guideline we recommend is to ask insight-provoking questions and then wait for at least a ten-count before saying anything else. Trust silence.

Using Minimal Encouragers

Minimal encouragers are those brief statements, questions, sounds that encourage the client to continue talking. Sometimes, clients come to a full stop in their dialogue. They've made a statement and are waiting for you to respond. However, you think there is more to what they have said, and you want to encourage them to continue talking. An excellent way to do that is to use one of these minimal encouragers:

✓ Can you tell me more?

✓ What else?

✓ How does that work?

✓ Say more.

✓ Um-hmm.

✓ Go on.

✓ Interesting.

✓ That's great.

✓ And then?

✓ What happened next?

Minimal encouragers can also be nonverbal. You might just nod, shake your head, or wave your hand in a "please continue" manner to encourage the client to keep going.

CLIENT   Where I grew up, in Japan, I learned to be respectful toward others and not to be direct. When I came to this country at seventeen, I was told that I had to be more direct, so I learned to do that. Now, that's how I prefer to interact with people.

COACH   (nodding)

CLIENT   You know, if you have a problem, you just say so. Maybe you fight, and then you kiss and make up later. But in this company, people aren't direct with each other, and they think I'm different for just saying what I think.

COACH   Hmm.

CLIENT   I'm convinced that's why they don't get anything done around here. Decisions don't get made because no one will just say what he means.

COACH   Never?

CLIENT   (pausing) You know, I think decisions sort of get made by default in this place. The culture is one where people avoid confrontation, so if you have a problem with someone, it's considered bad form to be direct with them about it. Instead, you're supposed to beat around the bush or something.

COACH   Tell me more.

You would not want to use minimal encouragers exclusively, of course. They are excellent tools at the right moment, especially with clients who are economic with their speech or who don't fully develop their thoughts. They are also useful when it's important to keep clients talking—perhaps because they are following an insightful line of thought or because you have observed or concluded something but would rather your clients discover it for themselves.

Pointing Out the Elephants in the Room

The elephant in the room is the big, ugly, hairy, smelly beast that everyone knows is in the room but no one wants to talk about. It's the "gross truth" that will cause discomfort or embarrassment if it's discussed, so people tend to talk around it or pretend it isn't there. Effective coaches know the elephant is in the room and point it out. The only way issues can be resolved is to discuss them, even if they are big, ugly, hairy, and smelly.

CLIENT   It's unbelievable that this team hasn't come together and done what it's supposed to do. I've put the best people there. I've given them all the resources they need. I've made it clear what they're expected to do. I won't do the job for them, but short of doing that, I don't know how the hell to get this bunch to perform like they should.

COACH   I think you are the problem.

In this case, Terry was coaching a hard-charging senior executive who tended to throw his weight around like the proverbial bull in the china shop. He was not used to people being so direct with him and was not ready to hear this feedback, so it was a pivotal moment in the coaching. In our view, coaches must be truth tellers, as they see it. Their value is in being as candid and forthright with clients as the clients can handle. Coaches who soften the blow simply to protect their clients' egos are not being helpful. There are times in the coaching dialogue when candor is all that will move the client's discovery process forward, and if you fail to point out the elephant in the room, then you fail the client.

Synthesizing Now and Then

One way to show that you've been listening is to synthesize the dialogue from time to time. A synthesis is different from a summary. In a summary, you merely repeat, in condensed form, what's been said. A synthesis is a wholly new formulation of what's been said. Literally, it means to combine separate elements into a coherent whole. When you synthesize the dialogue, you create a new picture from the elements of the dialogue, a picture the client may not have thought of previously. So synthesizing is one powerful way to develop and share insights, as the following example shows.

CLIENT   I don't think Eduardo has had much experience speaking before large groups of employees, and we will have nearly five hundred people at the event.

COACH   You seem anxious about that.

CLIENT   I don't want to put someone up in front of the group who isn't going to do a spectacular job. Marina has more public speaking experience, but very few people at the event will know who she is.

COACH   So what are your options?

CLIENT   I suppose we could videotape the chairman and show the video on several large screens.

COACH   What else?

CLIENT   We could look for an outside speaker, someone who has a marquee name and knows how to wow a large crowd.

COACH   Would your people find anyone like that relevant?

CLIENT   Probably not.

COACH   So if I put this all together, I'm hearing that you're not comfortable with any of the options you've considered, including the one you haven't talked about, which is you giving the presentation yourself. Is this about your own fears of public speaking?

Listening with Your Eyes As Well As Your Ears

How clients say things and what they do in between saying things is at least as important as what they say. Listening with your eyes means carefully observing your client's body language, gestures, pauses, and tone of voice, and then using what you observe to further the dialogue.

COACH   You look like you haven't slept. Are you all right?

CLIENT   I don't think it's important. It hasn't, . . . well, let's just say it won't be a problem in the future.

COACH	It hasn't what, John? You hesitated there.
CLIENT	I was going to say that it hasn't, uh, caused the kind of problem I thought it would.
COACH	I'm glad to hear that, but I'm a little confused. You don't sound relieved.
CLIENT	Well, you know I was hoping to be named manager of the design engineering group.
COACH	And you were.
CLIENT	Yes, but they've just announced a reorganization that means I'll still be at the same level. My new position was reclassified downward.
COACH	Hmm. So what won't be a problem in the future?
CLIENT	I won't have to worry about being promoted. Clearly, they've decided against it, and I'm stuck at this level.
COACH	Hmm. I'd like to know a bit more. What else did they say when you were told about the promotion?

It's difficult in words to illustrate a visual phenomenon, but we hope this brief sample of dialogue illustrates the importance of observing clients carefully and using those observations to deepen your and the client's understanding of the situation. Listening with your eyes means noticing when clients rub their hands, tap their fingers, fidget, look at their watch, scratch their chin, look off in the distance, smile, or do myriad other things that communicate pleasure, fear, discomfort, frustration, happiness, uncertainty, and so on. Clients are often unaware that they are doing these things. When you point them out, you often help clients gain insight into how they feel about what's happening to them.

Listening with Your Heart As Well As Your Head

Finally, you should also listen with your heart as well as your head, and this means listening for how clients feel, being attuned to their emotional frequencies, so to speak. When you listen with your heart, you empathize with clients and thus demonstrate that you understand how they feel and can put yourself in their shoes. In normal conversation among business people, *empathy* is a word that's often misunderstood and seldom practiced, in part because many business people confuse empathy with being "touchy-feely" and feel that connecting with someone else's emotions is inappropriate, at best, and scary, at worst. Given the widespread confusion over empathy, it would be useful to define the term. According to *Merriam-Webster's Collegiate Dictionary*, empathy is "the action of understanding, being aware of, being sensitive to, and vicariously experiencing the feelings, thoughts, and experience of another of either the past or present without having the feelings, thoughts, and experience fully communicated in an objectively explicit manner."

The complexity of this definition may explain why the term is so often misunderstood. Gerard Egan (1998), a professor emeritus of Loyola University of Chicago, offers a simpler definition in his book *The Skilled Helper:* "Basic empathy involves *listening* to clients, *understanding* them and their concerns to the degree that this is possible, and *communicating* this understanding to them so that they might *understand themselves* more fully and act on their understanding" (p. 81). The operative word here is *communicating*. Empathy occurs when coaches are able to communicate their understanding of their clients to their clients. Empathy is one of the key ways coaches reflect what they've heard or observed—verbally or nonverbally—and it often does reflect the emotional aspects of clients' stories.

CLIENT   (pausing) You know, I think decisions sort of get made by default in this place. The culture is one where people avoid confrontation, so if you have a problem with someone, it's considered bad form to be direct with them about it. Instead, you're supposed to beat around the bush or something.

COACH   And that frustrates you. [recognizing the emotion]

CLIENT   Absolutely! Why can't people just say what they mean? I keep leaving meetings with the senior executives wondering if I understood what they were saying. It's like you have to read between the lines because nobody will just tell you what they think. Is he okay with my decision or not? I don't know! Does he think I'm doing a good job or not? I don't know!

COACH   It must be very unnerving not to know where you stand. [Another way to empathize is to hypothesize how the client might feel.]

CLIENT   (nodding) I feel like saying, "If you don't think I'm doing a good job, then just say so. We can talk about it. If I disagree, I'll say so. If you disagree, you say so."

COACH	You would be happier if people were candid with you about how you're doing. [projecting how the client would feel if the situation were different]
CLIENT	Absolutely. It saves time. No beating around the bush.
COACH	Have you asked people for very direct feedback?
CLIENT	Yes. I mean I've said, "Tell me how I'm doing, and if you think I need to do something differently, just tell me." What I get in response are vague assurances that I'm doing okay, with maybe a suggestion or two, but then I hear through the grapevine that somebody's unhappy about my decision to let Simpson go, and somebody else thinks I'm too hard on my staff, and whatever.
COACH	You're frustrated because people won't be candid with you if they think you're doing something wrong. [The classic way to show empathy is to say, "You're feeling ____ because ____."]
CLIENT	That's right.
COACH	I wonder why that is. Are people not candid with everyone? Or primarily with you?
CLIENT	I don't know.
COACH	Perhaps we should find out.

We should note that being empathetic does not mean being nice, or trying to make the client feel better, or anything of the sort. It means understanding the client's emotions and communicating your understanding in a way that helps the client gain more insight. In this example, the client does move quite a distance—from "decisions get made by default" to "somebody thinks I'm too hard on my staff." In the end, however, the coach is not buying the client's conclusion that the entire culture is non-confrontational. What will eventually emerge in this dialogue is that the client discourages others from giving honest feedback because she resists hearing feedback and becomes antagonistic when people try to give her feedback. The coach's empathy enables her to accept this difficult truth about herself and thus begin to change.

In *Emotional Intelligence*, Daniel Goleman (1995) notes that "all rapport, the root of caring, stems from emotional attunement, from the capacity for empathy" (p. 96). When you empathize with clients, you show that you have heard them with your heart, not merely your head; that you have connected with them on an emotional level; and that you understand how they feel. These are the prerequisites of caring, which is itself a prerequisite of trust. For clients to trust you, they must know that you care about them as people and are committed to helping them succeed. Coaches who don't care remain at an emotionally detached distance. They may understand cognitively what the client's issues and opportunities are, but they will never truly grasp the essential person unless they can also understand the client's emotional landscape.

We will close this discussion of empathy with a brief note about *empathic accuracy*. Empathizing is important, but it must be accurate. After all, if you mislabel the client's emotions, you don't create an emotional connection; instead, you demonstrate that you are not attuned, that you don't get it. So if you have trouble reading other people's emotions or aren't sure what emotion the client is experiencing, then it's best to test your empathic accuracy with these kinds of questions:

✓ You seem _____. Is that how you feel about it?

✓ You seem to be _____ about this. Is that how you would describe it?

✓ You feel _____ about this. Does that seem right to you?

✓ You are feeling _____. Am I seeing this correctly?

Listening is largely a matter of patience and focus. You have to be patient enough to release your agenda and *be with* the client while you are coaching and focused enough to minimize distractions and truly hear what the other person is saying. It requires a degree of single-mindedness that many coaches lack, as evidenced by the kinds of suggestions that many of the clients we surveyed made to their coaches.

- *Strive to listen more empathetically (i.e., restate statements and the underlying meaning in a question format).*

- *Don't be afraid of being a bit more empathic when appropriate.*

- *Listen more attentively and demonstrate more that you truly are listening.*

- *Listen more to let the person know that he or she is being heard. Repeat back what is understood.*

- *Listen more instead of forming opinions first.*

- *Listen to what is being said before speaking.*

- *Listen well before giving feedback.*

- *Develop better listening skills. Do not be judgmental too early in the process.*

- *Listen completely before reacting to a situation.*

- *Listen carefully to what I am saying.*

- *I like her ambition to solve the problem, but Gloria does not always listen to all the facts before jumping in with suggestions.*

- *Releasing agenda: listen effectively. Know that you don't have to control every situation.*

- *Maintain genuine empathy for the people you coach and the situations you are asked to address. Listen with all of your senses.*

- *Listen, listen, listen.*

QUESTIONING

Albert Einstein said, "I have no special talents. I am only passionately curious." Although not intended as such, this quotation describes the finest coaches. They are passionately curious about the people they are helping, and they exercise their curiosity by asking probing questions. A good question can open a closed door. It can stir people's memories; stimulate them to think about things in ways they've never thought about them before; and provoke insight and change by causing them to examine their aspirations, motivations, choices, assumptions, priorities, and behavior. Questions are the most important tools in a coach's toolbox, and the skill with which coaches use questions reveals the difference between the novice coach and the master. As Egyptian author Naguib Mahfouz said, "You can tell whether a man is clever by his answers. You can tell whether a man is wise by his questions." Wise coaches have a repertoire of questions and know which kind of question to ask at any point in the dialogue to stimulate the client and move the dialogue toward insight.

Much has been written about the difference between *open* and *closed* questions. Open questions are those that encourage the respondent to provide expansive answers; closed questions are those that can be answered in one word or two. "Did you attend college?" is a closed question; it can be answered "yes" or "no." "What did you enjoy about college?" is an open question; to answer it, the respondent has to provide more information. We are not going to dwell on open and closed questions because the distinction itself is not straightforward. Yes, you should use open questions to encourage clients to open up and closed questions when you seek a simple, more definitive response. Beyond that, the open/closed distinction is not terribly useful.

More useful is understanding the types of questions that can help clients explore themselves and their motivations more deeply, or challenge and provoke them to question their own perspective, or encourage them to dream. These include motivation questions, ideal outcome questions, implication questions, sensory questions, and Columbo questions. However, to set up these kinds of questions, you often need to gather more facts, so you may need to start by asking some situation questions.

Situation Questions

Situation questions are the common, fact-gathering questions that Rudyard Kipling cited in his poem:

> I keep six honest serving-men
> (They taught me all I knew);
> Their names are What and Why and When
> And How and Where and Who.

Invariably, coaches need to ask some of these basic questions to learn more about the facts of clients' lives and their work, organization, role, plans, problems, and so on. However, situation questions do not provoke insight. They merely engage clients' memory. They are like oral fact sheets, and clients derive very little benefit from answering situation questions. Moreover, if you use too many situation questions in a row, you can start to sound more like an interrogator than a coach. For both of these reasons, then, we suggest keeping situation questions to a minimum. Use them when you need information, but then move on to the more provocative questions we discuss below.

Motivation Questions

Motivation questions include the following.

✓ What led you to do that?

✓ What were the factors in your decision?

✓ What would you prefer? Why?

✓ What is most important to you?

✓ Why is that important to you?

✓ If you had it to do over again, what would you do differently?

These types of questions are useful for exploring clients' motivations, decision processes, and priorities. They can yield considerable insight into how clients think and what is important to them. Consider the difference between these pairs of questions:

SITUATION   Where did you go to college?

MOTIVATION   Why did you choose to go there?

The situation question yields a simple piece of information. The motivation question can disclose the client's youthful dreams, educational interests, career goals, life ambitions, state or other affiliations, and so on. The situation question offers slim pickings; the motivation question yields tremendous bounty. It tells you a great deal about the person.

SITUATION   What is your primary goal for your business unit?

MOTIVATION   Why is that goal your most important one?

Again, the situation question yields nothing more than a simple fact. The motivation question can yield a response that tells you what challenges the business unit is facing, what the unit must achieve to meet those challenges, what resources or constraints the unit may have, how the client has prioritized among the various options, and so on.

You will notice that motivation questions often follow a situation question. First comes a fact, then an understanding of the thinking that led to the fact. For coaches, the value of motivation questions is that they reveal how clients think. For clients themselves, the value is that they stimulate an examination of motives, priorities, interests, and decision criteria. Moreover, you can use follow-up questions to deepen your understanding of the client's motivations and any changes that have occurred:

MOTIVATION   I'm curious. Why did you choose to accept that offer?

FOLLOW-UP   Knowing what you know now, would you still have accepted the offer?

FOLLOW-UP   What if the conditions had been different? What would have made it more attractive to you?

FOLLOW-UP   How do you think that experience changed you? What became more or less important to you afterward?

Ideal Outcome Questions

Ideal outcome questions, like the ones that follow, help coaches explore clients' goals, dreams, and vision of the future.

✓ What are your goals and aspirations?

✓ What is the best possible outcome?

✓ What would you ideally like to see?

✓ What would the best circumstances be?

✓ Where would you like to be in a year? Two years?

✓ If there were no constraints, what would be possible?

The real value of these questions is not just that they encourage clients to think about the future but that they ask clients to raise the bar and posit an *ideal* future. The difference between "What do you think you can achieve?" and "If there were no constraints, what would be possible?" is the difference between the mundane and the sublime, especially for people who see more barriers than opportunities, who lack self-confidence, or whose dreams have always been muffled by circumstances they have more control over than they imagine. These people may be sailing through life, so to speak, with a virtual sea anchor dragging behind them. Part of the value of coaching can be to help them dream again—and then explore ways to achieve more than they thought possible. To aid in this transformation, you need to follow up on ideal outcome questions with questions that help clients see options:

OUTCOME	What would you ideally like to accomplish?
FOLLOW-UP	What would it take for you to do that?
CLIENT	It's not possible.
FOLLOW-UP	Imagine for a moment that it were possible. What would you need to do?
CLIENT	But they won't let me.
FOLLOW-UP	Imagine that *they* weren't a constraint. If it were entirely up to you, what would you need to do?

In this sample dialogue, we've shown how you can respond to clients who are skeptical about reaching an ideal goal. Obviously, some goals are unattainable for some people because of real constraints that cannot be overcome, but in our experience clients imagine more constraints than they actually have, and accomplishing something less than the ideal goal is nonetheless a great outcome and is usually more than they thought possible. If your challenge in coaching someone is to raise her aspirations, then ideal outcome questions are a good tool.

A variation of the ideal outcome question is the *straw man* question. In these types of questions, you ask clients to imagine a situation that does not currently exist (much as we did in the previous example) and then figure out how to close the gap between that imaginary state and current reality:

CLIENT   It's pointless to even present this proposal. The board will never buy it.

STRAW MAN   What if they were open to it? Imagine for a moment that the board was open to this kind of proposal, what would they need to see from you in order to say yes? What would make this a compelling proposition?

Straw man questions are useful when clients perceive insurmountable barriers and are not allowing themselves to think beyond the barriers. We have found that straw man questions have an amazing ability to get people to release real or imaginary constraints long enough to problem-solve what they would do if there were no constraints. After they problem-solve, you ask clients how they could remove or overcome the constraints.

FOLLOW-UP   What could you [or others] do to make the board more open to your proposal?

Implication Questions

Implication questions ask clients to explore the potential consequences of actions or events.

✓ What would happen if [the event] occurred?

✓ If you do (or don't do) [this action], what could happen? What are the consequences?

✓ What are the implications of [doing one thing or another]?

✓ What would be the impact of [doing one thing or another]?

✓ How serious would it be if [this event] occurred?

✓ How bad could it be? [or conversely] How good could it be?

Implication questions are among the most effective types of questions for challenging clients. Implication questions can cause them to question their assumptions, enable them to envision a brighter or darker future, and contemplate the effects of taking or failing to take a particular course of action.

CLIENT	It's pointless to even present this proposal. The board will never buy it.
IMPLICATION	If you don't pursue this proposal, what's going to happen? *Or,* If you don't pursue this proposal, what will the company stand to lose?

Implication questions can be positive or negative. They can explore the upside of a potentiality or the downside.

UPSIDE	How big could this be? If you pursue this course of action, what's the best that could happen?
UPSIDE	What if you could achieve two or three times more than you imagine?
DOWNSIDE	How serious could this be? If you pursue this course of action, what's the worst that could happen?
DOWNSIDE	What if you achieve only half of what you expect? Then where would you be?

You can use implication questions to help the client calibrate the importance or significance of a course of action.

CLIENT	I'm not sure we can replace the team leader at this point.
IMPLICATION	Well, if you don't, what impact will that have on the team's performance?
CLIENT	Oh, not much, really. This team is functioning pretty well on its own.

The principal use of implication questions is to encourage clients to think through the consequences of their actions, both for themselves and for their team or organization.

IMPLICATION	If you could exceed your targets in Germany, wouldn't you be able to attract some heavy hitters to your initiative? What would be the implications for the division as a whole?

Implication questions encourage clients to think. They are probably the most thought provoking of all questions.

Sensory Questions

Questions like the ones listed below invoke the senses and help clients explore their feelings.

✓ How do you see [this situation]? What do you envision? How do you look at this?

✓ How does that sound to you?

✓ What does that feel like?

✓ What are your feelings about [this person, thing, or situation]?

Sensory questions provoke a more visceral response from clients, one that is grounded in what they have sensed or experienced or could imagine sensing or experiencing. Appealing to a client's sense of sight, sound, or touch engages parts of the brain not normally engaged in discussion. Sometimes, to help clients re-create the sensation, you might even ask them to isolate the sense.

SENSORY   I'd like you to sit back and relax for a moment. Close your eyes and try to remember what happened when you heard the news. Where were you? Imagine that you're back there now. What do you see?

SENSORY   Close your eyes for a moment and imagine that you've already achieved the goal. What does that look like?

SENSORY   Close your eyes for a minute. Just rest your head in your hands and try to remember what you heard during the meeting. What were people saying?

These kinds of questions may seem touchy-feely, and we suppose they are. But they are an often powerful way to help clients re-create an important moment and remember facts or feelings they had forgotten. Long-term memories often form because the situation produced strong emotions when it occurred. When you ask clients sensory questions, you often help them reconnect with those emotional events and thus remember things more clearly than if they don't make the sensory connection.

Columbo Questions and Statements

Finally, we refer to the following group of questions and statements as Columbo questions. We remember Peter Falk's Lt. Columbo as the disheveled detective who people tended to underestimate because he was so unassuming. But if Columbo seemed dumb to some perpetrators, he was dumb like a fox. Columbo questions work because they are a way of asking for clarification of something a client has said. They are also a way to be skeptical without appearing to be skeptical. Here are some examples.

✓ How does that work?

✓ Do you think they'll go along with that? I'm really curious about why they would. What's in it for them?

✓ Why would you approach it *this* way rather than *that* way?

✓ Help me understand that. [This and the next statement are better than asking *Why?* because they don't sound challenging or evaluative.]

✓ I don't understand. *Or,* What I don't understand is why [this situation] is true [or not true]. Help me out with that.

✓ Please explain. *Or,* Tell me more about [the situation or problem].

Of course, you have to use the proper tone when making Columbo statements and questions. You have to be genuinely intrigued by or interested in something the client has said.

What Else?

One final question deserves its own heading: *What else?* We sometimes see coaches who are satisfied with the first response they get to a question and don't probe further. Many times, the best second question to ask is "What else?" You can keep asking this question a number of times to encourage clients to keep thinking and dig deeper.

COACH   As you think about your future, Jane, what would you like to do next?

CLIENT   I'd like to lead a product development team. I think I'm ready for that, and I have some ideas I'd like to explore that could take us in some new directions.

COACH   What else?

CLIENT   At some point, I'd really like an overseas assignment. I think international experience is an important step on the road to advancement in a global company. I don't want to be seen as one-dimensional or knowledgeable only about domestic markets.

COACH   What else?

CLIENT   Hmm. I don't know. (pause) I hadn't thought about it, but I guess I'd like to work directly for a CEO, someone who could teach me about running a large corporation.

COACH   You'd like to be a general manager someday?

CLIENT   You know, I would. And I think I have what it takes, but I need more experience.

Asking this simple question repeatedly indicates that you think there's more gold in that mine and that you're not willing to stop digging until you've found all the ore there is to be found. It forces clients to go beyond the easy answers and develop ideas that had been undeveloped and articulate thoughts they had not articulated before. This is a simple but powerful way to continue the dialogue and force clients to work a little harder.

COLLABORATING WITH CLIENTS

Collaboration means to *co-labor*, to work together toward the accomplishment of a shared goal. Coaching is (or should be) a collaboration between the coach and the client, a journey undertaken by mutual consent in which the desired result is the client's development, growth, or enlightenment. For it to be a collaborative process, coach and client must jointly discover the relevant facts and perspectives and their implications for the client's life and work.

We have been arguing that dialogue is the principal vehicle for this mutual journey, and in this chapter we have discussed how two primary skills—listening and probing—help coaches guide the process of discovery without overcontrolling it. In the next two chapters, we will discuss the coach's complementary skills: sharing observations with clients (chapter 9) and pushing and pulling (chapter 10). It takes this entire suite of skills to create a dialogue that informs, enriches, and engages clients enough to help them change.

9

Sharing Your Observations with Clients

Continue to encourage others to expand beyond their current comfort levels.

Give more positive feedback. Focus on what was done right and not always on what was done wrong.

Help the coachees see where they could have done something different. When you see for yourself what other options there were, it forms a more lasting impression.

Suggestions to coaches from the "Coaching Effectiveness Survey,"
Lore International Institute, Inc.

I n chapter 8, we argued that much of the art of coaching lies in listening and asking insight-provoking questions. Indeed, in nondirective coaching, you may spend more than 90 percent of your time doing just those two things. However, clients will also want to know what you think and what you have observed about them, and in this chapter and the next we discuss how to share your perspective with your clients. *Asking* and *listening* may be the primary tools you use to manage the dialogue, but you also need to do the right kind of *telling* at the right time. In directive coaching, ways of telling (giving feedback, advising, teaching, etc.) play a more prominent role in how coaches help clients learn and grow, but even with the nondirective approach, it's important for coaches to observe their clients and use various telling tools to advance clients' understanding of themselves, build their skills, and modify their behaviors.

As you observe clients, either in their work settings or in your sessions with them, you will develop a perspective on what they are doing well and what they need to change. You share your direct observations of them through feedback. You also observe clients by noting how they talk about themselves, their environment, and their experiences, and you sometimes share those observations by *reframing* something a client says or believes. Reframing typically means using language that is different from your clients' to create a different picture for them. They see something one way, and you reframe it in a way that gives them a new perspective on it. In this case, your observations are not on the behavioral level, as with feedback, but on the cognitive or conceptual level. Finally, one effective way to observe clients is to synthesize your observations of them in a way that may create a totally new picture for them. We call this *reflecting*, which means, in effect, "to hold up the mirror." In this chapter we discuss effective ways to give feedback, reframe, and reflect.

Giving Feedback

On the field of play, coaches typically give very direct feedback based on their observations of players: "You're not following through with your racket, Donna! Swing all the way through the stroke." "Jensen! Keep your eye on the ball. Whatsa matter with you?" This kick-in-the-butt style of feedback is, fortunately, less common in business but still occurs. Terry recalls staying at a hotel some years ago and walking behind two businessmen down a hallway. They had just left a conference room, and one man said to the other, "George, you need to keep your mouth shut. You're making everybody mad." Feedback is sometimes very direct and very frank.

Some business coaches adopt this macho, in-your-face style, and it seems to work for them, but in our view this approach is more about imposing upon and intimidating people than it is about coaching. Some clients may want to be abused by their coaches, but in our experience most prefer a mutually respectful relationship in which feedback is given with a certain amount of grace, tolerance, and understanding. That said, figure 6 shows a framework for giving feedback that we have found to be simple, practical, and effective.

Observation

Good feedback is based on observation, not opinion. It is factual rather than evaluative. It is given as close to the event as possible so clients can

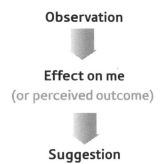

Observation

Effect on me

(or perceived outcome)

Suggestion

Figure 6 Giving Feedback

recall it. Finally, it is behavioral, concrete, and specific so clients can understand exactly what you are referring to. Here are some examples of
good observations:

COACH   John, I just saw you talking to Carolyn. When she asked how
the tests were going, you responded in a composed, thoughtful manner. I didn't see any of the frustration or anger we
talked about last week.

COACH   Fran, I have an observation about the meeting we just left.
I noticed on three occasions that you interrupted the client
when she was speaking. First, you cut her off when she was
explaining their strategy for marketing in the Midwest. Then
you interrupted her when she was responding to John's question about their IT systems. You cut her off again toward the
end of the meeting when she was summarizing the next steps.

Bear in mind that these statements are not feedback—they are merely
the observations that form the first part of feedback. An entire feedback
sequence has three parts: observation, effect, suggestion. When you make
the observation, you are simply stating what you saw, but this is an important first step.

Effect on You or Perceived Outcome

Next, you should say what effect the client's behavior had on you or the
outcome you think it may have had on others.

COACH   You came across as much more cooperative and less moody
and volatile than I've seen you in the past. And Carolyn
seemed to appreciate it. When you interact with people that
way, you build more trust and more willingness to work with
you. That's how I felt, and I think it's how Carolyn felt.

COACH   I found your interruptions annoying and, although I can't speak for the client, she seemed to be annoyed, too. When someone interrupts you repeatedly, it feels disrespectful.

Citing the effect on you or the perceived outcome on others of the client's behavior does several important things. First, it indicates why you think the observation is important. After all, if there were no significant positive or negative outcomes, there would be no point to the observation. You chose to observe *this* behavior because it had real or apparent consequences on you or others. That makes it important to the client. Second, citing the consequences of the behavior helps clients better understand what effect their behavior is having. They may not have known that they were doing whatever it is you observed, or they may not fully appreciate the impact their behavior has. In any case, the *observation* and the *effect* raise their awareness, an important first step in learning.

Suggestion

Finally, feedback is not complete until you close the loop by suggesting what they should continue doing (if it's positive) or what they should do differently (if it's negative).

COACH   I don't know if you felt frustrated or angry about the tests, but you managed your emotions well. You should keep doing that.

COACH   I suggest you try to be more aware of "turn taking" in conversations and allow the other person to finish completely before you start talking. And if you catch yourself interrupting, apologize to the person and ask her to continue.

Sometimes, as in the first example, you are observing something the client did right, and your suggestion may be nothing more than "keep doing it." Otherwise, your suggestions should be as specific and actionable as possible, as in the second example. The point is to help the client see behavioral alternatives. If you don't know what the client could have done differently, then say so. In our experience with coaches, the part of feedback most often neglected, oddly enough, is the suggestion. We often have to coach the coaches by saying, "So what do you suggest?"

Putting It All Together

Actual feedback is not quite as rigid or one-sided as our examples above imply. Generally, feedback occurs as part of the dialogue and is an exploration that includes the client's thoughts, as shown here:

COACH   John, I just saw you talking to Carolyn. When she asked how the tests were going, you responded in a composed, thoughtful manner. I didn't see any of the frustration or anger we talked about last week.

JOHN   Thanks. I was really trying to control myself. It's damned hard, I can tell you. It's not how I felt.

COACH   Well, you came across as much more cooperative and less moody and volatile than I've seen you in the past. And Carolyn seemed to appreciate it. When you interact with people that way, you build more trust and more willingness to work with you. That's how I felt, and I think it's how Carolyn felt.

JOHN   Yes. At least she didn't run the other way when she saw me coming.

COACH   I know you're still frustrated or angry about the tests, but you managed your emotions well. You should keep doing that.

Similarly, dialogue with Fran might run something like this:

COACH   Fran, I have an observation about the meeting we just left. I noticed on three occasions that you interrupted the client when she was speaking. First, you cut her off when she was explaining their strategy for marketing in the Midwest. Then you interrupted her when she was responding to John's question about their IT systems. You cut her off again toward the end of the meeting when she was summarizing the next steps.

FRAN   I didn't realize I was doing that.

COACH   As you think back on the meeting, do you recall the moments I'm referring to?

FRAN   Yes, I guess so. But it's just the way I am. I get into the conversations and just blurt out what's on my mind.

COACH   Be that as it may, I found your interruptions annoying and, although I can't speak for the client, she seemed to be annoyed, too. When someone interrupts you repeatedly, it feels disrespectful.

FRAN   Yes, I can see that.

COACH   I suggest you try to be more aware of "turn taking" in conversations and allow the other person to finish completely before you start talking. And if you catch yourself interrupting, apologize to the person and ask her to continue.

FRAN   Well, like I said, I just get immersed in the topic. It's not like I'm trying to interrupt people.

COACH   So the challenge for you is to become more aware when it happens.

FRAN   Yes.

COACH   Okay, let's work on that.

We suggest that you don't give people too much feedback at once, even if you have numerous observations. A lot of feedback can be overwhelming and, if too much of it is negative, it can be discouraging. It's best to prioritize your feedback and give people only the most important two or three observations at one time. Be sure to engage in enough discussion around each point so clients are able to explore the behaviors thoroughly and understand what they can do differently. If you have given someone feedback on a particular behavior before, especially in an area where the client should do something differently, and the same ineffective behavior occurs, then you need to emphasize that this is more feedback on the same issue. If clients have had the same feedback repeatedly and have not changed their behavior, then you need to explore why.

People sometimes ask us if they should always give positive feedback before giving negative feedback. The answer is that you should always give positive feedback if you have any to give, but it's dangerous to fall into a pattern of *positive then negative.* Clients are smart and will detect the pattern. Some of Karen's former students called this pattern "the poison sandwich." Soon, they'll start discounting the positives because they are waiting for the negatives. If you have only negative or corrective feedback to give, then give it. You can still be encouraging without having to fish for a compliment the client knows is false. Similarly, if you have only positive feedback, then give it. In any case, try to give feedback as close as possible to the event so it's fresh in clients' minds as they hear your observations and suggestions.

Ineffective Feedback

Feedback that is not immediate or rooted in observation can be maddeningly ineffective and unhelpful to clients. Following are some examples.

COACH   You did a poor job on that report, Clark. [This is evaluative and insulting. It doesn't help Clark understand what he did;

it merely disparages his efforts. Evaluation is not observation, and people can't change unless they know what to change.]

COACH   Clark! Great job on that report! Way to go. [Although this is positive and encouraging for Clark, it is also evaluative and fails to enlighten him about what he did well. Positive feedback is great, but without specific observations it is not helpful to clients. Again, evaluation is not observation.]

COACH   Fran, you interrupted the client all through that meeting. Everybody was really annoyed with you. [They might have been annoyed with Fran, but you can't speak for everyone. Generalizing how everyone felt is dangerous. Stick with what you have observed and felt, although it is fair to observe what you saw others do: "After you interrupted her the third time, the client glared at you and then glanced at her watch. She didn't say anything else after that."]

COACH   You need to do a better job of managing your time. [Evaluative and too vague.]

COACH   David, several months ago, I noticed you . . . [Forget about it. That's too long ago.]

COACH   Fran, how do you think you did in that meeting? [A good question but not as a setup for negative feedback. We've heard a number of coaches use this gimmick. The idea is to get clients to surface the pros and cons themselves. However, this ploy feels manipulative—and is! Clients don't like being led around by the nose. If you have feedback, be candid and give it.]

Getting Feedback from Others

It's often useful to ask clients to solicit feedback from the people they work with and then summarize for you what they've heard. Clearly, this is especially useful if your clients are doing something important and you can't observe them yourself. So you suggest they ask for feedback from people who did observe them. Later, when you meet with your clients, you can ask these kinds of questions:

✓ What feedback did you receive? *Or,* What did people say?

✓ What do you make of the feedback? How useful was it? What did you learn?

✓ What could you have done differently?

✓ How would you do it next time?

The important role you play in debriefing clients' feedback is to help them extract the lessons learned and identify what they can and should do differently next time (or what they should continue doing that worked well). You can also help them identify themes emerging from feedback they receive from diverse sources or resolve inconsistencies if the feedback seems contradictory. Coaching is an important learning experience for clients; however, they may not fully appreciate what they've learned until they discuss it with a coach.

When Clients Resist or Reject Feedback

Some clients do not want to hear what they perceive as bad news, or their defense mechanisms kick in when they feel they are being attacked. In truth, it's difficult for most people to hear negative feedback. It can be a threat to our identity and our self-esteem. Bear this in mind as you give feedback to others. The cliché is that "feedback is a gift," but in truth it isn't always a gift, and even when it's offered in the right spirit, some people find feedback very difficult to hear. The fact that you have a coaching relationship with your clients implies that you have permission to give feedback, that feedback is at least in part what clients want from you. So clients are more likely to accept feedback from you. Nonetheless, some will argue about it, explain the "special circumstances" in which the event happened, or attack the feedback giver ("He's always had it in for me"). When this happens, it's generally best to use the occasion to focus on how they are accepting feedback rather than the specific feedback itself.

COACH   David, I don't know whether this person's perception is accurate or not, but you're rejecting the feedback out of hand. You may be missing an important opportunity for learning. What if there is some truth in this perception? Would you be concerned if other people saw it the same way?

COACH   Well, let's assume for a moment that the feedback does have some merit. What would that imply? [This is the straw man approach. You try to get the client to accept the possibility that the feedback could be accurate and then move beyond the accuracy question to the implication question.]

COACH   Accurate or not, this is how one person saw it. Remember that feedback is not reality; it's just one person's perception. But let's focus on that for a moment. Why do you think Susan saw it this way? [In this approach, you clarify that feedback is not reality; it's just a perception. Then you move on to the reason for the perception.]

COACH   Lisa, I need to observe something. In our last three meetings when we've talked about feedback you've heard from people, I've noticed that you tend to explain it away. You always have reasons why the feedback is wrong, why the person didn't understand what you were trying to do, and so on. You don't resist hearing feedback from me, but I observe you resisting it when it comes from other people. I think this is a serious issue. People are trying to help you, and you're not hearing them. What's going on? [Sometimes, the best approach is to confront the resistance head on. In this example, the coach is also being confrontive, which we will discuss in the next chapter.]

In giving feedback, you must be *gentle* enough to be perceived as caring and yet be *candid* enough to be perceived as caring. The apparent contradiction in this statement contains the art of giving feedback. Feedback is often as difficult for the coach to give as it is for the client to hear. It's hard to sit across from someone you are trying to help and give them feedback that you know may be hurtful and cause them distress. Yet if you soften the feedback and avoid giving people the tough messages they sometimes need to hear, then you protect them at great expense. The only way to be helpful is to be candid in a caring way. You do that by empathizing, by showing that you know the feedback is hard to hear, by staying with them after giving the feedback so you can help them process it, and by being encouraging and supportive.

REFRAMING

Reframing is like looking at the moon or the large planets in our solar system through a telescope and then using different color filters to see the image in a different perspective. Different filters show a completely different picture of the same thing, and that's what you do when you re-frame something a client has said or a perspective the client holds. In ef-fect, you put a filter on the image so clients can see it in a new light. When you give clients *feedback,* you are responding to what you have observed of the clients' *behaviors.* When you *reframe,* you are responding to how you have observed the client constructing or "framing" a picture of reality.

When clients tell their story, they are selecting some parts to tell (and are leaving other parts out) and are putting the parts they've chosen to-gether in a meaningful way that supports their interpretation of reality. Consider, for example, how one client, Camilla, frames this event:

CAMILLA   The copier outside my office jammed, so I ran up the stairs to the next floor and finished copying and assembling my re-port. Twelve copies. So I got to the meeting about five min-utes late. Mark was annoyed with me about that. He wouldn't even make eye contact. Jim had to introduce me to the client, Sue Bernard. The rest of the meeting went downhill. They lis-tened politely to my presentation, and then it turned out that a few pages in my report were upside down. I don't know how that happened. Anyway, at the end of the meeting Mark went to lunch with Sue and never did talk to me.

Camilla's sequence of events here includes some of what happened but not all of it. She left out the following:

- Two other people in her company were also late to the meeting and in fact arrived after she did.

- Mark, her boss, was meeting with a new client for the first time and was focusing on the client as the meeting began. He later indicated that he had not noticed that Camilla was late and was not annoyed at her or anyone else.

- Mark complimented Camilla on her work as he introduced her part of the presentation.

- The client asked Camilla several questions about the area she re-ported on. Mark smiled at Camilla several times as she responded to the client's questions, but Camilla didn't notice because she was speaking to the client.

- The meeting ran over its scheduled time, and at the end of the meet-ing Mark and the client had to leave quickly to get to the restaurant, where they were scheduled to have lunch with three other client representatives.

Camilla's situation is probably familiar to all of us. In the Myers-Briggs® typology, she prefers Judging and hates being late to meetings. She felt guilty because she was running late, even though the reasons were beyond her control. Nothing seemed to be going right that morning, so she painted the gloomiest picture of people's reactions when she came in. Her guilt was the filter that caused her to view the situation the way she did. Moreover, she worries obsessively about Mark's view of her. She wants to do a good job and is probably more concerned than she ought to be about what her boss thinks of her. The coach had been working with Camilla for a while and knew how she tended to frame reality, so this is how he reframed it:

COACH Sounds like you had a really bad morning.

CAMILLA To put it mildly.

COACH But I'm not sure about your reading of Mark. Maybe he was just focused on the client the whole time. [reframing her interpretation of Mark]

CAMILLA I don't think so. He looked annoyed.

COACH Did you ask him if he was annoyed with you? [checking her perception]

CAMILLA (pause) No.

COACH Then you are assuming he was annoyed but really don't know for sure.

CAMILLA I guess.

COACH Could it be that you just had a bad morning and everything seemed doom and gloom? You know, things didn't go right. You hate being late to meetings. So you feel badly going in. Then you've inadvertently turned some pages upside down in your report. You were probably embarrassed about that. Am I right?

CAMILLA Yes! I couldn't believe I'd done that.

COACH Because you want everything to be perfect.

CAMILLA (nodding)

Differing with the Client's View

As in Camilla's case, what coaches often do is reframe a client's bleak view of reality. "I see you painting a very bleak picture," the coach might say. "Maybe it's not so bleak." On occasion, you may witness the same event your client does and have a very different view of it. When that happens, you should not contradict the client's perspective by saying something like, "Oh, that's not what happened at all." Instead, you want to acknowledge the client's perspective and then differ with it: "Hmm. That's interesting. You felt that Mark was annoyed with you when you came in. I guess I didn't see it that way at all."

Sometimes, you differ with the client's perspective by putting yourself in someone else's place. For example, if a client said the following, you might differ as we've indicated below.

RAMESH   Everyone on the team wants a quality solution. No doubt about it. They might not like working late every night, but it's the price we have to pay to get the highest-quality solution. Everyone knows that. And if we have to redo some piece of analysis, then so be it. They'll keep redoing it until they get it right. That's not too much to ask, believe me.

COACH   I don't know, Ramesh. You're working your team fourteen hours a day and sometimes more, five days a week, and you've required them to work some weekends. If I were on your team, I would see that as excessive, and I'd be questioning whether we need a 100 percent perfect solution. Maybe 80 percent would do.

RAMESH   They can take it. It's only for four months.

COACH   Maybe they can't. If I were working for you, I would not be happy about the lack of balance in my life. You are seeing yourself as a leader who is uncompromising on quality, but others might see you as uncompromising with people. Day after day after day. If I were on your team, it would be too much, and I wouldn't sign up to be on another team with you.

As this example illustrates, a more confrontational reframing is sometimes necessary, and we will have more to say about this in chapter 10. The coach can't speak for the people on Ramesh's team, but she can imagine herself as a member of the team and imagine how she would feel. To do this, you have to use your understanding of human nature to imagine how the client's behavior would feel to others. Of course, it's best if you can also talk to those other people and ask how they feel, but this is not always possible. When you put yourself in someone else's shoes, however, you have to feel certain that your view of the situation represents the view that the people actually in the situation are most likely to have.

Using Implication Questions to Reframe

One way to reframe is to state your differing perception. Another way is to ask questions that pose a reframed reality and ask the client to consider it. Probably the best form of this question is the implication question. As we noted in chapter 8, implication questions are ones that take the form "If [something] happens, what would the consequences be?" Another way to pose an implication question is to say, "What would be the implications if [something] occurred?" When you use an implication question to reframe the client's view of reality, you ask the client to imagine the consequences, favorable or otherwise, of moving forward with a course of action.

CLIENT   I've decided to move the entire staff from Charlotte to Kansas City. We have eighty-three people in Charlotte, and I'm sure not all of those people will choose to move, so I'll have to hire replacements in Kansas City, but in this labor market that should be no problem.

COACH   How many of those eighty-three do you expect will move to Kansas City?

CLIENT   I'm confident that at least half of them will. Maybe three-quarters.

COACH   What if only a handful agreed to move?

CLIENT   I'm sure that won't happen.

COACH   What if it did? What would the implications be? For you and for the company?

This kind of reframing works best with clients who form conclusions or make decisions too quickly and on too little evidence. You become a helpful thought partner by reframing the situations so clients are forced to think through them more deeply. Over time, you will help these clients become more thoughtful by helping them learn how to explore different perspectives. We have found that clients often view their situations from such a narrow perspective that they fail to see how other people will react or how others are affected by what the clients do. They sometimes don't consider all the possible outcomes of their actions, so reframing is a very useful coaching tool.

The sharper the contrast in perceptions, the more powerful reframing tends to be, but remember that it's best to offer alternative viewpoints as a means of exploration, not as a way to refute the client. Whenever you state or imply that someone's beliefs or perspectives are wrong, you invite an argument and may make them defensive. So the best approach is to pose questions or alternative viewpoints as a *different* perspective rather than *the right* perspective.

Generalizing and Specifying

Finally, you can sometimes help clients see a different perspective by generalizing from their particulars or specifying from their generalizations. Generalizing is a good way to help clients see the bigger picture and to test their perceptions.

CLIENT   I told Connie last week I didn't see any reason why we couldn't change the logo. We need something fresher and more hip than the look we have.

COACH   How did she feel about it?

CLIENT   She's worried about losing brand identity, but I don't think that's an issue. I think customers are ready for a change.

COACH   I think one of your strengths is challenging tradition. You seem to be good at taking a creative look at areas other people wouldn't question. [generalizing from the client's behavior to a trait or ability; this may give the client a new view of himself and may reframe how he views his capabilities and potential contributions]

Generalizing is particularly helpful for clients who clearly prefer Sensing on the Myers-Briggs typology. People who prefer Sensing tend to be practical and concrete in their orientation. They are more detail minded than their opposites types: Intuitive types tend to focus on the big picture and sometimes don't attend to the details. Conversely, specifying is often a more insightful form of reframing for people who prefer Intuition, precisely because they sometimes do not make the leap themselves from the general to the particular. They sometimes overgeneralize and don't test their assumptions by examining the particulars.

CLIENT   I'm not going to work with that group anymore.

COACH   Why not?

CLIENT   You can't trust them.

COACH   Well, I know you had a legitimate problem with Ted, but I wasn't aware of any other instances.

CLIENT   No, there haven't been, but that one was enough.

COACH   You're assuming the whole group can't be trusted just because of what Ted did. Maybe they're not all like him. Have you had any problems with Tom? Or Rudy or Marianna?

CLIENT   No.

COACH   So the problem may be Ted, not the group as a whole.

CLIENT   I guess you're right.

Reframing is a tool for challenging the client's assumptions, beliefs, conclusions, and views of situations and people that do not seem accurate or well thought out. Sometimes, unless clients examine their assumptions, rethink their beliefs, and question the conclusions they've come to, they will not change, and this raises an important point. Coaching is about helping clients change. Generally, clients need to change their behavior, but they frequently will not or cannot do that unless they also change how they view themselves and the world around them. Reframing is one of the most powerful tools coaches have to help clients think about and revise their perspective.

REFLECTING

Reflecting means to "hold up the mirror" to clients and give them a view of themselves they might never have seen otherwise. When you reflect, you synthesize your observations of a client in an image that ideally illuminates the client's needs and leaves an indelible impression in the client's mind. The best reflections are powerful and memorable. When you can create the right image for clients, you coalesce all your observations around a single perspective that helps clients work on what they need to change. To illustrate reflecting, we will offer some cases from our coaching experiences, beginning with the woman who made herself small.

The Woman Who Made Herself Small

Gina was an accomplished young woman with a Ph.D. and excellent job skills, but the coach noticed in working with her that she had the peculiar habit of scrunching down in her chair when she met with people. She would fold her arms in front of her, as though in self-protection, and seemed to pull back into the corner of the chair to keep distance between herself and others. After observing this behavior for a while, the coach told Gina what he had observed and then gave her a reflection.

COACH   You are a woman who makes herself small.

GINA   You think I do this all the time?

COACH   I can't say that, but every time I've seen you, you've been scrunched over like that. Also, you tend to discount yourself when you talk to others.

GINA   How do I do that?

COACH   You say, "I'm not sure about this," or "I may be wrong," or "That's only my opinion." You diminish yourself by qualifying what you say. You make yourself small.

To help her see this, the coach arranged for her to be videotaped interacting with other people, and when they watched the tape together, Gina saw how she "withdrew" physically from people and how self-effacing she was in her speech. This insight enabled her to deal with some serious self-confidence issues, and she eventually stopped making herself small. During the period of her coaching, however, the idea of "making yourself small" became a theme that she and the coach discussed frequently. In fact, it became the main focus of her coaching.

The Tin Man

Like the Tin Man in *The Wizard of Oz,* Paul H. had no heart. He was a senior administrative manager in a large corporation and had frequent complaints from his staff about being insensitive. Turnover in his group was high, and many of those who remained said they went through the motions but hated the job. It paid well, so they stayed, but they did what they had to do and left as early as they could. Paul knew that he needed to do something differently but didn't know what.

PAUL   I'm not sure what these people want.

COACH   Have you asked them?

PAUL   I'm not as insensitive as people think I am. I know what's going on, but work is work. You keep your personal life at home. (pause) Jeanine was crying at her desk last week. I guess I was supposed to stop and ask her what was wrong, but I don't know what to say in a situation like that. I'm not everybody's parent. I'm the boss. When you have work problems, bring them to me. If it's not about work, deal with it on your own.

COACH   Paul, let me tell you how you're coming across. You're like the Tin Man in *The Wizard of Oz*. You have no heart.

PAUL   That's not true. I have a personal life like everybody else.

COACH   That may be, but you're coming across like the Tin Man. Did you stop and ask Jeanine what was wrong?

PAUL   No.

COACH   Was she aware that you noticed her and didn't say anything?

PAUL   I suppose so.

COACH   Was anybody else aware? Did they see you looking at her and then moving on without stopping to ask what was wrong?

PAUL   Probably so. We have an open office environment out there.

COACH   Well, you gave a classic demonstration of being insensitive. You're the Tin Man.

As you can see, the coach was not particularly subtle in delivering this reflection, but Paul was the type of person who needed to hear it bluntly and plainly. The coach knew Paul would not be offended by the observation, so he repeated it a number of times. The image stuck, and in their further work together, Paul talked about getting a heart. One of the values of a good reflection is that it crystallizes the client's development needs and gives both coach and client an image to refer to as they continue their work together.

Joan of Arc

This client was the classic martyr. She sacrificed everything for others. She would volunteer to work late if others couldn't because they wanted to go watch their children play soccer. She agreed to work weekends to revise reports. And she turned down a promotion because it would have meant more travel, and she didn't want to inconvenience her husband. She did not view what she kept doing as extraordinary, but after listening to her story for a while the coach made this observation:

COACH   You're Joan of Arc.

JOAN   What do you mean?

COACH   You keep sacrificing everything so you can please others.

JOAN   Anybody else would do the same.

COACH   I doubt that. Besides, you're the one working weekends all the time, and then going home to take care of your family.

JOAN   I don't think I'm doing anything special.

COACH   I disagree. The people you're doing this for should erect a monument to you in the town square. You're sacrificing a lot for them. What are you doing for yourself?

Images like this one can sometimes be so startling that they jolt clients into a sudden insight. Joan fought this image for a while but agreed to start making a list of the things she did for others and the things she did for herself. Initially, she saw the things she did for herself as "being selfish," but as she compiled the two lists she came to realize that her standard mode of being was to please others regardless of the cost to herself. Once she saw the pattern, she was able to break free of it.

The Funambulist

Jessica H. was a very bright young professional who carefully weighed her words and actions. She came across as very thoughtful, but people felt that she had much more potential than she was realizing. When you talked to her, you had the sense that she had enormous untapped potential, that whatever she showed you was merely a fraction of the talent she had available but did not use. After working with her for a while, the coach made this observation:

COACH   Jessica, a word that comes to mind when I think of you is
          funambulist.

JESSICA   What does that mean?

COACH   Literally, a funambulist is a tightrope walker. But it also
          means someone who is mentally agile. That's you. You're
          bright and mentally nimble. But you also walk the tightrope.
          You're cautious, as though you're afraid to lose your balance.
          I don't see you taking risks, for instance. You haven't in your
          career or your work, and you don't with me. Everything is
          measured and careful. I think your caution will prevent you
          from having the impact you could.

JESSICA   I guess I'm afraid of falling.

COACH   Yes, you could fall. You could also soar.

As it so happened, Jessica feared success. The funambulist image
opened a door for her, however, and she was then able to explore her caution through the rest of the dialogue.

The Jackhammer

Jack was an executive who drove his own perspective relentlessly. People
complained that Jack was not a good listener, but the coach felt that poor
listening was only part of the problem. After observing Jack interact with
other people in meetings, the coach reached a conclusion:

COACH   Jack, you're like a jackhammer in the meetings I've seen you
          in. I can understand why people have told you you're a poor
          listener. You drive your point of view relentlessly.

JACK   Yeah, I guess I do that.

COACH   You're amazing to watch because you're tireless.

JACK   (nodding) When I have something to say, I say it.

COACH   No kidding.

JACK   So it's too much, I guess.

COACH   Well, if I were on the receiving end of it, I would feel like I
          couldn't get a word in edgewise. That's for sure.

Some people might have been offended at the jackhammer analogy, but Jack had a tough veneer and got the message. The solution, which was "seek to understand before seeking to be understood," was right for him but hard for him to implement. Eventually, he learned to turn off the jackhammer and listen, but it took constant reminders because his natural style is to drive, drive, drive.

The Black-or-White Woman

Another interesting case involved a woman who viewed herself as being at odds with the culture of the company she worked in. She saw herself as a very direct person ("If I have a problem with you, I'll tell you; if you have a problem with me, you tell me") in a culture where people were not that direct. She was frustrated by the fact that things got done in a circuitous manner with a lot of private conversations and negotiations. In her view, the culture was highly political, while she preferred direct confrontations. Other people in the company, however, saw her as combative in her interactions with people, and they felt that she was not collaborative. In sorting through this, the coach had an insight.

COACH   Cory, I think you tend to see things as being either black or white. There are no shades of gray for you.

CORY   What do you mean?

COACH   You want people to be direct as opposed to indirect, but others don't see the same distinction. To them, disagreement is not about conflict or avoidance, black or white; it's about approaching people the right way, raising issues so they don't offend anyone and yet get resolved, and working harmoniously so that goodwill and cooperation are preserved. You're a black-or-white woman working in a world filled with shades of gray.

This image helped Cory see the either/or distinctions in the way she thought. It was a pretty subtle learning point for her, and the coach needed to show her other instances in which her thinking tended to be black or white. She was uncomfortable with ambiguity and tended to disparage anything she couldn't readily understand. However, this became the overriding theme of their work together, and she later developed more of an understanding of ambiguity if not outright comfort with it.

The Screensaver

Our final case involves Peter. His presenting problem was that he was not an inspirational leader. A few interactions with him helped the coach understand one of the fundamental problems: Peter showed very little affect when he spoke to people. No matter what the conversation was about, Peter's face was like a blank slate. There were no facial expressions or reactions. If you joked, he did not smile. If you were angry, he did not react. If you were sad, he showed no concern. No matter what happened in a conversation with Peter, his face did not change. His coach told him this, but it had little impact. Finally, his coach said the following:

COACH   Peter, you're like a screensaver. When you talk to people, your expression never changes. If you had a screensaver of your face, you could be talking to someone, leave the room for coffee, come back later, and no one would know you were gone.

This example illustrates an important point about reflecting. You should never use an image that will be insulting or damaging to the client. However, your images should be accurate and provocative. The more provocative they are, the more likely the client is to find them memorable and to work on the problem. In this case, Peter was shocked by the image but not offended by it, and the coach knew Peter would not be offended because he had worked with him long enough to accurately judge Peter's ego strength and resilience. The image was shocking enough, however, for Peter to work seriously on the problem. He practiced conversations in front of a mirror, worked with a voice coach, and learned to be more visually expressive in his conversations with people. Peter hadn't grasped the magnitude of the problem until the coach observed that his expressionless face was like a screensaver.

Whether you are giving clients feedback, reframing their view of the world, or reflecting an image of them that may provoke insight, you are using your observations of them to enhance their understanding of themselves and rethink how they behave, how they present themselves, and how they interact with others. When you combine observation with listening and asking insightful questions, you have a powerful repertoire of skills for coaching. In the next chapter, we will discuss how you can use additional telling skills to push and pull clients through the dialogue. We will also discuss the important use of process checks to ensure that your coaching remains adaptive and relevant to your clients' needs.

10

Pushing and Pulling

Give more detailed hints for improvements.

Provide suggestions to the people who are being coached to help them identify what they need to do to improve.

Be more straightforward in communicating the "not quite so nice" feedback instead of sugarcoating it so much.

SUGGESTIONS TO COACHES FROM THE "COACHING EFFECTIVENESS SURVEY,"
LORE INTERNATIONAL INSTITUTE, INC.

I n the previous chapter, we focused on one of the most powerful ways in which coaches share their perspective with clients: observing their behavior and giving them feedback, observing their thought processes and reframing how they view themselves and their world, and giving them reflections of themselves that synthesize the coach's impressions and give clients a potent image that can help drive change. In this chapter, we examine additional forms of telling: advising and teaching, confronting, and encouraging clients. We also discuss a critical tool in adaptive coaching: the process check.

Advising, teaching, and confronting are ways in which coaches can *push* clients. When you advise or teach clients, for instance, you are giving them a perspective that you hope will *move* them from one place to another—from one attitude to another, from one skill level to another, and so on. The driving force behind this movement is your knowledge, expertise, experience, or authority. When you confront clients, you are trying to move them by directly contradicting or challenging them, and the driving force is your will.

You can also move clients by *pulling* them, so to speak, and you do this primarily through encouragement. When you encourage people, you reward their successes (and sometimes their noble failures) and give them positive reinforcement for the things they've done right. The word *encourage* comes from the Old French *cuer,* which means "heart." When you encourage clients, you are filling them with courage; giving them heart; imbuing them with the mental or moral strength to venture, persevere, and withstand danger, fear, or difficulty. Encouragement has a powerful effect on clients and is probably not used enough.

ADVISING CLIENTS

Everyone loves to give advice. People enjoy feeling like experts and being valued for what they know (or appear to know). Ann Landers and her sister, Abigail van Buren, made careers of it. Solving other people's problems is one of life's great vicarious pleasures. Of course, this begs the question: Who gets the most from advice—the giver or the receiver? Nineteenth-century American writer Josh Billings said, "Most of the advice we receive from others is not so much evidence of their affection for us as it is evidence of their affection for themselves." The principal danger of advice giving is that it can be a self-administered aphrodisiac, doing more to satisfy your own ego than to help clients. So we will borrow our advice on advice giving from the Roman poet Horace, who said, "Whatever advice you give, be brief." Here are more tips on giving advice.

Don't Offer Advice Too Early in the Relationship

Clearly, there is a role in coaching for advice giving. Sometimes clients ask for it, and in some types of coaching relationships, advice giving is expected. When professors coach students, for instance, the professors are expected to offer advice because of the explicit master-novice relationship. The same is true in parent-child relationships and in many supervisor-subordinate relationships. Whenever one person in a relationship is presumed to know more than the other and when one purpose of the relationship is to convey knowledge or build skill, then advice giving is not only acceptable, it's expected. In other types of relationships, such as colleague-colleague or friend-friend, advice giving *may* be part of the relationship, but some level of trust must have been built before this is true.

In a master-novice relationship, there is a presumed or implied *right to advise;* however, in a relationship between peers there is no such right. It must be earned. If you and I are colleagues, I may not believe that you are a credible advisor. If I don't and you offer me advice, I will reject it and think less of you for not being savvy enough to know that I wouldn't accept advice from you. This is also true in coaching relationships. There *may* be an implied right to advise, depending on the extent to which the client views the coach as a "master," but there may not be. The coach may have to earn the right to advise by first being a good listener and a capable and insightful thought partner. For this reason, it's best not to offer advice too early in a coaching relationship unless a client specifically asks for it.

COACH   Maria, you said that the two groups are really not aligned.

MARIA   That's right. Everyone would claim to be customer focused, but the engineers are really more concerned about the elegance of their designs. They always see more potential functionality than the finance team thinks customers are willing to pay for.

COACH   So you have another meeting on Thursday. Right?

MARIA   Thursday from three to five, right.

COACH   How are you going to handle that issue?

MARIA   I'm not sure. I've tried discussing it rationally, but each group thinks the other group doesn't understand the problem. What would you suggest?

Feed the Hunger

Clearly, when clients ask for advice or a suggestion, you should give it. However, we've seen coaches who instead ask another question:

COACH   Well, what are your options? *Or,* I have some thoughts but I'd like you to come up with some alternatives first.

Neither of these responses is adequate. The coach may legitimately want the client to do most of the brainstorming, but it still seems unreasonably coy to avoid answering a direct question. When clients are hungry, you need to feed the hunger. In other words, when they ask you a question, answer it!

Resist Telling War Stories

Next, be cautious about offering advice that is entirely grounded in your experience.

COACH   How are you going to handle that issue?

MARIA   I'm not sure. I've tried discussing it rationally, but each group thinks the other group doesn't understand the problem. What would you suggest?

COACH   You know, I faced a similar situation several years ago when I worked for Atlantic General. I was a division manager at the time and was responsible for the Southeast region, including Florida, which I loved, by the way. Have you ever been to St. Petersburg Beach? Anyway, I had a marketing group then that was totally at odds with our product specialists. What I did . . .

Maria can only hope the coach's story doesn't go on too long. Coaching is not a license to tell interminable war stories or provide oral histories of your life. Too much of that can feel to clients like going to a friend's house for dinner and having to sit through their three-hour, six-hundred-slide presentation of their last vacation, complete with humorous narration. When you give in to too much personal storytelling, you risk boring your clients and diminishing your value. It's best to confine advice to best practices or lessons you've learned from your experience.

Don't Put Yourself in the Client's Place

Some coaches have the annoying habit of assuming that they are the client. They presume to put themselves in the client's place and offer advice on what they would do.

COACH   How are you going to handle that issue?

MARIA   I'm not sure. I've tried discussing it rationally, but each group thinks the other group doesn't understand the problem. What would you suggest?

COACH   Maria, if I were you, I would get both groups together and ask them to present their point of view. You might even ask each group to defend the other group's perspective, so they step into each other's shoes for a while.

The advice being given is a reasonable option, but it is framed in a way that undercuts its value. The "If I were you" construct is annoying to a number of people and limits the client's options to the single path the coach would choose. You aren't the client and can't presume to be. Moreover, there is a danger in presuming to be the client, which is that you risk assuming the problem is yours to solve, and you may convince yourself that your way is the only way to do it. Ex-CEOs who become coaches, for example, run a great risk when they coach other CEOs. They may miss "the thrill of the hunt" so much that they not only *put* themselves in their client's place but start wishing they *were actually* in their client's place and start acting like the CEO. Some coaches have trouble separating the "If I were you" construct from actually wishing they were the client. It's best to keep some distance.

If You Know You Don't Know, Say So

Next, resist the temptation to offer advice when you don't know what you're talking about. Some coaches seem to be confident that they can "wing it" if they're asked a question they really don't know the answer to, but it's best to be totally transparent.

COACH	How are you going to handle that issue?
MARIA	I'm not sure. I've tried discussing it rationally, but each group thinks the other group doesn't understand the problem. What would you suggest?
COACH	I don't know. I've never faced that problem. Why don't we think it through?

Obviously, "faking smart" when you really don't know the answer is risky because you may steer clients in the wrong direction. If you give advice and it's wrong, you may lose all of your credibility with the client, and "faking smart" is a good way to be wrong. Acknowledging that you don't have all the answers often builds trust because you've been honest and you're showing that you're human. If you're candid about what you don't know, then clients will have more trust in what you do know.

Be Culturally Sensitive in Your Advice Giving

Finally, it's important to consider the cultural differences between you and your clients when you offer advice. Differences between you and your clients in culture, gender, age, nationality, and so on can affect how clients view what you tell them, how appropriate your advice is, and whether the advice is accurate for that person. We have much more to say about diversity and coaching in chapters 12 through 15. Suffice it to say here that if you advise someone from a culture that values harmony to be a lot more assertive, you may be giving them inappropriate and culturally insensitive advice. When you are not sure whether your advice is culturally appropriate, it's better to ask rather than tell. When you *ask* clients how they might handle a situation, they automatically invoke their own cultural filters. When you *advise* them, you have to invoke the cultural filters and may be wrong.

Advice giving is fraught with danger. In Shakespeare's *Hamlet,* Polonius was a character who seemed compelled to give people advice. Look what happened to him.

TEACHING CLIENTS

When clients need to learn something the coach knows or need to build their skills, then the challenge for coaches is to teach them (or find someone else who can). The latter is often the right answer. If you lack the knowledge and skills yourself, then your responsibility as a coach is to help your clients find the right teacher, master, program, seminar, or other learning aid. However, if you do have the knowledge or skills to be helpful, then you need to know how to teach clients effectively. Teaching is obviously a complex topic, but coaches who are not professional teachers can nonetheless do an adequate job by keeping in mind a few basic principles.

Different Learning Styles

First, people learn in different ways. For the sake of simplicity, we will call these learning styles know, show, and throw. Some people prefer to learn by *knowing:* they read about the topic; absorb the subject matter cognitively; and then deepen their knowledge by discussing the subject with others, researching the subject, and sometimes writing about the subject. These kinds of people might say that they don't know what they think about something until they write it down. The act of writing (or speaking to others about the subject) is their way of processing their learning and synthesizing it in ways that are meaningful to them. Knowers typically respond well to content-based lectures, books, and thoughtful discussions. If you are teaching this type of person, then you should provide books or other written materials as well as a bibliography or list of other resources. Other people learn best by being *shown* how to do something. They thrive on models and often describe themselves as visual learners. They need to see how things work and prefer coaches who can model the skill or behavior for them. People who prefer to learn by being shown how to do something typically enjoy demonstrations and other forms of instruction that walk them through the steps or illustrate what must be done.

Finally, some people like to learn by doing whatever it is they need to learn. They are generally very tactile people and prefer to touch, handle, and manipulate the thing in order to learn how to use it. They may want to see it done first, but they are generally impatient during any demonstrations and just want to "jump in and get their feet wet." The mantra of people who prefer to learn by being thrown into the situation is, "You can't learn to swim by watching from the side of the pool while the coach swims."

Knowers are the people who buy a new DVD player and study the manual before doing anything else. Showers are the people who buy a new DVD player and then ask someone else to show them how to use it. Throwers are the people who toss the manual aside and try to figure out how to use their new DVD player by experimenting with the buttons on the remote. To some extent, of course, each of us has the characteristics of the knowing, showing, and throwing types of learners. However, we do generally prefer one form over another. When you are coaching and need to teach a client a skill, you first have to consider what kind of learner the client is. Then adapt your approach accordingly.

Reducible and Nonreducible Skills

Another important consideration in teaching clients is the subject matter itself. Some subjects can be reduced to logical parts or sequential operational steps. For instance, if you are teaching someone how to operate a drill press, you can reduce the operation of the drill press to a series of steps, a sequence in which things must be done, or a series of steps required to operate the equipment safely. If the thing to be learned can be reduced to a sequence of steps, then you teach by teaching the steps, following the logic required to operate the thing so learners can grasp the bigger picture of its operation and learn what should happen in what order. One caution is important, however: often what looks to an experienced practitioner like a series of steps is really a more complex activity to a novice, and countless educational mistakes have been made by people trying to teach complex skills in a step-by-step fashion.

The process is not so simple with nonreducible subjects such as learning how to build strong client relationships, how to resolve conflict between groups, or how to develop an effective business strategy. With nonreducible subjects, there generally is no single right way to do things and no order in which things must be done. People take individual approaches, and although there may be principles and best practices regarding how best to do a particular task, doing it well still requires some art and judgment. There is no formula for building client relationships (although a few authors might suggest otherwise).

The Two Basic Approaches to Teaching Clients

When you are teaching clients a subject that can be reduced to steps, then you should show them the subject, explain how it works, and then have them practice it. Show, explain, practice. Showing gives people the big picture and aids the visual learners. Explaining helps people understand the principles behind the operation of the thing. Practicing gives them the visceral feel of the thing and reinforces what they saw you do. Because practice makes perfect, as the old saying goes, it's important for clients to practice doing the thing as many times as is feasible, and they should practice it with you observing and giving feedback and encouragement. When they falter, tell them specifically how and where they did so and how to do it right. When they succeed, pat them on the back and reinforce what they did correctly.

When you are teaching a subject that is not reducible to steps, it's often best to begin by observing what the client has already done. Look at his previous work or observe him doing whatever it is you want to teach. Then share your observations, talk about what's working and what's not working, and discuss and explore alternatives. It's often good to model the skill and talk about what you're doing and why you're doing it as you are performing. You may also have some best practices or general principles to share, but clients by and large are going to learn by doing, getting feedback, and doing again. Your observations about their past performance in the areas they want to improve is critically important to this learning process.

Confronting Clients

Advising and teaching are relatively benign ways to *push* clients (unless you bore them with unwanted advice). However, confronting can be direct, dramatic, and, well, confrontational. It is the maximum strength form of *pushing* clients. As we are using the term, *confronting* means to deliberately and directly challenge or contradict clients in ways intended to compel them to rethink an attitude, perspective, or conclusion. Confrontation is likely to be a little-used tool in your coaching toolkit, but it's an important one on the rare occasions when you might need to use it.

When to Use Confrontation

Three circumstances may occur during a coaching dialogue in which the correct coaching response could be to confront the client: when a client is deceiving herself, when a client is doing or saying something contradictory, or when the client is too facile at explaining away an issue. The first of these, self-deception, is not unusual. To one degree or another all people engage in some self-deception. We overlook our own blemishes and selectively ignore indications that we are not as smart, attractive, professional, generous, and right as we like to think we are. Some self-deception is not only normal; it's probably healthy. It becomes debilitating, however, if it shields us from uncomfortable truths and prevents us from accepting a real need for change. When you are coaching someone and observe an inordinate amount of self-deception on the client's part, then it may be appropriate to confront the client by pointing out the self-deception.

CLIENT   I don't have any problem sharing power.

COACH   I have to say, Dennis, that's not what I've observed. On the contrary, you seem to worry most when you don't have total control over a situation.

↜

CLIENT   That was primarily my idea! How did Bob Franklin become team leader?

COACH   Correct me if I'm wrong, but didn't Bob develop the prototype?

CLIENT   Yes, but he used my ideas to solve the design problems that kept us from creating a working prototype in the first place.

COACH   Maybe they don't care where the ideas came from. Maybe they only care about who was able to make the concept workable.

CLIENT   It still doesn't feel right to me.

COACH   Maybe not, but Bob Franklin may deserve more credit than you're giving him.

You may also choose to confront clients when they contradict themselves—when what they say is inconsistent with what they do or when they contradict something they said previously. You need to be careful not to point out a contradiction as a way of saying, "Gotcha!" The purpose is to help clients see when their thinking is muddled or when contradictory behavior is a source of the client's problems.

PATRICIA   I am a firm believer that you have to treat everyone fairly. You can't show any favoritism or bias toward anyone on the team.

COACH   I know you feel strongly about that, but how does it look when you always award the highest bonuses to the same three people?

PATRICIA   They're consistently the highest performers.

COACH   I have no doubt that's true. But let's be candid. Don't you always give them the best assignments? And didn't you tell me that you spend more time coaching them than anyone else on your team? I think you mean well, Patricia, but I also think you set up those three people to succeed.

Without this confrontation, Patricia may not have realized her unconscious bias in managing her team. It's not uncommon for people to espouse certain theories but have other "theories in use." In other words, they say one thing but do something else. Pointing out these inconsistencies can be illuminating to clients.

Finally, confronting clients is a useful tool when their explanations of their behavior are too facile and they aren't accepting responsibility for something they clearly are responsible for.

DAN   I'm glad she left.

COACH   I thought she was one of your top performers.

DAN   She was, and that's the worst part of it. But in the end she just wasn't a team player.

COACH   I don't buy it, Dan. I spoke to Kathy several times. I've seen her in action. She was very much a team player in my book.

DAN   You didn't know her like I did.

COACH   That's true, but I still don't think that's why she left. I think she had trouble with your management style. And, let's be totally candid here: I think you were threatened by her. She was a strong succession candidate.

DAN   You're way off the mark here.

COACH   Maybe so, but you keep losing good people, and we need to understand why. If you can't retain your top people and build some solid successors to your position, where does that leave you?

As the previous examples illustrate, confronting clients can be gentle and less forceful ("Correct me if I'm wrong, but didn't Bob develop the prototype?") or bolder and more forceful ("I think you were threatened by her"). There are a number of ways to confront clients. Generally, coaches should err on the side of gentle, less forceful methods, but occasionally clients will not respond to anything other than a direct confrontation. To explore this idea further, we will describe a continuum of ways to confront clients.

Ways to Confront Clients

Figure 7 illustrates the ways in which coaches can confront clients. On the left side of this continuum, at the number 1 position, are question and reflect. These are the milder, more indirect ways to confront. In this mode, you express curiosity about inconsistencies between the client's words and actions or may interpret the client's behavior in a way that is mildly challenging to his point of view. The purpose is not to put the client on the spot but to call something into question that you believe needs to be reexamined. Here are some examples of what you might say to mildly question or challenge clients:

COACH   Jim, you told me last week that you were determined to see this through. What's changed?

COACH   Liz, you have very high standards and are one of the most success-oriented people I've ever met. But I have this image

Figure 7 Continuum for Confronting Clients

of a turbine engine that just never stops. How much risk is there that you'll burn yourself out or burn out the people on your team?

COACH   Fernando, do you think the other district managers are deliberately excluding you, or are you pushing them away? How much of your own behavior is causing the isolation you feel?

Mild confrontations like these are easier for clients to hear than more challenging ones, so there is less likelihood of defensiveness or other reactions in which clients resist your perspective and push back in ways that make it even more difficult for them to listen to and consider the challenge. As we suggested earlier, the mild, indirect mode of confronting is preferable in most circumstances because it is less likely to engender a defensive reaction. You give clients more latitude to disagree with you, more room to maneuver, so to speak, so they don't feel cornered. Most people are more willing to entertain a contrary notion if they don't feel *compelled* to accept it but instead are *invited* to think about it.

In the middle of the continuum is disagreement and outright challenge. Clearly, these are stronger forms of confrontation. You use them when clients are not responding to milder forms of confronting and when you believe they need a stronger antagonist to question their position or viewpoint. Here's how disagreements and challenges might look:

COACH   Jim, last week you told me you were determined to see this through. Now you're saying it doesn't look feasible. Some things have come up that will prevent you from moving forward. That just doesn't seem right to me. I don't see any reason why you shouldn't continue.

COACH   Liz, you have very high standards and are one of the most success-oriented people I've ever met. But I'm concerned about you burning yourself out and burning out your team.

In my experience, people have trouble sustaining the kind of pace you've set. Are your recent health problems related to this?

COACH   Fernando, you and I have been talking about this problem for several months now, and I know the other district managers. I just don't think it's true that these people are deliberately excluding you. I just don't see it. What else could be happening?

In the middle part of this continuum, you are essentially saying things like, "That doesn't sound right to me," "I don't think that's true," or "That hasn't been my experience." In disagreeing with clients, you are challenging them directly and encouraging a more vigorous debate about the ways in which you disagree with them. In fact, the purpose of this kind of confrontation may be either to cause a debate or get clients to rethink something they believe. Your tone should be respectful, not combative, and you should focus more on the ideas than the person.

The far right part of the continuum, the number 3 position, is the most forceful and direct way to confront. Here, you are consciously opposing the client's perspective and perhaps even evaluating the client. This level of confrontation is "in your face" and bold.

COACH   Jim, last week you told me that you were determined to see this through. I'm not seeing you do that. What I'm seeing is the same old pattern we've been talking about. You back down when you run into roadblocks. What's it going to take for you to break that pattern?

COACH   Liz, you have very high standards and are one of the most success-oriented people I've ever met. But you are burning yourself out and you're burning out your team. People just can't sustain the pace that you've set, and your own recent health problems are evidence enough that you can't continue at this pace, either. You need to let up before something really serious happens.

COACH   Fernando, you and I have been talking about this problem for several months now, and I disagree that the other district managers are deliberately excluding you. On the contrary, I think you do a lot to push them away. You're blaming others for a problem that is largely of your own making.

Confrontations like these are among the most dramatic things coaches can do, and you can't be this confrontational unless you have already established a very high level of trust with clients. Being this bold too soon in a coaching relationship would destroy trust (because the client would rightly question your judgment). You have to earn the right to be this bold with clients. What gives you the right is that 1) you have already demonstrated that you care about the client and are acting in her best interests, 2) you have shown that you maintain confidences so she knows that whatever you say to her will not go elsewhere, and 3) your purpose in being so bold is to be helpful, not harmful.

Even when you have a high degree of trust, you should not be this bold unless you know the client is resilient. Resilient people have the power to endure difficult messages and bounce back when things are tough. If you choose to be strongly confrontational with a client, you must know beforehand that she will not disintegrate under the onslaught to her ego. The key factor is the client's ego strength. Resilient people have a strong enough self-concept to endure negative messages. Someone with less ego strength may crumble under a strongly negative message, begin to question her worth, and enter a negative spiral of self-doubt and vulnerability to other negative messages. The key questions to ask yourself are, "Can this person take a direct message?" and "Will she rebound from it and, in fact, come out stronger?" If you have any doubts yourself, do not use the bolder forms of confrontation.

In our experience, the strongest forms of confrontation are used very infrequently. In Terry's two decades of coaching, he has had to do it only about a dozen times. The milder forms of confrontation work well enough in most cases. In coaching, as in medicine, it is wise to adhere to the main tenet of the Hippocratic oath: "Above all, do no harm." Always err on the side of milder forms of confrontation first. Then, if necessary, escalate to the stronger forms. What follows are two case examples of confronting clients. Note in both examples that confronting clients does not entail being rude or mean. In every form of confrontation, you should always be respectful and considerate.

An Inauthentic Life

In this case, the coach worked with a partner in a professional firm who appeared to have withdrawn from his fellow partners. He was mentally disengaged from the partnership and was not contributing at the level he had previously. Moreover, he was isolating himself socially from the firm—he had stopped attending partner meetings and even informal social gatherings. His behavior was puzzling, so the firm engaged a coach. As they began working together, the client revealed to the coach that he was having trouble in his marriage. He had been having an affair, he said, and was about to file for divorce. As the coach listened, he realized that this client was very conflicted about his behavior and the choices he'd made. He'd withdrawn from the partnership partly to hide the affair and partly because he was ashamed of what he'd done. In the course of their discussion, a picture coalesced in the coach's mind:

COACH   I think the fundamental issue, Charles, is that you've been leading an inauthentic life.

CHARLES   How do you mean?

COACH   I think much of your life has been about taking the moral high ground. You've been a highly principled person, both in school and in your profession. But recently you've made some decisions that you are clearly conflicted about. You've been living a lie in your personal and professional life, and I think the shame you feel has caused you to withdraw from your partners and friends, in a sense to isolate yourself from people you care about and respect because you're ashamed of what you're doing.

Note that the coach balanced "you've been living a lie" with statements like "much of your life has been about taking the moral high ground" and "you've been a highly principled person." The purpose in this confrontation was to show how the client's recent behavior was at odds with his fundamental character. The notion that he had been leading an inauthentic life was a profoundly disturbing one to this client and caused an abrupt about-face in his behavior. Shortly after this confrontation, the client put an end to the affair and tried to reconcile himself to his wife. He had been feeling, but could not articulate, the deep ethical dilemma that he felt. Once the coach surfaced it for him, he radically changed the direction he'd been taking and eventually reconciled himself to the partnership as well.

A Matter of Time Management

In this case, Bernard, an office manager for a large company, was receiving coaching on his leadership in the office. However, during one meeting with the coach, Bernard opened the discussion by saying, "I'd like to talk about my wife." He revealed that they were having trouble in their marriage. His wife felt that he was not spending enough time at home, and Bernard worried that she might leave and take their three-year-old son with her.

COACH   You're clearly feeling anxious about that.

BERNARD   Yes, I'm worried about it.

COACH   Tell me more about her complaint that you don't spend enough time at home.

BERNARD   Well, she's right, of course. This is a new office, and I have a lot of responsibility. I've been spending probably twelve hours a day here. I come in at six, typically, and leave at seven or seven-thirty. Sometimes later.

COACH   Which, if I do the math, is more than twelve hours a day.

BERNARD   Yes, well, I guess that's right. I do what I have to do. It's a new office, as I said. We have only eight people now, but the company expects us to generate as much revenue as offices with two or three times that number. Last year, we grew by more than 300 percent! Can you believe it? This year won't be as much, certainly, but we are still the fastest-growing small office in the company.

COACH   You seem really proud of that.

BERNARD   We all are. It's a huge accomplishment, especially because we're in a relatively undeveloped market.

COACH   So you're very busy at work.

BERNARD   Constantly. There's never enough time to do what I *need* to do, much less what I'd *like* to do. We need to hire more people, but I can't do that until we increase our customer base.

COACH   So you're doing your own job plus—

BERNARD   Plus building the business, plus servicing some new accounts, right. It's overwhelming sometimes. I spend a lot of weekends just catching up on e-mails.

COACH   And your wife thinks you're spending too much time working.

BERNARD   She complains about it all the time, and I can see her point, really, but I'm doing all this for her and Josh. At this point in my life, I have to do what I'm doing, you know, but I'm making good money and building a lot of security for our family.

COACH   Uh-huh.

BERNARD   It's a time management issue, and that's what I guess I need help with. I really do want to spend more time with my family.

COACH   (pause) Hmm. I don't think that's true.

BERNARD   (pause; shocked)

COACH   I think you're fooling yourself, Bernard. If you wanted to spend more time with your family you would be.

BERNARD   But I *do* want to spend more time with them!

COACH   No, in a strange way, you don't. If you wanted to do that, you would be. You're making choices. No one's twisting your arm. You are choosing between your wife and work, and you're choosing work.

BERNARD   That's not true.

COACH   It might make you feel better to think it's not true, but it is. All the evidence says that you find work much more satisfying than spending more time with your wife and son.

This was one of those moments in coaching when absolute candor was required. Bernard needed to be shocked out of his complacent notion that he was doing the right thing for his wife and son and that somehow he had a "time management" issue. The fact is that clients do make choices, and those choices are revealed in the decisions they make. Bernard needed to see how he was deceiving himself, and the coach felt that a strong confrontation was necessary. It worked. In the dialogue that followed, Bernard accepted the fact that he was making a choice and that if he wanted to save his marriage he had to rethink his priorities.

ENCOURAGING CLIENTS

As we said at the beginning of this chapter, encouraging clients is a way to *pull* them, to motivate them to go forward and to reward the progress they've made, which encourages them to make even more progress. That clients want more positive reinforcement than they are getting is evident from these client responses on our *Coaching Effectiveness Survey*. Remember that these are suggestions from clients to coaches about how the latter could be more effective.

- *Increase the amount and frequency of positive feedback to individuals.*

- *Recognize excellent performance and superior effort, even if they fail.*

- *Recognize good performance on a more regular basis.*

- *Be more supportive and give out "atta boys."*

- *Always highlight the positives of situations and then explore how to improve.*

- *Continue to encourage others to expand beyond their current comfort levels.*

- *Have more positive feedback. Focus on what was done right and not always on what was done wrong.*

- *Use more encouragement and "pats on the back."*

- *Recognize achievements.*

- *Be more open to offering praise as well as helping with problems.*

- *Compliment successes both large and small.*

- *Attempt to express approval and encouragement more frequently when specific jobs have been well done.*

People hunger for encouragement, although they don't want mindless cheerleading or false praise. Pats on the back and encouraging words from coaches must be perceived as genuine and deserved. They can't be so frequent as to defy credibility, nor so lavish as to provoke doubt. What people want is an authentic acknowledgment when they have done something well and an appreciation for their efforts, even when those efforts result in a noble failure.

Encouragement *fills the heart with courage.* It gives people the inner resources to keep trying and the strength to endure hardships and barriers. It's important to recognize wins, even if they are small ones. Small wins accumulate, but without ongoing encouragement, clients may become disheartened if the wins seem too small or too infrequent. Some coaches excel at giving encouragement; others are much more parsimonious with their praise. The right answer is to read each client's need for encouragement and adapt accordingly. The error most coaches make is to encourage too little. So err by encouraging too much.

DOING PROCESS CHECKS

In this chapter we have discussed ways of moving clients by pushing and pulling. In truth, we've spent more time on pushing than we have on pulling because the former is considerably more difficult to carry off with finesse. Pulling by encouraging clients is almost second nature to most coaches (although they still may not do it enough). Another way to pull clients is to engage them in reflecting on the coaching process itself, to make them willing accomplices in the shaping of the ongoing dialogue, and you do this through process checks.

The simple principle operating in the process check is to make the coaching process transparent and adaptable to the client's needs and wishes. You do this in part by telling clients what you're doing or what you think the process should be:

✓ Before discussing the results of your feedback surveys, I'd like you to tell me how you view yourself as a leader. That may help both of us understand the feedback better.

✓ I'm not sure we've fully defined the problem yet, Sean. What do you think?

✓ In your development plan, I think we ought to identify not only what you want to achieve but how we will measure progress. That way, we'll both know when you've accomplished your goals.

You also make the process transparent by asking clients how they feel about it:

✓ What do you think we should discuss next?

✓ Where would you like to go from here?

✓ How useful was it for me to review your business plans?

To keep the dialogue on the right path, the most helpful path, you have to know which path you are on, and your assumptions about how helpful you are being may be wrong. In our work with coaches, we have seen numerous instances in which the coach was heading off in a direction that did not seem productive. Often, the coach started offering advice on a problem that seemed peripheral to the client's actual needs. In our roles as coach supervisors, we would sometimes stop the process and ask the coach to do a process check using these kinds of questions:

✓ Is this helpful to you? *Or,* Am I being helpful?

✓ Should we be doing anything differently?

✓ Are we on the right path?

✓ Are we focusing on the right topic?

✓ What would be most helpful to you right now?

The answers to these questions would frequently be, "No, this isn't helpful," or "No, we're really not talking about the right thing." You have to remember as a coach that, along with the dialogue you and your client are having, the client is having an interior monologue or stream of consciousness that may parallel what the two of you are discussing but often sidetracks into related memories, assumptions about where this discussion is going, thoughts or emotions that stream from something that's been said, and even thoughts about the drive home or dinner that night. The client's interior monologue often holds the key to the real issues and problems, as well as real but unspoken barriers, fears, hopes, and dreams. The way to tap into this stream of consciousness is to step away from the content flow of your discussion and ask a process question: "Is this helpful?" By asking if the process is helpful, you invite clients to make midcourse corrections that are usually more helpful to them than what you were doing. Making those midcourse corrections is fundamentally what adaptive coaching is all about.

What if you ask clients if what you are doing is helpful to them and they say that it's not? Are there risks inherent in process checking? We don't think so. No matter how clients answer process questions, there is no bad news. If you are on target and are being helpful to your clients, that's great. If not, then at least now you know and can change your approach. The worst thing you can do is assume you're on target and assume you're being helpful and then learn later that the client felt the coaching was a waste of time.

Being transparent about the process and being willing to adapt to your client's needs and wishes have other benefits: they build trust and help ensure that your coaching will have real impact. There is also tremendous value in admitting when you are lost, when you don't have the answer or an opinion, or when you lack experience. You may be the coach, but you don't have to have all the answers. You just have to be a thoughtful dialogue partner and a good listener. Don't assume that you always know the right way to go or that your assumptions are always correct or that the path you're taking is the right one. Instead, do a process check and then adapt accordingly. That will keep you on the right track.

11

Closing Coaching

Keep your promises. You are a highly skilled listener during coaching sessions. These listening skills are in large contrast with the follow-up, which gives people the impression you don't care about their development.

Actively follow up the actions agreed upon.

Allow the people being coached to make the final decision for what they need to do and take responsibility for their decisions.

SUGGESTIONS TO COACHES FROM THE "COACHING EFFECTIVENESS SURVEY," LORE INTERNATIONAL INSTITUTE, INC.

ome coaching relationships end without closing. The coach and client become busy, and the coach doesn't follow up. The best of intentions evaporate in the midst of problems, competing commitments, telephone calls, e-mail messages, meetings, and dozens of other daily distractions that result in whole populations of workers having more starts than finishes. As we said at the end of chapter 6, it doesn't have to be that way. The most effective coaching occurs when the process reaches a satisfying sense of closure, and this is as true for individual coaching meetings or events as it is for the coaching relationship as a whole. Managing closure is a key coaching skill.

In chapter 7, we said that dialogue is an act of exploration that helps clients determine what they must do to navigate the rest of their journey safely and successfully. In coaching relationships that extend for months or even years, the dialogue forms a continuous—and sometimes discontinuous—chain of interactions that, together, constitute the journey. Each of these dialogues should conclude in a satisfying way and yet form a bridge between the previous dialogue and the one yet to come. This is to say that each dialogue should have a distinct opening, middle, and ending. In chapter 6, we talked about how each dialogue should begin. In this chapter, we discuss how each one should end. We also discuss the follow-up that should occur between meetings and, finally, how effective coaches bring closure to the coaching relationship itself.

Closing Individual Coaching Sessions

Fitness experts recommend that every workout begin with a warm-up and end with a cooling down period. Coaching sessions are like this as well. In the warm-up, you reengage, remind each other where you ended last time, review commitments and action steps, and warm up to the main body of the session, which is the helping dialogue. Toward the end of the session, the coach needs to sense the "winding down" in the energy or flow of the discussion that signals the need to start closing. Sometimes you sense closure when the client seems to have exhausted her capacity to explore further; sometimes, the agreed-upon time for the meeting has elapsed; and sometimes, a natural break occurs when you have fully explored a topic and neither of you has the time, energy, or willingness to begin exploring another. When you sense that the time has come to close the dialogue for now, you need to start "cooling down" the discussion and bring it to a satisfying conclusion. Our key point here is that closure is a process you should manage. It should not *just happen.*

In our experience, a satisfying closure has these four elements: 1) identification of the key points or learnings in the preceding dialogue and a synthesis of them into a shared perspective on what emerged from the dialogue; 2) an articulation of any new commitments the client has made; 3) identification of next steps each person agrees to take, including when you will meet again and how you will follow up; and 4) a process check on this session, and sometimes on the coaching process as a whole.

Synthesizing Learnings

As you sense the dialogue winding down, it's important, first of all, to recapture and synthesize the key points of the discussion. You need to review the ground you have covered together and reach a mutual understanding of the lessons you learned, the key discoveries you made, or the insights you reached. One reason for summarizing the key points is to ensure that you don't lose track of something important, something you need to remember or may need to follow up on. Another reason is to ensure that you have a *shared view* of what took place. It's not unusual for two people who have had the same conversation to remember it differently. So when you summarize the key points of the dialogue you are, in a sense, *negotiating* a shared understanding of what was important and what should be remembered. Finally, if you ask your clients to summarize the key points, then you also gain some insight into what they considered important—and it may differ from what you considered important, as this example shows:

COACH   Richard, we said we would stop at eleven o'clock, and it's nearly ten till. As we wrap up, would you summarize what we talked about today? From your standpoint, what were the key things we talked about this morning?

RICHARD   I think the key thing is that I just need to step out as the new leader of this company and not worry so much about being second-guessed.

COACH   Uh-huh.

RICHARD   I'm not entirely comfortable with the role yet, and I'm not sure everyone else is comfortable having me in the role. Until a few months ago, I was one of their peers.

COACH   Yes, but now the decision's been made. You're the new president.

RICHARD   (nodding) I just need to get my own self-doubts behind me and not worry about what people are thinking.

COACH   People are waiting for you to really take charge.

RICHARD   (nodding) So I just need to get on with it. The other thing we spoke about was my comfort, or lack of it, in being visionary. I'm not going to be the charismatic leader Stuart was, but I understand the need to set a clear direction and get everyone behind it.

COACH   We talked about how you might do that.

RICHARD   Right. I need to go out into the offices and talk about where I see the business going. And I need to do that with more energy and optimism than I usually convey. Not that I'm not optimistic, but my natural style is not to wave the flag and lead people in the company cheer.

COACH   No, and you don't need to go to those extremes to motivate people. They mainly want to feel that their leader is positive about the future and is confident that the company will attain its goals.

RICHARD   Exactly. Well, I'm comfortable with that. (pause) So those are the two key things I want to take away from this morning.

COACH   Those were two key points. I recall one more. We also talked about the fact that you tend to avoid conflict if you can, and people have interpreted this as being indecisive.

RICHARD   (laughing) I was trying to avoid that one.

COACH   Sorry about that.

RICHARD   Well, it's true, I don't like conflict. I do everything I can to put it off and then hope it will go away on its own. (pause) No, it's clear that I can't keep doing that. In some ways, this will be the hardest thing for me to overcome. It's just not something I enjoy doing.

COACH   Most people don't enjoy conflict. In your new role, however . . .

RICHARD   I know. I'm going to have to fight those fights when they happen.

This synthesizing process should not be just a mundane summary of the key things you talked about but instead a real search for a shared understanding of what emerged from the dialogue. In effect, you are jointly answering the questions *What did we just talk about?* and *What insights did we gain?* Notice that in response to each of the client's comments in this example the coach helped shape their joint understanding. Sometimes, the coach's comments were supportive: "People are waiting for you to really take charge." Sometimes, the coach reminded the client what they did: "We talked about how you might do that." And sometimes the coach reinforced a key learning point: "You don't need to go to those extremes to motivate people. They mainly want to feel that their leader is positive about the future and is confident that the company will attain its goals." As clients synthesize what they gained from the dialogue, coaches have a prime opportunity to shape their mutual understanding of the outcomes and to reinforce key lessons learned or behavioral changes the client should make.

We have found that it's generally best to keep your own notes during a coaching session so you have a record of the key points, insights, or conclusions as you saw them. You should have your own perspective on what's important and what isn't. However, it's best to ask clients to summarize and use your notes to determine whether they've left anything out.

Articulating Commitments

Next, if clients have reached any conclusions during the dialogue about what they will do differently or how they will change their priorities, then it is useful in closing a session to ask them to articulate those new commitments. As we noted earlier, the moment when clients decide to change is both pivotal and fragile. Decisions have a way of disintegrating unless they are reinforced and acted upon reasonably quickly. Life events, work distractions, and the sheer difficulty of change may weaken clients' resolve. To counter this tendency, it helps if clients express their commitments out loud. It often helps further to put those commitments in writing. It helps even more to share those commitments with others. The more public the commitment, the more likely the client is to stick with it because of peer pressure and the desire to be seen as someone who has the discipline and perseverance to see things through. Here's how it might look:

COACH   Richard, what are you going to do differently as a result of our talk this morning? What commitments are you willing to make?

RICHARD   (reflecting) I suppose the most important one is that the next time I'm faced with a conflict situation I'm not going to put it off. As much as I don't like it, I'll jump in to resolve it as soon as possible.

COACH   Do you have any conflicts right now? Anything that needs to be fixed immediately?

RICHARD   Yes, I've got a district manager I've got to deal with.

COACH   What's the issue?

RICHARD   He's retiring in place. (pause) He's just not showing the energy or commitment to the job anymore, and I either need to turn him around or ask him to leave. It's causing morale problems in his district. I know it's been going on, but I just haven't wanted to confront him about it.

COACH   So that's one situation you could deal with tomorrow.

RICHARD   (reflecting) I'll get it on my calendar.

Moving clients to concrete action steps is an important step in making commitments real. You need to strike while the iron is hot and convert intentions to actions. As you get clients to articulate their commitments, you can also return them to their personal development plan and reinforce what they are trying to accomplish. As we have discussed, clients' personal development plans should consist of their goals based on their developmental needs, the steps they have agreed to take to reach those goals, and how they will measure success. After clients have established their personal development plan in the first place, you should revisit that plan in subsequent sessions and 1) gauge their progress toward their goals, 2) reinforce those goals, 3) problem-solve if they are encountering barriers, and 4) renew their commitments to the plan.

Agreeing on Next Steps

In closing your coaching sessions, you should also agree with clients on the next steps both of you will take. Clearly, these next steps may include the kinds of commitments we just discussed. They can also include actions or exercises you ask clients to complete before your next meeting. In our coaching engagements, we frequently give clients "homework" to do before the next meeting. This homework might include the following:

- Asking the client to meet with each of her key stakeholders (superiors, peers, or subordinates) to ask what they expect from her and what she could do to work more effectively with each of them.

- Having the client record each instance in which he lost his temper and the circumstances that led to that event.

- Asking the client to find ways to recognize and reward any of his direct reports who do something noteworthy between sessions, to justify why he did not recognize and reward some employees, and to identify what he could do to support the performances of those he did not recognize.

- Asking the client to read a book and respond to a self-test in the book in order to better understand some issues she is facing. Some books we often assign as homework include *Emotional Intelligence* by Daniel Goleman (Bantam Books, 1995), *Reinventing Your Life* by Jeffrey E. Young and Janet S. Klosko (Penguin, 1994), and *Learned Optimism* by Martin E. P. Seligman (Pocket Books, 1990).

- Asking the client to complete a "life timeline" that helps him identify the parts of his life when he was most and least satisfied and the types of life and career choices that are most rewarding to him.

- Having the client analyze his executive team and determine the appropriate leadership response to each team member according to each person's level of skill and will.

- Having the client complete a psychometric instrument, such as the *California Psychological Inventory*™ assessment or the *Myers-Briggs Type Indicator*® personality inventory, and reflect on the implications of her results. (You must be qualified to administer these instruments. If you aren't, you may find someone in your organization who is qualified. Both instruments are available from CPP, Inc., formerly Consulting Psychologists Press.)

We have used these and many other assignments between sessions to help clients learn more about themselves, explore alternative behaviors, and gain insight into where they are effective or ineffective in what they've been doing. We don't have a standard set of homework assignments that we take off the shelf, so to speak. Instead, we invent the right assignments for each client during the coaching session, and after some sessions there may be no homework for clients to do. It depends on the client, the client's needs, and the circumstances. As with everything else in coaching, you have to be adaptable.

In addition to doing homework, clients may have a number of additional next steps to take between coaching sessions, including practicing a new behavior (or trying to modify or eliminate a current behavior), meeting with other people in their "ecosystem" to get feedback, writing a report on their progress, and so on. In our view, every coaching session should end with some commitments on the client's part to do something next. Coaching sessions are way stations on the path to development, but they are not development itself. Clients may learn a lot during the coaching dialogues, but their development largely takes place in how they act and what they try to do differently in between those dialogues. So it's important that clients not view the time in between sessions as "time off."

Doing a Process Check

The final element in effective closure to every session is doing a process check. Essentially, you want to ask the following:

✓ Was this session useful to you?

✓ What would have been more helpful?

✓ What would you like to do next time?

These kinds of questions help you understand if you are being effective as a coach and if the client feels you're on the right track. As we said earlier, there is no bad answer to these questions, because if you're not being helpful or you are on the wrong track, it's better to know that sooner rather than later. Of course, these questions also help you adapt to your clients' preferences, so they are fundamental to adaptive coaching. Next, you might also ask some broader questions about the coaching relationship.

✓ Am I being helpful overall?

✓ Should I be doing anything differently as your coach?

✓ Could I do anything that would be more helpful to you?

These questions serve as a sort of midterm coach evaluation and, again, there is no bad answer. You should ask these questions periodically just to gauge whether you are providing the kind of value as a coach that you hope to provide. We've also used another form of this question:

✓ Am I being helpful overall? Please be candid with me because I really want to be helpful to you. On a scale of one to ten, with ten being the highest, how would you rate my effectiveness as a coach?

We've found that some clients are uncomfortable with this question, but most aren't and will tell you truthfully what they think. If their response is anything less than a ten, then your next question is:

✓ What could I do to reach a ten?

The purpose of this question is not really to receive a quantitative evaluation. You're really trying to discover what more you could be doing that would be helpful to the client. However, we have worked with some coaches who are uneasy about this question, particularly when they are not employed as coaches but are instead going out of their way on the job to coach a colleague or a direct report. Their attitude is, "I'm the one doing the helping. Why should I be evaluated for something that is essentially voluntary on my part? I don't have to do this." We believe that whether coaching is or is not part of your job, and whether or not you are a volunteer, if you're going to provide the greatest value to the people you're coaching, you should ask these kinds of questions. First, having the feedback helps you become a better coach. Second, it helps you understand how each particular client wants to be coached, and if you can learn to adapt to their needs and preferences you have a better chance of having real impact with each person.

FOLLOWING UP
COACHING SESSIONS

In between coaching sessions, the client's development journey continues, and coaches should follow up on their clients' progress in various ways. In programmatic coaching, it is especially important to be structured and systematic in your follow-up, but we believe that even circumstantial coaching should include a reasonable degree of follow-up after every coaching session or event. A number of the coaching clients we surveyed in our research indicated a greater need for consistent follow-up.

- *Establish documented goals and completion dates for your coachees and follow up regularly with those individuals.*

- *Jeanine is very good at helping with problems or finding out what is happening, but she needs to follow up on what the resolution was for the problem.*

- *Follow up completely on agreed action items.*

- *Improve on following up with coachees after coaching sessions.*

- *Follow through with all aspects of your coachees' goals.*

We suspect that a number of coaches are not good at following up because they are unpaid volunteers, so to speak. They have their own job priorities and many other responsibilities and demands on their time. No matter how well intentioned a coach may be, after the coaching session ends, real life then intrudes upon the coach, and it may be difficult to follow up consistently when there are so many other demands on the coach's time. Be that as it may, if you are going to be effective as a coach, then follow-up is necessary.

Of course, following up with clients can be as informal as dropping by the client's office to see how things are going. Telephone calls, voice messages, and e-mail messages are also good tools for following up. Face-to-face meetings and telephone calls allow for interaction, but we have found that many clients appreciate voice or e-mail messages as well. An e-mail reminder before a client goes to an important meeting can be the kind of reinforcement of behavioral change that he finds helpful. Some clients may not want to clutter their e-mail with messages from their coach, but in our experience these clients are rare. An e-mail message from one's coach is different from the unwanted "spam" messages that truly do clutter people's mailboxes. It's best, of course, to talk about how clients would prefer for you to communicate with them, but you should not neglect these informal kinds of periodic follow-up.

One important reason for following up is to check on clients' progress, especially when they are trying to make behavioral changes. Generally speaking, the greater or more critical the behavioral change, the more frequent and persistent your follow-up should be. Is the client sticking with the program? Is she doing the things she said she would do? Is she running into any barriers or roadblocks? Is she maintaining her commitments? Besides asking the client these questions, you may also talk to the people who work with her. With her permission, you may want to interview selected colleagues or direct reports or other members of the "ecosystem" surrounding your client and ask these kinds of questions:

✓ Has the client told you what she is working on?

✓ Have you seen any change? If so, what?

✓ What is this person doing differently? Is it more or less effective?

✓ What else could this person do to be more effective?

Naturally, follow-up discussions with people who work with your client must be treated sensitively and confidentially (unless by prior agreement with your client they will not be). Furthermore, the client should know that you may be following up with people who work with her. In talking to the people who work around your client, you are essentially returning to the poles of the needs compass that we discussed in chapter 3 and calibrating the client's progress by returning to your original sources of information on the client's needs.

In our research on effective coaching, we learned that a great many clients prefer a more systematic and disciplined approach to coaching. As we shared earlier, one client's lengthy suggestion to his coach describes almost perfectly the programmatic approach to coaching:

Create a long-term plan of action that goes through the following process:

> a) *Highlight areas of improvement.*
>
> b) *Highlight long-term goals—both personal and professional.*
>
> c) *Create a specific plan of action to address the weaknesses and move toward the goals.*
>
> d) *Create a structured mechanism to review the above.*

The last item in this wish list is about following up. It's insufficient, really, to help clients determine where they need to improve, help them establish goals, help them create an action plan for their development—and then not follow up on their progress and provide ongoing support, encouragement, and modeling. You may be an excellent coach in most respects, but if you don't meet with clients more frequently than once a month, and you are absent in between meetings, you will be much less effective in helping clients change. Following up after coaching sessions is a crucial part of the process.

BRINGING CLOSURE TO THE COACHING RELATIONSHIP

Inevitably, the curtain must fall. You will have reached your agreed-upon objectives, or your clients will have gone as far as they can with your help, and it's time to end the coaching relationship. We would hope these relationships close with feelings of gratitude, satisfaction, and accomplishment rather than relief, regret, and disappointment (if the latter occurs, you could not have been doing good process checking along the way). If indeed the coaching relationship has been a good one, then it is beneficial for both coach and client to end the coaching relationship in a way that gives each person a satisfying sense of accomplishment and closure.

In successful coaching relationships, the coach and the client will both have invested a lot in the success of the effort, so it makes sense to review what you *hoped* to accomplish and what you *did* accomplish. Reviewing goals and outcomes is important, because it helps bring closure to the goals you achieved and reminds you of the client's continuing developmental journey if there is more to be done. Professional coaches often ask clients for an evaluation of them at this point, and we think this is a good idea, too. If coaching is an important professional activity for you, then you should seek as much feedback as you can. Coaches have ongoing developmental needs, too.

The last words in the coaching relationship should be positive and encouraging. There should be a sense of the distance clients have come, the changes they've made, and the goals they've achieved. There should also be a sense of the continuing journey. Learning and development are lifelong pursuits, although some people may choose to sit out the journey. The clients who benefit most from coaching are those who recognize that no matter where they are in life and their career they will never reach a place where they have nothing left to learn and no place left to grow. Indeed, the people who decide they have nothing left to learn are virtually uncoachable anyway and are unlikely to have successful coaching relationships in the first place.

For the fortunate clients whose outlook allows them to seek help from a coach and continue to develop themselves, the conclusion of a successful coaching relationship should be a cause for celebration. It is one more positive step on a journey that may take them far and may help them be more successful and happier than they would otherwise. So the best way to bring closure to the coaching relationship is to celebrate. Obviously, people do this in different ways, depending on what is meaningful to them. A simple handshake and a smile may be celebratory enough, but some coaches and clients do a celebratory dinner or something similar. If the coaching has resulted in real change for clients and an improvement in their work and lives, then acknowledging and celebrating those results is a fitting way to bring the coaching relationship to a satisfying and rewarding sense of closure.

PART 3

COACHING SPECIAL POPULATIONS

Coaching is not a platform for you to mold people in your image, getting them to behave the way you would behave and make the choices you would make. It's about helping them find what is right for them. When you adapt your coaching style and approach to the needs and preferences of the people you are coaching, you show that you accept and respect who they are and are willing to coach them on their own terms and within their own context. Those contexts include their culture, gender, ethnicity, socioeconomic class, age, and role in the organization.

In this final part of the book, we offer an overview of key concepts in the literature on diverse populations to help guide the adaptations you must make when you are coaching people who differ from you in some fundamental ways. We include these chapters on special populations because the coaching literature is virtually silent on the matter. The implication of this silence is that authors and practitioners alike behave as if coaching is coaching is coaching and clients are clients are clients. These assumptions are simply untrue. The theme of all four chapters in this section is that populations who are different, whether in society in general or in particular business units or organizations, have unique backgrounds that affect their experience, performance, and advancement at work. Yet our society tends to avoid these differences except in the most simplistic ways, such as meeting diversity goals in hiring, and even then the subject is often contentious and resented. Sometimes, ignoring the lived experience of difference is done out of politeness or discomfort, and sometimes it is out of ignorance or fear, even though those very differences profoundly shape the day-to-day experience of many nontraditional employees. In many cases, in their efforts to fit in, those who are different also try to ignore or deny their experience. Even C-level executives, who are in some ways the consummate insiders, experience a degree of isolation within their organization that can greatly undermine their effectiveness and even longevity in their position.

Coaches need to be both sensitive to the individual and deeply knowledgeable about the kinds of marginalization that individuals of a particular group tend to experience. This combination of coaching expertise and cultural expertise can help coaches identify issues in performance, job satisfaction, and cultural fit that tend to go unnoticed except in the most outrageous instances.

We begin this section with a chapter on coaching cross-culturally. When you coach someone in your own culture, you more or less share a worldview, a set of values, and a set of assumptions that allow much to remain unspoken. You know how to interpret what you hear and can be reasonably accurate in assessing the relevance of any suggestions you might make. However, when your clients are from a different culture, you need to be sensitive to such differences in worldview as beliefs about the collective versus the individual, achievement versus ascription, objective versus subjective, and so on. These differences can be so profound that if you are unaware of and ignore them, you may seem, at best, irrelevant to your clients and, at worst, laughably inept.

Chapter 13 explores the work experiences and work values and conflicts of women and minorities and teases out the coaching implications for these groups, including the variations in socioeconomic class that also appear more often among these groups. Far more than most mainstream white males realize, the internal conflicts and frustrations that women and minorities have over their role and experience at work is never far beneath the surface, even though people choose to deal with these conflicts in quite diverse ways.

Chapter 14 looks at generational differences between the two key age groups in the differences in values, goals, and basic approaches to work—groups who may also lack the most basic vocabulary for articulating what they are experiencing. The result is a workplace rife with tension between the two groups, with frustration and resentment on both sides of the generational divide. Finally, chapter 15 explores the unique challenges of C-level executives and what coaches should and shouldn't do in coaching these very senior leaders.

Not every coaching situation that involves members of these groups will begin with difference as the presenting problem, and the issue may not come up at all. Individuals within each of these groups vary considerably with regard to how much they think about their status, color, gender, class, or ethnicity—either consciously or unconsciously. Coaches should, however, be prepared to take an objective and informed look at what their clients are going through, and how they are dealing with it, so they can help to surface issues of difference when they seem to be a significant if unacknowledged theme.

At the heart of adaptive coaching is a willingness on the part of coaches to adapt their coaching style and approach to the needs and preferences of the people they are coaching. Not only is this good coaching; it's also good business, because if you fail to adapt to the needs of your clients, you will not be giving them the help they need and are less likely to help them achieve their goals. When you are coaching someone who is different from you in some fundamental way, you really have no choice but to be sensitive to those differences and do your best to understand their perspective, their preferences, and their needs as they pertain to the context in which they live and work. Moreover, it doesn't matter whether you are a man coaching a woman, a woman coaching a man, a Boomer coaching an Xer, an Xer coaching a Boomer, an American coaching a Mexican, a Mexican coaching an American, or any other variation on difference. Your worldview is unique to who you are—and so is theirs to who they are.

12

Coaching
Cross-Culturally

Throughout the exchange between Europeans and their "others" that began systematically half a millennium ago, the one idea that has scarcely varied is that there is an "us" and a "them," each quite settled, clear, unassailably self-evident.

EDWARD SAID, CULTURE AND IMPERIALISM

California, and especially Los Angeles, a gateway to both Asia and Latin America, poses the universal question of the coming century: how do we deal with the Other?

CARLOS FUENTES, THE BURIED MIRROR:
REFLECTIONS ON SPAIN AND THE NEW WORLD

W hen you coach someone from a shared cultural background, it's a one-on-one encounter. But when you coach someone from a cultural background different from your own, there are more than two of you in the room. The history of relationships between your culture and your client's poses an invisible filter between you, peopled by the generations who have gone before who affect your perceptions, preconceptions, expectations, and perhaps even biases toward each other. If you are a Euro-American coach working with a client whose cultural history includes a colonial relationship with people from your cultural history, it's practically unavoidable that the power imbalance of that past colonial relationship will influence your client's perception of you, and it will probably influence your perception of your client as well. And, since the colonial dominance of the West over the rest of the globe spanned most of Asia and India, the Middle East, Africa, the Caribbean, the Pacific Islands, and South and Latin America, not to mention the indigenous and other minority populations of the United States (see Edward Said [1993, p. 8], who notes that by 1914, 85 percent of the earth was under European control), this age of global business evokes and potentially reenacts those past colonial relationships of dominance and exploitation by the people whose history you represent.

Much of the literature on conducting global business makes a good-hearted gesture toward cross-cultural understanding by focusing on the externals of cross-cultural communication: gestures, customs, careful use of language, etiquette, avoidance of idiomatic expressions when talking with someone whose native language is different from yours, and so on. This chapter attempts to get closer to the heart of cross-cultural relationships, because the coaching relationship goes deeper than the levels of functional cooperation that are necessary to do business. The coaching relationship requires the deep levels of trust, mutual respect, and understanding that facilitate self-revelation and exposure, as often of one's failures and weaknesses as one's successes and strengths. To arrive at this level of intimacy, the coach must have deep knowledge of the cultural and psychological structures that form what anthropologists call the "worldview." As Eduardo Duran and Bonnie Duran (1995) caution: "Without a proper understanding of history, those who practice in the disciplines of applied social sciences operate in a vacuum, thereby merely perpetuating this ongoing neocolonialism" (p. 1). Or, as R. D. Laing (1970) observes, "If I don't know I don't know, I think I know" (p. 55).

Understanding worldview requires more than intellectual knowledge. It requires an emotional intelligence that is rooted in a deep understanding of difference. The kind of deep understanding we are describing resides in an open, nondefensive, and nondominant attitude to ways of constructing and being in the world that can be sharply at odds with each other. Such intelligence encompasses self-knowledge of the cultural blinders we generally don't even know we have. It includes the kind of empathy that can pick up interpersonal and intercultural tensions and surface subterranean identity conflicts over living at the interface of seemingly incompatible worldviews. All of these operate in the invisible domain of culture that nevertheless shapes our beliefs, values, predispositions, preferences, definitions of truth, our identities—in short, nearly everything about us—in ways we never fully realize until we work closely with someone who lives across a cultural divide.

This chapter explores and interweaves data from the research literature on three "cultures": global business, anthropology, and clinical psychology. The goal is twofold: to help coaches develop a mind-set and the background knowledge that will help them develop the intellectual and emotional intelligences mentioned above and to suggest productive techniques for coaching clients who work with people from diverse cultural backgrounds. To accomplish these goals, we first present five dimensions of cultural variation and their implications for coaching:

- Collective versus individualistic cultures

- High-context versus low-context cultures

- Achievement versus ascription cultures

- Objective versus subjective cultures

- Present-oriented versus traditional cultures

Since a coach can never know all the subtleties that distinguish one culture from another, understanding cultures in terms of these themes is a more efficient and effective way to begin to reckon with one's own cultural predispositions and to help make them more transparent to clients who work in cross-cultural situations.

This section concludes with a consideration of the unique challenges that face a person who is bicultural. For the large numbers of business executives whose advanced education and business practices are Western but who also live, work, and define themselves according to the worldview of their home culture, biculturalism is a daily and often ambivalent reality. The chapter concludes with a discussion of how cross-cultural contexts challenge conventional understandings of coaching and push toward an enlarged definition of what's involved. The lessons of global business increasingly point toward finding synergies between cultures instead of polarities. Coaching cross-culturally is a laboratory for these larger organizational processes.

COLLECTIVE VERSUS INDIVIDUALISTIC CULTURES: AGENCY AND RESPONSIBILITY

Some years ago when Karen was serving as a dean at a public liberal arts college, the governing board mandated that all pay increases, including cost-of-living, were to be merit based. While this is a standard business practice, it was new to the college because funds had been scarce in previous years and salaries across all disciplines and ranks were below average. So the practice had been to give across-the-board pay increases. While some of the academic departments were overjoyed with the change, others were quite resistant. To the governing board, it seemed only "natural" to reward exceptional individual performance and silly, even unthinkable, to reward average or below average faculty the same as the stars. Put this way, it's a hard proposition to argue with. But for the faculty members who were resistant to the new mandate, reality looked much different. Their departments had developed strong collective identities. The faculty believed that outstanding individual performance was a result of a supportive group culture, and that singling out any individual for special recognition would disrupt the harmony of their group.

The governing board had issued an all-or-nothing mandate that was rooted in deeply held but unexamined and unchallengeable "truths" that were then universally applied. The reality was that instead of either/or, the merit pay issue could have been better handled as both/and. As a result, what we'll call the "group identity" departments resorted to subterfuge by agreeing to rotate the merit awards among members of the department from one year to the next and to fabricate the required justification. Sadly, the culture clash between the unquestioned individualistic position of the board and the collective position of these departments resulted in the departments acting dishonestly toward the institution rather than disrupt deeply held, internal values. Viewed as an isolated instance, one might shrug it off. But the larger ramification was that institutionalizing one act of dishonesty in the departments' dealings with the administration (which was seen as simply the enforcement arm of the governing board) opened the gates to other acts of dishonesty in other spheres of interaction, because trust and mutual respect were undermined. Consequently, the departments' group identity became even more oppositional to their identity as members of the college community, and their overall relationship with the administration seemed to them more justifiably antagonistic, both overtly and covertly.

We open with this example to illustrate three things: 1) the invisible nature of culture and the unquestioned values and worldview that go along with it; 2) the multiple groups to which the concept of culture can be applied, from national to corporate to religious to work group, each of which has the capacity to construct a unique and in many ways binding culture; and 3) the relationship between culture and power, particularly when a dominant culture exercises its will over a minority culture, sometimes out of a paternalistic sense that the dominant group knows what is best for the minority group, but sometimes without ever recognizing the role of power in the relationship. Therefore, we use the term *culture* advisedly, recognizing that it operates at multiple levels of inclusiveness and that for every generalization about culture, such as "Western culture," there will be individual or subcultural exceptions. Despite these cautions, the concept of culture is a necessity for naming the very real differences that shape—or distort—one group's interactions with another. Without this very useful concept, one would tend to view the story related above merely as an instance of uncooperative individuals, a bunch of people who refused to be "team players," which, sad to say, is pretty much how they were viewed at the time.

An understanding of this cultural variation between individualistic and collective cultures is useful in coaching, particularly in two situations: 1) in coaching relationships between a coach who holds values largely individualistic in orientation and a client who may lean more toward a collective worldview (or vice versa), and 2) in coaching clients whose subordinates may vary along this dimension but who do not necessarily perceive either the immediate or long-term ramifications of their different worldview.

In terms of coach/client interactions, these observations open up a number of dilemmas that are culturally grounded.

- What if you have a client, say from a traditional Chinese family, who has been taught that achieving insight is a foolish waste of time, that what counts is keeping busy, not dwelling so much on yourself, and keeping your mind on more productive activities, that is, activities that benefit others?

- What if you have a client, again from an Asian culture, whose performance history indicates that a lack of assertiveness is holding him back, but for whom assertiveness is regarded as undesirable self-promotion?

- What if you have a client, say a Native American, who experiences deep ambivalence over abandoning the home culture as the price of success in corporate culture, and this ambivalence shows up in a career plateau?

- What if you have a client, say a Nigerian, who experiences her identity not as a unitary self but as a member of an extended family, clan, or tribe, yet she works in an organization that defines value, responsibility, and accountability along individual lines?

■ What if you have a client, say a Japanese, who is responsible for supervising a number of subordinates but whose cultural background
views criticism as the worst kind of humiliation and praise as an inappropriate singling out of individual merit from the efforts of the
group?

Even defining the coaching challenges this crisply implies that they are
easy to spot. But more likely, until a coach can recognize the cultural roots
of the problem and articulate them as such, coach and client are likely to
talk past one another, if they talk at all. Research on persistence in conventional counseling/therapy shows that more than 50 percent of minority clients terminate the relationship after only one meeting, compared
with 30 percent of white clients, and they are much less likely to seek help
in the first place (Sue and Sue 1999, p. 11). While we have argued at some
length that coaching and psychotherapy are quite different, in the absence
of similar research on minority persistence in coaching, it's not unreasonable to assume a similar outcome.

In *Counseling the Culturally Different,* David Sue and Derald Wing Sue
(1999) argue that the prime reason for these low persistence rates is that
counselors are not trained to meet the needs of culturally different
clients—that, in fact, Western psychology as it is taught today is still pre-
disposed to characterize non-Westerners as genetically, intellectually, or
culturally deficient with little understanding of what it means simply to
be culturally different. All the examples above illustrate very different
conceptions of individual agency and responsibility between individualistic and collectivist cultures. These are based not just in different geographic cultures but even within subcultures of a specific organization.
Coaching clients through these challenges requires both understanding
and imagination to create a third way that accommodates both cultural
traditions in a business setting.

HIGH-CONTEXT VERSUS LOW-CONTEXT CULTURES: ACHIEVING MEANINGFUL COMMUNICATION

Anthropologists and communication theorists distinguish cultures in
terms of the degree of explicitness they attach to communication. Some
cultures, mostly Western, are low-context cultures that practice explicit-

ness and directness in their communication style. They depend on the people in the immediate communication situation to convey meaning and create a unique context. The purpose and outcome of the communication—the transaction—take precedence over the interpersonal relationships involved. Making assumptions transparent, preparing detailed legal agreements that anticipate all contingencies, defining terms, getting down to business: all these are ways in which low-context cultures practice communication.

High-context cultures, on the other hand, prize subtlety and indirectness. China, Japan, Saudi Arabia, and Spain are examples. They depend on a shared cultural context to carry meaning. Instead of getting down to business, high-context cultures tend to rely first on existing relationships outside the business arena so that shared understandings make explicitness unnecessary. Or they take time to build relationships if the participants are strangers—often maddening amounts of time to a transactionally minded, low-context person. To a low-context culture, this style of communication can look undisciplined, evasive, untrustworthy, uninformed (dare we say "stupid"?), or just plain lazy, and a waste of precious time. To a high-context culture, the explicitness of low-context communication can look boorish, pushy, patronizing, indelicate, distrustful, unnecessarily detailed ("stupid"?), and insensitive.

The distinction is closely related to what Trompenaars and Hampden-Turner (1998) call specific versus diffuse cultures: "In specific-oriented cultures a manager segregates out the task relationship she or he has with a subordinate and insulates this from other dealings [i.e., low context].... However, in some countries every life space and every level of personality tends to permeate all others" [high context] (p. 83). Thus, in a high-context society, there is little separation between business and personal life or between business and social life. To do business, you get to know the other person and establish ties outside the business context. Conversely, in a low-context society, the business deal is the basis for forming a relationship, but the business comes first.

With their different standards for getting to know one another, individuals from high-context and low-context cultures strongly influence the coaching relationship. A coach who tries to zero in on the issues with a high-context client will end the relationship before it can begin. Despite whatever pressures the coach may feel to make the relationship efficient and cost-effective, a high-context client needs and expects time to build the relationship outside the coaching engagement, and the coach needs to slow down, back off, and let things unfold. Conversely, an extremely low context client will want to cut to the chase and may have little or no interest in forming a relationship with the coach.

Coaches who understand these cultural differences can also be extremely effective in helping clients who work in multicultural situations read and respond to the cultural imperatives of individuals with whom they work. The coaching situation can become a place for the client to name and to unravel cultural knots that get in the way of communication, job satisfaction and effectiveness, and productivity.

ACHIEVEMENT VERSUS ASCRIPTION CULTURES: STATUS AND TRUST

Cultures also vary widely in terms of who has status and where status comes from. In ascription-oriented societies, factors such as age, gender, social connections and social class, family background, and religious or spiritual position define status and thus whom one might look to for advice. These societies define status based on who the person is. On the other hand, achievement-oriented societies tend to define status based on what the person has achieved: educational credentials, both in terms of degrees earned and where they came from; stature in the business hierarchy; amount of experience.

In actuality, these two distinctions can be rather tightly intertwined. A wise elder can give such consistently bad advice that no one seeks it anymore, or a talented, educated, high-potential fast-tracker can get derailed because he didn't go to the right schools or because she is a she. Some "ascriptions" are harder to cross than others: social class, even in a country like the United States in which everyone claims to be middle class, can be hard to work one's way out of, especially when compounded with race, ethnicity, or gender; it can be harder still when the local culture or business culture denies the existence of these factors but clearly makes decisions based on them. Likewise, even the most achievement-oriented culture still looks for certain markers of ascription: the right references, the right schools, the right dress, even the right physique. There is a tendency to think of ascription-oriented cultures as traditional and achievement-oriented cultures as more modern and progressive, but it is more useful to see how sources of ascribed value change and continue to influence all societies.

One of the challenges of coaching is to establish credibility with the client, even after the client organization has accepted a particular coach based on whatever criteria it uses. What if you have a client, say from a staunchly religious Latin American country, who believes that discussing personal problems, including work performance, is the province of the clergy? How do you establish credibility as a coach? Or a client from an Asian country who doesn't recognize that your Ph.D. makes you a real doctor or who believes your training in counseling or coaching is meaningless because psychology is not something worthy of study? In cases like these, where a client places great weight on authority, the coach may need to take extra steps to be sure the client's superiors convey their respect for the coaching engagement, or to ferret out other sources of authority that the client holds in high regard and ally herself with these.

Understanding clients in terms of cultural variation can be quite useful in helping them uncover biases and predispositions that may be limiting how they work with subordinates or even how they present themselves. The executive who conceives of nearly all work-related issues in terms of sports or war and talks about them this way, for example, may fail to engage a significant number of his subordinates, if not alienate them altogether. The ascribed value being placed on these two activities may carry little meaning to someone who has participated in neither or who has moral, cultural, or political reservations about their worth. An executive who places too much emphasis on ascribed values may overlook the talent that is right in front of him. Or an executive who does not recognize a client's predisposition for working with certain kinds of people based on ascribed values—elder statesman, respected educational background, correct community or international ties, nationality, and so on—may undermine the client's confidence in the business relationship. See the text box "Implications for Cross-Cultural Coaching" on page 244.

Objective Versus Subjective Cultures: Knowing and the Role of Emotions

Western culture conceives of itself as having a rational, empirical, objective relationship with the world. Western intellectual history points with pride to the Age of Enlightenment as a turning point in the birth of this orientation and its subsequent elaboration during the Scientific Revolution. These historical shifts made for rapid advances in technological and

IMPLICATIONS FOR CROSS-CULTURAL COACHING

1. Allow cultural differences to be visible, self-conscious, and acknowledged.

2. Recognize that in coaching, as in any communication situation, the message that ultimately counts is the message the other person creates in her mind, not the one you intended to send.

3. Getting at the real meaning:

   a. Pay unusually deep attention to the person as well as to the words being said. Empathize to understand the other person's context in order to build rapport and trust.

   b. Frequently paraphrase the message you think you heard; ask questions.

   c. Suspend judgment about the other person; assume good intent.

4. Recognize that the other person is more willing to forgive error than arrogance.

5. Finding synergy:

   a. However unsettling, own up to yourself any notions you may hold of cultural superiority so you can begin to accept and value difference.

   b. Recognize the multiple meanings of a situation from the perspectives of different cultures.

   c. Articulate the multiple assumptions that are being made based on cultural differences.

   Use differences creatively to seek solutions from multiple perspectives and find one that is mutually acceptable.

economic advancement and set the stage for the age of Western Imperialism, which treated the world as a kind of laboratory (or object) for the spread of Western ideologies and a resource for the development of European culture. This is the outward-looking, progressive West that, in its purest form, seeks deliverance from the intrusion of messy and untrustworthy emotionalism. Western societies have epitomized the scientific method as the purest form of knowing.

Although we have used the term *emotional intelligence* to describe the cross-cultural sensitivities that good coaches need, it's interesting to observe that it wasn't until the scientific-sounding word *intelligence* was coupled with *emotions* that Western intellectuals inside and outside the business community began paying serious attention to the role of emotions in a worldview that, on the surface, has traditionally found emotions highly suspect. Even more paradoxically, one does not have to go as far afield as Eastern religion and mysticism to find cultures more aligned with subjectivity. Southern European and Latin American cultures accept and expect emotional intensity as a marker of engagement and a mode of conducting serious business.

For someone bound up in objectivist ways of knowing and interacting, emotions simply cloud the issue and waste time. Emotional outbursts can make people extremely uncomfortable and induce a kind of flight response, most often manifested in the suggestion to take time out and let people compose themselves in private. The associated value judgment is that this is someone who lacks self-control or who is unprofessional. For a person for whom a subjective emotional response is a gauge of something worth attending to, something worth putting your heart in, detached objectivity signals disengagement or unimportance, coldness, and distance. The associated value judgment here is "Why waste my time and energy in something that you obviously don't care about?" or "This person is hiding something behind that cool façade, and I can't trust her." Emotions are something you work with, not something that you work against.

Consider the opposite extreme. The long silences that are part of Asian communication patterns are meant to convey respect for what the speaker had to say, by providing time to reflect and make a considered response. But to a Westerner, who is uncomfortable with silence and accustomed to fast-paced conversation with the frequent interruptions that signal a high level of excitement about the discussion, silence can seem detached, uninterested, disengaged. Ironically, the self-defined objective, unemotional, cool professionalism of the Westerner is undone by the silent contemplation of the Asian.

The cultural distinctions between objectivism and subjectivism are probably most familiar to coaches and clients because these distinctions are closely related to those between preferences for thinking or feeling, which have become prevalent in the business community through the widespread use of the *Myers-Briggs Type Indicator*® personality inventory. Nevertheless, it's one thing to perceive these polarities as individual traits and another to understand their embeddedness in culturally determined values and behaviors. The difficulty here is that what looks like out-of-control emotion to one person is just a normal form of expression to another. How much play is given to emotions can thus affect the amount of trust in a coaching relationship because of the value judgments attached to emotionalism or the lack of it. The clinical detachment that helping professionals strive to develop in their demeanor with clients may very well be derived from a Western value that prizes objectivity and neutrality as ways to truth. To someone from a subjectivist culture who expects a high level of emotionalism, this value may instead convey messages about lack of care, lack of engagement, lack of empathy, and lack of trustworthiness.

The difficulty is that this cultural dimension, like all the others, is largely invisible, even though the inferences and value judgments that result when people at opposite ends of the spectrum confront each other are immediate and keenly felt. In coaching clients about how to deal with their own and others' emotions in business settings, Trompenaars and Hampden-Turner (1998) offer a useful analysis of questions about the role of emotions in business:

> *Americans tend to exhibit emotion, yet separate it from "objective" and "rational" decisions. Italians and south European nations in general tend to exhibit and not separate. Dutch and Swedes tend not to exhibit and to separate. . . . There is nothing "good" or "bad" about these differences. You can argue that emotions held in check will twist your judgments despite all efforts to be "rational." Or you can argue that pouring forth emotions makes it harder for anyone present to think straight. Similarly you can scoff at the "walls" separating reasons from emotions, or argue that because of the leakage that so often occurs, these should be thicker and stronger.* (p. 74)

There are two challenges for the coach. The first is to help the client (or perhaps the coach herself) recognize when the value judgments related to objectivism versus emotionalism kick in, and thus learn to set them aside. The second, and more difficult one, is to help the client see that the two approaches are simply different and that there may be strengths in the opposite approach that one's own cultural biases have precluded the client from seeing.

PRESENT-ORIENTED VERSUS TRADITIONAL CULTURES: TIME AS AN ARBITER OF VALUE

The final cultural dimension has to do with how cultures vary according to their view of time. Perceptions of time cover a variety of extremely fundamental issues:

- Time as a limited commodity that cannot be wasted, as opposed to time as a synchronous experience that meshes past, present, and future

- Time as a repository of value—whether value lies in the past or the present

- Time as a repository of knowledge—the reverence for preserving traditional knowledge and customs versus the quest for new knowledge and a critical view of present knowledge and its limitations

- Time as the medium of change, as opposed to time as a preservation of the past

- Time as linear, always leading to the future, as opposed to time as circular, always taking one back to the past

- Time as something to be measured and doled out, as opposed to time as something to be experienced

- Time as a future that threatens vital relationships formed in the past, as opposed to time as a promise of better things to come

- Time as short term and time as long term

On the surface, these orientations toward time would seem to have little to do with the conduct of business—but only among people who share a common conception of time and its value. Our sense of time is so deeply embedded in our definitions of ourselves and in our relationships with the world that time is truly something we often cannot see and whose value we cannot grasp except when it is handled in ways that are not consistent with our expectations. However, since our conceptions of time define how we use it and hence the values we attribute to it, human beings' constant negotiations with each other are typically, at the heart of things, negotiations about time.

Consider, for instance, the value placed on punctuality. To be late for an appointment is the height of rudeness in present-oriented cultures, largely because it wastes other people's time, showing disrespect and costing money. But time is not the supreme value in some ascription-oriented cultures, if for instance, one must choose between being on time and finishing up a conversation with a respected senior colleague. Nor would it be at the top of the hierarchy in collective cultures when one must choose between being on time and reaching consensus on an important issue with one's work group. This is not simply a decision to spend time in one way rather than another way. It is about differing experiences of time and differing hierarchies of value.

Helping clients in a cross-cultural environment reframe their perspective on their work through the lens of time can be hugely valuable because time is so fundamental. How much of the organization is devoted in one way or another to time: managing it, policing it, dividing it up and parceling it out, measuring performance against it, determining its value by what activities or people receive more time and what or who receives less? Does this organization seem optimal in terms of business and cultural values? When is time the highest value and when does it give way to other values? How is the use of time related to other interpersonal difficulties that the client needs to resolve at work? What value judgments does the client attach to other people's use of time? Are these evaluations legitimate or simply culture blind? How does the client's own perception (perhaps even preoccupation) with time help or hinder his management effectiveness? What conflicts are, at their root, conflicts over time? When do traditional orientations to time offer solutions to problems that present orientations can't imagine? And vice versa. Is it possible to negotiate a shared perspective on time for purposes of operating the business? Obviously, coaches can, and should, ask the same questions of themselves when dealing with clients whose orientation to time is not the same as theirs.

BICULTURALISM AND THE WESTERN WORLDVIEW

In today's global business environment, many international managers and executives were raised in the home culture but educated in the West. They live simultaneously in two cultures, often experiencing a psychological push and pull to live according to two different and sometimes conflict-

ing sets of norms. The built-in conflicts of inhabiting a bicultural psychological space are present not just at work but also at home. South
African scholar Amina Mama (2002) raises the question: "But what
should Africans be adjusting to in the era of globalization? As young
urban Africans rush to embrace the often violent and misogynistic North
American ghetto cultures of rap, hip hop, and Rambo-style machismo,
their elders cannot but view this as a form of maladjustment!" (p. 10).

India and Japan are useful as case studies for helping coaches understand the limits of the Western worldview as it is embedded in assumptions and values regarding adjustment and identity. This all-too-brief
analysis is useful, nevertheless, because the same themes are similarly
played out throughout postcolonial states around the globe.

The two centuries of British occupation of India were characterized
by an attitude of contempt for all things Indian and a conscious effort to
eradicate Indian culture through reeducation of the young in the British
mode. The goal was to replace Indian values and lifestyles with all things
English, just as the federal Native American boarding schools of the
United States during the early 1900s were part of a highly conscious attempt to eradicate native cultures in America. Indians were viewed as un-
clean, dishonest, dishonorable, and completely inferior to Europeans. In
his study of Indian and Japanese cross-cultural psychology, Alan Roland
(1988) maintains that "the reverberating effects of this educational system
are still felt today, and greatly affect Indian identity" (p. 19). These effects
include conflicts between very different value systems, different ways of
relating to others socially, and different standards and assumptions about
healthy psychological functioning and are most intensely experienced
among upper-class males. (Women's more sheltered role in society tended
to isolate them from the daily onslaught of British prejudice and reeducation programs.) Bound up in these conflicts is considerable ambivalence toward those who represent Western value systems, in this case, an
outside, non-native coach. As Roland points out:

> *The intense denigration of Indian culture and Indians under the
> colonial regime resulted in profound consequences to the Western-
> educated Hindu upper castes and upper-class Muslims, and compli-
> cated the processes of acculturation and assimilation of foreign ele-
> ments into the Indian framework. . . . So powerful have been these
> kinds of identity struggles generated by British colonial rule that they
> continue even some forty years after Independence. Sudhir Kakar has*

*remarked that beneath the guise of many overtly held value positions,
deep down, Western-educated Indian men must to this day make a
decisive choice between being Indian in identity or Western. Whenever the identity investment is more Western, there is inevitably a
subtle or open denigration of many things Indian.* (pp. 20–22)

Thus, for many Indian people today, working at home or abroad,
marriages are still arranged; educational choices, career choices, and all
other major life decisions are made in close consultation with parents
whose guidance dominates decision making; social ties and friends become part of an extended family; and a holistic Hindu worldview is pervasive. The individual lives a highly reciprocal and interdependent life in
which the ongoing approval of others is central to maintaining a sense of
self-worth. One strives to become "a person centered in a spiritual consciousness and being, so that there is an inner calm amid the stresses and
pulls of close familial and other group hierarchical relationships" (p. 60).
Roland describes the Indian sense of self as a "we-self" that imposes quite
different meanings on educational and professional achievement than is
typical in the West. "Skills and motives for achievement tend to be sub-
sumed under a we-self and familial embeddedness rather than acquired
for self-actualization. The central cultural ideals . . . revolve around the
gradual realization of the spiritual self, wherein subtle differences and nuances in inner makeup, temperament, and inclinations are all utilized in
the spiritual quest" (p. 331).

Though the Japanese do not have the heritage of cultural denigration
that Indians bring to life in a global society, they attach similar values to
work. Achievement is not about incurring individual distinction and self-
actualization in a Western sense but is part of a larger journey toward
inner cultivation that is as much aesthetic as functional and is realized
only in connection with a family or other group. Self-containment, verbal and otherwise, is characteristic of this deeply interpersonal orientation. Functionally, containing oneself is a necessity to maintain harmony
with others in one's family or work group. Spiritually, it is a necessity in
cultivating the inner psychological space needed for spiritual development. The Japanese response to a Western-style global environment has
been to develop what Roland refers to as "a two-layered personality: a
deeper core associated with traditional Japanese culture, and an upper
layer associated with acculturation to American and Western influences
in Japan" (p. 21). The coach who treats any of these native practices as
quaint, or who romanticizes them by reducing them to caricatures of

Eastern mysticism, will fail utterly to establish a working relationship with an Indian or Japanese client.

The difficulty in getting beyond these reactions, though, is more complex than adopting existing prescriptions for cultural "tolerance" or "respect." At the heart of the matter is a deeply embedded Western view of the meaning and value of work as an expression of psychological maturity. For Western cultures, the normative pattern of individual growth is developing autonomy, or what therapists call "individuation." This is achieved by breaking away from the family and striking out on one's own, achieving independence as a decision maker so one becomes free to craft one's own identity. Individual freedom of all sorts—physical, interpersonal, verbal, intellectual, emotional—is the supreme value and is assumed to be necessary to reach one's full potential. Affiliation with others is not a responsibility; it is an independent choice that marks maturity.

As an applied social science—specifically, a branch of psychology— the very concept of coaching is an expression of this uniquely Western worldview. With a family tree that reaches back through Western philosophy and American psychology, coaching embodies assumptions that are fundamentally Western:

- Coaching is based in a one-on-one relationship between client and coach.

- The reason for coaching is change in the client to help the person become a more effective individual, to continue along that path of normative development.

- Change comes about through rational insight, and self-understanding is the basis for subsequent behavioral change.

- The coach helps the client change, and the client, in turn, becomes more capable of effecting change in himself and the client's organization.

- Coaching, while it explores emotions, is an inherently rational, empirical process.

- The medium for coaching is dialogue, and verbal discursiveness is necessary to achieve the desired changes.

Given these characteristics, Duran and Duran (1995) characterize psychology and its applied offspring as having "roots so deeply entrenched in classic Western philosophy that many scholars agree it is simply a footnote to Plato.... In no way does Western thinking address any system of cognition except its own" (p. 17). David Sue and Derald Wing Sue (1999), arguably the most authoritative scholars and practitioners of cross-cultural counseling, go one step further. Based on an extensive review of the literature, they draw the persuasive, if somewhat uncomfortable, conclusion that "American. . . . psychology has been severely criticized as being ethnocentric, monocultural, and inherently biased against racial/ethnic minorities, women, gays/lesbians, and other culturally different groups" (p. 31). The very normative invisibility of the Western worldview, they argue, is what makes it so impregnable. As such, they contend,

> *it is well-intentioned individuals who experience themselves as moral, decent, and fair-minded that may have the greatest difficulty in understanding how their belief systems and actions may be biased and prejudiced. . . . Perhaps the greatest obstacle to a meaningful movement toward a multicultural society is our failure to understand our unconscious and unintentional complicity in perpetuating bias and discrimination via our personal values/beliefs and our institutions.* (p. 34)

Understanding that neither the medium nor the purposes of coaching are value-free is a first step toward effective cross-cultural coaching. The various dimensions of cultural difference presented here are intended to help coaches working with minority and international clients develop broader understandings of cultural practices and values and to help their clients do the same. However, it is also true that these clients likely face quite different challenges at work than do mainstream clients. Stereotyping, prejudice, and discrimination are alive and well in the business world just as they are in society at large. The problems that surface in coaching minority or international clients may not be the client's problems but the organization's, and the coach, not the client, may need to become the change agent within the organization. Thus, it may mean that the coach ultimately works in a broader context than that of the coach-client relationship to help business organizations themselves become the models of globalization that they need and ought to be.

13

Coaching
Women and Minorities

I truly believe you don't know how frustrated I am—how frustrated
we African Americans are—by the lack of acknowledgment or
apparent understanding of how our experience in the workplace
differs from yours, and how it affects not just our own morale but
the health of the organization over all.

KEITH A. CAVER AND ANCELLA B. LIVERS, "DEAR WHITE BOSS"

Too often, women were passed over for certain assignments because
male partners made assumptions about what they wanted. . . .
Usually we weren't even conscious of making such assumptions.

DOUGLAS M. MCCRACKEN, "WINNING THE TALENT WAR FOR WOMEN"

In *Coaching for Leadership,* Laurence Lyons (2000) of Executive
Coaching Network argues that "with a sound appreciation of business and interpersonal dynamics, a good coach is simply a process person
who can establish rapport; is informed about the executive's immediate
environment; is honest and courageous in providing feedback; is a good
listener; asks good questions; is visionary and analytic; and is a good plan-
ner who seeks follow-up and closure" (pp. 6–7). Most people would agree
that these attributes are essential in an executive coach. In addition, the
coaching relationship demands of the coach objectivity, insight, the ability to distinguish facilitation from advice giving, open-mindedness, and
creativity, along with the mainstays of any counseling relationship: gen-
uineness, empathy, warmth, and unconditional positive regard. But for

executives who are women or members of a minority, these are necessary but not sufficient conditions.

Participation of women and minorities in the executive ranks remains marginal, and although their numbers are growing slowly, senior executives continue to cite pipeline problems as the chief cause for their continued absence (see Catalyst 2000). Although the pipeline explanation is debatable, the lack of gender, ethnic, racial, and even social class diversity poses special challenges for women and minorities who either have made it to the executive track or are on their way to it. Coaching for women and minorities requires special knowledge of the unique needs and challenges of these groups. This chapter describes these challenges and the role of executive coaches in helping their clients, and sometimes their organizations, to meet them.

Although the literature on coaching has exploded in recent years, research on coaching for women and minorities is essentially nonexistent. Researchers seem to assume that coaching is coaching is coaching. Like the early research on leadership, and much of the literature on human development, the person that researchers have in mind is ostensibly gender and ethnically "neutral" but is most likely a white, middle-aged man. For instance, the influential book by Morgan McCall, Michael Lombardo, and Ann Morrison (1988), *The Lessons of Experience: How Successful Executives Develop on the Job,* never identifies the gender or ethnic backgrounds of the executives the authors studied. In fact, all but one of the executives in that study were male. A follow-up study, *Breaking the Glass Ceiling: Can Women Reach the Top of America's Largest Corporations?* (Morrison et al. 1992), which was also sponsored by the Center for Creative Leadership, was launched to correct the overrepresentation of male experience. "Our goal," say the authors, "was to match as best we could the group in this study to those in the earlier interview study of male executives so that responses could be compared" (p. 9). This and subsequent research on the professional experiences of women and minorities has made it clear that these populations face very different challenges as they move upward in the executive ranks. Successful coaching outcomes for women and minorities depend on an informed sensitivity to those challenges and an ability to frame them in a way that is helpful to the client.

Even if the coach happens to be a woman or a member of a minority group, there is no guarantee that the client's gender, race, class, or ethnicity will factor into the coaching relationship. It is more likely that the same assumption of gender and ethnic neutrality that we see in the general literature on executive development will dominate the underlying framework of the coaching, unless very concrete issues related to these factors are at the root of the client's coaching needs.

The early days of the women's movement focused on various forms of consciousness raising precisely because understanding the experience of being a woman was shrouded in denial and resistance. The civil rights movement for blacks, Native Americans, and other minority groups followed much the same pattern: first to name the condition (of being female, black, Native American, Hispanic, and so on) before you could begin to consider the ramifications. Scholarship in women's studies and ethnic studies continues to elaborate what it means to be black or Asian or Native American or Hispanic, and/or female, and has recently broadened its focus to include analysis of how social class also significantly influences professional opportunities and how organizations and individuals respond in the corporate environment and other settings. Sensitivities are not genetically encoded in the gender or ethnicity of the coach but result only from a combination of academic study, practical experience, and raised consciousness about difference.

EMPATHIC ACCURACY

Perhaps the greatest challenge for an executive coach, regardless of background, is to ensure empathic accuracy. A white, male, upper-middle-class coach working with a black, female executive raised in a rural environment may sympathize with that individual's struggles in the academic and corporate world, as well as in society in general, but that coach may never fully understand the internal frame of reference through which that client interprets her experiences. Nevertheless, the more informed the coach can be of what it means to be the only black face at the conference table, or of the legacy of suspicion that you were really an affirmative action appointment, or of the psychological conflicts of crossing cultural boundaries, the more able that coach will be to hear what the client is saying, to unearth unnamed conflicts, and to help guide the process of executive development.

On the other hand, a white, female, upper-middle-class coach working with a white, female, upper-middle-class executive may overempathize by too readily mistaking her own struggles as a woman for the client's. Inevitably, women and minority coaches and consultants who fully engage the literature on workplace issues discover a deep-seated anger, and however constructively they may channel that anger, it can still interfere with their ability to understand and empathize with the particular circumstances of the executive sitting in front of them. Meanwhile, many women and minorities who are just trying to succeed and to advance in their jobs often expend just as much energy trying to ignore differential treatment or rationalize it or cope with it or deny it. In any case, accurate empathy is more likely to come about through the combination of close listening, careful analysis, and deep knowledge of oneself and one's limits and of the other, as both an individual and a member of a particular minority group.

In this chapter, we examine three categories of difference that tend to set women and minorities apart from mainstream work culture: appearance differences, work values differences, and interpersonal differences. Implications for coaching are discussed in relation to each category.

DIFFERENT APPEARANCES

Let's start with the obvious: women and minorities look different from white men. Although organizations talk about being gender-blind or color-blind, at best this talk is metaphorical—a statement of values. At worst, this metaphor blinds organizations to the very reasons they sought diversity in the first place: to seek multiple perspectives and experiences as a way to enrich the work that goes on.

Discussion

The reality is that people who look different from the majority stand out. Their work is more visible, which means that their achievements, but more often their mistakes, are magnified. Study after study reports the same conclusion: women and minorities are held to higher performance standards than the mainstream population, and they derail more often. In a recent interview, a young Native American executive working for a major technology firm stated, "As a minority, you always have to be twenty times better, and they still keep upping the bar." A new study confirmed this perception: "The two career advancement strategies most frequently cited by executive women were consistently exceeding performance expectations, and developing a style with which male managers are comfortable, suggesting that women have to work harder to prove themselves for consideration for opportunities and that they have to make many adjustments to 'fit in' to the corporate culture" (Catalyst 2000, p. 47).

Physical difference sets up a chain of differential expectations and differential reactions to those expectations among those who are different. First, there is perfectionism. Women managers and executives tend to become highly perfectionistic in their work, perhaps because of the double standard discussed above. Although perfectionism has its obvious plus side in accounting for successful women's tendencies to exceed performance expectations, it does seem to play heavily into the glass ceiling phenomenon. The downside of perfectionism includes the following.

- Perfectionism makes people averse to risk. They disregard the important intuitions and subtle internal cues that are often our best sources of insight.

- Perfectionism keeps people isolated from the formal and informal cultures of the organization because they bury themselves in their work. For women and some minority groups, this is particularly damaging, because the research on difference tells us that it's through connection with others that their best work is done (see Rosener 1995 and Belenky et al. 1986).

- Perfectionism often blinds us to the big picture, making us slaves to the microscopic world of details. Perfectionists often come to be typecast as detailers or micromanagers, unable to take on a larger scope of responsibilities.

- Perfectionism induces high levels of stress and burnout because it is often used as a mask for the lack of self-confidence that women and minorities experience in their professional life. It's as if "by narrowing the boundaries of my world, I can control it and feel confident in it"—at the very time that, as an executive, one needs to reach out, branch out, break out.

- Perfectionism hinders work-life balance. It interferes with the necessary executive ability to decide what's important, to know when 110 percent is required and when 80 percent is good enough.

Perfectionism also adds to another significant career barrier for women and minorities: isolation. Personal and professional isolation starts with physical difference. However, isolation has different causes for women and minorities. For women, isolation often results from a number of factors.

▨ The social constraints and stereotypes around working with clients and colleagues outside the work setting continue to be problematic for women. Men can take clients to dinner and it's a dinner meeting. Women who take a male client to dinner are arranging a date. Women who take a woman client to dinner are just engaged in girl talk. Karen has worked with several female partners in a mainstream professional services firm who have never taken a male client to dinner because of these social stereotypes.

▨ The constraints of managing domestic and professional duties put special pressures on women, giving them little discretionary time for socializing or networking, despite the documented advantages of these out-of-office activities for professional advancement.

▨ The relatively small numbers of executive women within many organizations means that there are few colleagues with whom to spend what little time might be available. This problem becomes especially acute when it keeps women from finding the support systems they need—whether in the form of mentors who provide the informal coaching and contacts that drive advancement or peers with whom they can seek advice, try out ideas, or simply vent frustrations.

▨ The orientation of work culture, both inside and outside the office, continues to reflect male experiences and interests. In a recent Lore study of senior banking executives, respondents were asked to identify the kinds of rewards they would value for exceeding revenue goals. Men consistently requested perks like cruises, golfing, hunting, resort stays, and so on. Women just wanted time to stay at home and get caught up.

▨ Women tend to believe that merit is its own reward, that the harder you work the more recognition you will receive. Perhaps because of their traditional exclusion from the informal networks that bind men together, or perhaps because they don't see the value of those networks—whatever the reason—women executives have over-bought what Penina Glazer and Miriam Slater (1987, p. 227) term "the ideology of merit."

The same causes of isolation affect minorities but to an exponentially greater degree because their numbers in the executive ranks are even smaller. To these causes must be added the continuing legacy of social segregation. From elementary school through high school and college, and on into graduate school and entry-level jobs, few white people can count on more than one finger the number of people of color whom they consider friends and with whom they socialize regularly. Although executive salaries tend to erase economic segregation so that white, African American, Hispanic, and Asian executives live in the same neighborhoods, decades of social segregation are not so easily erased—on both sides. As will be discussed later, the gap between home culture and professional culture is also far greater for minorities than it is for whites, and the need to preserve home culture is often stronger.

Implications for Coaching

Generally, it's helpful to distinguish between the long-term, insider aspect of mentoring and the short-term, outsider dimension of coaching. But these lines need to blur somewhat in coaching women and minorities. The coach is often the mentor as well, because no one is available within the organization to be the anchor who keeps the minority person connected. To serve this dual role of coach/mentor, the executive coach must be intimately familiar with the ramifications of physical difference. Women and minorities live a complicated juggling act of denial and acceptance, of standing apart and fitting in. The coach becomes the objective lens that helps the executive gain insight into how and how well the juggling act is working. The coach is a trusted confidante who provides the sounding board and support that are unavailable in the executive ranks. The coach is also a teller of truths who uncovers and explores the impact of denial, who challenges the efficacy of perfectionism, or who helps the executive explore when asserting difference can make a difference organizationally or personally—and when it can hurt or hinder. The coach seeks entrance into that private space of difference that mainstream culture resists or—in its efforts to be blind to gender, ethnicity, and race—finds too impolite or incorrect to talk about. The coach is also a behavioral resource to help women executives figure out how to push against the stereotypes of working closely with men or to help African American executives feel comfortable socializing in all-white situations.

DIFFERENT WORK VALUES

Women in particular attach very different values to work than men do. *Fortune* magazine's 2000 listing of the "Fifty Most Powerful Women in Business" reiterates a frequently reported finding, that a key cause of the hemorrhage of women out of the corporate world and into the entrepreneurial world is that "guys just don't get it." For men, *Fortune* argues, power tends to be about authority—measured by titles, perks, and pay. To highly successful women, power is about "influence"—being part of a meaningful inner circle, making a difference, doing work that matters, and continuing to learn and grow personally and professionally (Sellers 2000, p. 148).

Discussion

Preliminary research at Lore with executive women in a professional services firm is consistent with *Fortune*'s findings. Top sources of job satisfaction for these women include respect and support of colleagues, a sense of accomplishment, doing work that is worthwhile in the larger scheme of things, and achieving a workable balance between home and career. The lowest-ranked source of professional satisfaction is "achieving visibility outside the firm." These findings reinforce the persistent theme in the literature on gender that women, in particular, value collaborative, connected, holistic, relational, nonhierarchical modes of leadership (see Helgeson 1985, Lipman-Blumen 1996, and Fletcher 1999).

Different work values also surface around questions of identity. Interviews with executive women, both white women and women of color, consistently revolve around such questions as: Who am I? Do I like the person I am becoming? Am I being co-opted in ways that I don't like? Am I selling out? As one executive woman of color said recently, "Let's face it. My job is about making rich people richer, and I'm not sure that's how I want to spend my time." The Native American woman quoted earlier talked about being plagued by the question of how much she was willing to give up. Another young executive woman tearfully confided that her nine-month-old baby didn't seem to know that she was its mother.

This is not to say that male executives don't struggle with questions of values or conflicts between roles, but the socialization patterns for young men and women point them in very different directions, and men are much more prepared for and supported in opting for work over home. As relative outsiders to organizational life, and as the member of the family who usually takes responsibility for working out the details of balancing home life and work life, women experience and must reconcile these conflicts daily.

The effect of this disaffiliation by women and minorities on the corporate world is an unprecedented exodus into entrepreneurship, where they can put into place business practices that more closely reflect their values. The number of women-owned businesses grew by 103 percent between 1987 and 1999, according to *Working Mother* magazine (June 2000), and they are opening at twice the rate of male-owned businesses (see Business Women's Network 2001). Among women-owned businesses, 15 percent are owned by ethnic or racial minorities. According to a Milken Institute Research Summary (October 2000), women today own 9.1 million of the 24 million small businesses in the United States, employing about 52 percent of the private sector workforce and generating 51 percent of private sector revenue. Minority-women-owned businesses account for the highest percentage increase in entrepreneurial start-ups. All this is particularly significant given that far less venture capital is available to women and minorities than it is to men (Business Women's Network 2001, pp. 84, 91).

The dearth of leadership talent available to large corporations and the war for talent that has resulted mean that coaching is a particularly important consideration for women and minorities. A recent McKinsey study reports that 75 percent of a group of seventy-seven large companies said they were "chronically talent-short," and 40 percent said they were "not able to pursue growth opportunities because they are 'talent constrained'" (Chambers et al. 1998, p. 47). Yet only 10 to 20 percent of these organizations made development of existing talent a priority (ibid).

Women and minority populations have long been identified as the untapped talent pool for American business, if for no other reason than that their demographic heft combines with their history of underrepresentation. A *Fortune* 2000 study, for example, reported a survey of network managers in which 335 had never hired a woman and 375 had never hired a member of a minority group, yet only 20 percent believed that minorities were underrepresented on their staffs. Nevertheless, within the first decade of this century, 85 percent of new workers are projected to be women, minorities, and immigrants, meaning that only 15 percent of entrants into the workforce will be white, Anglo-Saxon males (Business Women's Network 2001, p. 328).

Yet as the figures on entrepreneurship indicate, women and minority groups are most likely to leave the corporate world—at considerable cost to their former employers. And they are most likely to be lost in corporate reorganizations. A Hay Group (2001) study reports, "One out of every three employees working for a typical company will be gone in two years" (p. 1). The report goes on to document that each manager or professional who leaves costs the company the equivalent of eighteen months' salary, not counting the hidden costs in lost productivity, employee dissatisfaction, customer dissatisfaction, and the domino effect of departing employees taking other employees and/or customers along.

Implications for Coaching

Coaching is an economically viable retention mechanism and may be just as important in nurturing junior executives as it is in supporting senior executives. The Native American woman quoted previously provided an interesting perspective on the retention problem for women and minorities more generally. As newcomers to the corporate world, they start out at a disadvantage because they aren't automatically part of the informal culture that teaches beginners what's important.

- They don't know how to distinguish the career-advancing assignments from the dead ends.

- They have been taught that it's rude to assert what you want.

- They believe that if you are good enough, your work will be recognized.

- They don't have preexisting social networks, often family connections, to call on for help within the organization.

- Too often, they are tapped to recruit other women and minorities, which further erodes their presence in the real work of the organization.

It takes time to learn the ropes—time that their more privileged peers are spending getting promoted early in their career. The result is that those on the outside are quickly seen as stagnant because they are not moving up the ladder. The experience reported here is reinforced in the research on executive careers: those who move to the top receive high-visibility assignments early in their career, almost always through the intervention of a devoted mentor.

This is one of the ways that the glass ceiling affects women, and it is even more true for minorities—none of whom have women or minority mentors higher up in the organization, because their numbers are too small or they just aren't there. The result is that women and minorities see that they are going nowhere, become frustrated with the corporate system, and seek opportunities in the entrepreneurial world or simply stagnate in their jobs—playing out all the stereotypes about their capabilities and limitations that are out there waiting for them.

This discussion of retention and career paths may seem like a digression from the topic of coaching for women and minorities, and in a narrow sense it is. But in a larger sense, coaching women and minorities to become executives and to move forward in the executive ranks, is one of the best ways to ensure that there will be executives to coach.

The role of the coach in this instance is multifaceted because it involves the individual as well as the organization. The vexing questions of identity and work values need to be explored and resolved. For instance, the experienced coach who can articulate the broader social importance of the business may be able to place business impact in a larger and more meaningful social context that a younger person doesn't see. The coach may be able to offer advice and feedback on how to identify and access the informal networks where the real action is in the organization. The coach can teach how to ask for an assignment or ask for help or call attention to one's successes in ways that will still feel culturally authentic to the client. The coach can help to identify potential mentors, and perhaps even intervene to secure mentors, who can take up the task of shepherding the individual through the early and middle stages of an executive career. The text box "Principles of Effective Coaching for Women and Minorities" on page 264 provides helpful reminders in coaching these populations.

DIFFERENT INTERPERSONAL STYLES

Beyond the demographic imperative, the most compelling argument for a diversified executive pool is that people with different backgrounds bring new and different perspectives. Although in practice, businesses continue to shortchange themselves by more of the same kinds of people, the theoretical grounds for diversity are beyond debate. When we talk about the dearth of leadership talent, what is often underneath the complaint is a deeper need for leadership that can envision and enact change. Yet the double bind for women and minorities has to do with when to assert difference and when to fit in, and how to feel confident and comfortable with that difference when everything we know about human psychology tells us that human beings find change severely disruptive.

PRINCIPLES OF EFFECTIVE COACHING FOR WOMEN AND MINORITIES

1. Know the research on difference and the workplace regarding women, people of color, sexual orientation, and socioeconomic class.

2. Ensure accurate empathy (that your issues don't override their issues).

3. Recognize the ambivalence over difference: Is it my problem or other people's? Is it a personal shortcoming or a systemic flaw? What can I do about it?

4. Help clients name their experience.

5. Help clients understand the expenditure of energy it takes to be different, whether they work to fit in or work to stand out.

6. Use coaching as an opportunity for exploring and rehearsing behavior change.

7. Use coaching as a pipeline to network clients with others who experience the isolation of difference.

8. Recognize that coaching is as much about the system as it is about the client.

Discussion

Karen worked recently with a young woman executive in a leading professional services firm who grew up as an impoverished sharecropper's daughter in Oklahoma. Her ability to see things from a new and fresh perspective, to cut through the garbage (as she would put it), was uncanny, but working among the blue bloods from Harvard and Stanford and Oxford was a constant challenge to her self-confidence and a constant reminder of her sense of social inferiority. For all the talk in the leadership literature about the importance of self-disclosure, it was a real question for her about how much of her personal history to disclose and what the consequences of such disclosure would be.

Like many members of minority groups, she too struggled with the lack of fit between the values of her home culture and those of the corporate world. Back home, if you had a serious argument with someone, you took it outside and settled it with your fists. And, in her childhood years, as a big girl with bigger brothers, she had done just that.

There is an emerging autobiographical genre that has come to be called "literacy narratives." These personal accounts offer searing insights into the psychological and social struggles of those from working-class backgrounds trying to make it in the buttoned-down, white-collar world. Most are written by academics and tend to be focused around the transition into academic culture, whether as a student or a professional or both. But all of them describe the painful sense of loss of family and friends as one culture is exchanged for another; the sense of alienation and discomfort in the professional world; and the sense of inauthenticity, even fraudulence, that working-class people, regardless of gender or ethnicity, experience as not really belonging where they've ended up (see, e.g., Rodriguez 1982 and Hooks 2000). In all these examples, there's a palpable tension of living in two different, often contradictory worlds and trying to forge both a private and a public identity that yield integrity and coherence. If ever there were a role for a coach to help such people negotiate this complex psychological terrain without losing the gifts that brought them to it in the first place, this is it.

Implications for Coaching

The most constructive use of coaching for women and minorities is to help the individual name, understand, and accept his or her identity. Too often, these individuals feel that they are the only ones to struggle with their differences from the mainstream, and they start to question their abilities, even their sanity. You need a respected outsider to tell you that just because you're different from many people in the organization, you're not crazy, when all the signals may suggest that you are.

Learning through coaching that you are not alone is an empowering achievement. In *Tempered Radicals: How People Use Difference to Inspire Change at Work*, Debra Meyerson (2001) concludes that if individuals who are unique in their organization are to realize their capacity for change, they need to understand the systemic roots of differential treatment rather than seeing it as a result of personal shortcomings:

> *As people see their issues as theirs alone, they do not seek out natural allies for support. Leanne has kept her struggle to herself, which has prevented her from sharing her experiences with other women. . . . Her isolation has prevented her from seeing patterns and developing*

an alternative perspective on her situation, which may suggest new ways to address it. At the very least, talking to others might help her see that she is not alone, and that she is not necessarily to blame for many of her struggles. (p. 30)

Although Meyerson is not writing about coaching, the implications of her research point in the direction of finding ways for those with "marginalized identities" to connect with other professionals (such as executive coaches) who can help them accept, and capitalize on, their differences.

One example of the value of uncovering the systemic roots of differential treatment in order to use difference rather than deny it is explored in the influential monograph "Feeling Like a Fraud." Here, Peggy McIntosh (1985) probes the meaning underlying men's and women's approaches to communication. She argues that communication for men is often an act of demonstration, of making a point. For women, it's more often an act of initiating a conversation or an invitation, of putting an idea on the table for others to examine and explore. The result is that women are often considered tentative, apologetic, unsure of themselves, and therefore not worth listening to. Women come to believe that, and they *become* tentative, apologetic, and unsure of themselves, when in reality they are starting out with a different set of assumptions about the purpose of business communication. If an executive comes into coaching with the sense that she is not being forceful enough in meetings, that she is not being heard, a coach can help interpret the experience and explore ways to maintain the underlying value without being denied the authority to speak and be heard.

On a larger scale, the coach can be critical in helping women and minority clients figure out the meanings they attach to work. We've all heard, "It's not personal; it's business." But for women, and perhaps for minority males, the maxim is reversed: "It's not business; it's personal." Three popular films dramatically illustrate the intense personal/business link for women: *You've Got Mail,* in which the cut-rate, big-volume bookstore edges out the little bookstore around the corner that the owner inherited from her mother; *Erin Brockovich,* in which Erin angrily tells her boss, "You're damned right it's personal," when he calmly recites the business reasons for turning her case over to another, bigger law firm; and *Miss Congeniality,* in which a young woman quits her job as an FBI agent so she can keep watch over the contestants in a beauty pageant rather than following orders to pack up and go home. These films pick up two of the major tensions in women's professional worlds: the need for work to be personally meaningful to oneself and others, and the need to work in close-knit settings in which relationships with others are paramount.

In *What's Holding You Back,* Linda Austin (2000) sheds some light on the paradox: "Unlike men, who at times display one set of traits at work and a very different set at home, these [high-achieving] women seemed to be guided by a unified set of values in all spheres of their lives" (p. 13). An effective coach can help the client figure out the nature of her unique attachment to her work and analyze the impact of it in terms of her response to career successes and setbacks.

Finally, and what is perhaps the most sensitive issue of all, the coach needs to provide the objective distance to help clients interpret, from the perspectives of difference, their relations with their co-workers and with the organization itself. For example:

- *Was this interaction an expression of prejudice or not?*

- *Was that interaction sexual harassment or genuine liking or just clumsy insensitivity? Is it worth doing anything about? What will be the consequences if I do?*

- *Does this practice reveal yet another barrier, or is it simply a realistic approach to what it will take to get the job done?*

- *Am I just another affirmative action appointment? If I think I deserve to be where I am, how can I elicit the respect I deserve?*

- *How do I develop a level of trust in this organization to be who I am without feeling that I risk being labeled or marginalized?*

- *How do I go about supporting other women or minorities without being perceived as biased or having an exclusionary, single-issue agenda?*

- *How can I work to make this organization reflect a more inclusive set of values and practices—or should I just leave?*

It's hard to imagine that someone within an organization can have the trust and objectivity needed to help answer questions like these, but such questions mark the daily experience of women and members of minority groups at all levels.

COACHING FOR DIFFERENCE, COACHING FOR CHANGE

Research has uncovered many more differences in values, belief systems, and behaviors between men and women, between social classes, and between the dominant culture and minority cultures than we have identified here. This brief discussion is intended to call attention to the significance of these kinds of differences throughout executive careers in order to highlight the special role that coaching can play for these populations. Although much of human experience is certainly universal, it's also undeniably true that the lived experience of being a woman or part of a minority group is also unique and little understood by mainstream corporate culture. If difference and diversity offer at least one route to change, and if change is the route to a richer, more creative and effective, more fulfilled and fulfilling workplace, then coaching is an essential ingredient to developing and sustaining executive talent. Coaching can enhance and bring into play the unique perspectives of those who still stand on the margins.

14

Coaching Across Generations

Bitter clashes of interest and heated exchanges over rival claims for power and status have poisoned the relationship between Xers and Boomers.

Clashes of personality and culture . . . have made the two generations unintelligible, offensive, and ludicrous to each other.

Xers feel anxious, exploited, and betrayed, . . . Boomers feel misunderstood, unappreciated, and put upon.

BERNARD CARL ROSEN, MASKS AND MIRRORS

B oomers and Xers are the two major population segments in today's workforce. They will dominate the workforce for the coming decades. Boomers, who significantly outnumber Xers demographically, will continue to dominate their younger colleagues for some years as shrinking (or disappearing) retirement portfolios require that more and more Boomers extend their careers, enjoying the good health and longevity to do so. As both groups age, the struggle for power is likely only to intensify as Xers chafe to succeed Boomers in key policy- and decision-making positions while Boomers jealously hold fast to control a workplace that they, in many ways, have created. Studies of their generational differences agree that the two groups are deeply at odds with each other because of profound differences in their worldview, in their childhood and adolescent experiences, and in their value systems.

Recent studies, such as Bruce Tulgan's (2000) *Managing Generation X* and Hank Karp, Connie Fuller, and Danilo Sirias' (2002) *Bridging the Boomer Xer Gap,* argue that despite their differences, the two generations can work together productively. Tulgan, an Xer spokesman, writes as a defender of his Xer peers for their energy, talent, and creativity. Karp, Fuller, and Sirias write to dispel stereotypes of Xers as solitary, egocentric slackers who are both unable and unwilling to participate in the team-based environment of today's business culture. These arguments notwithstanding, the workplace itself is full of generational tension as the two groups encounter each other on a daily basis. As they come together in the special relationship of coach and client, it is essential for the coaching relationship to find a value-neutral zone for dialogue. To be able to grow, clients need to be able to see connections between their generational predispositions and the choices and consequences that stem from them. Coaches must understand their own generational mind-sets in order to see the client clearly, not through the haze of a set of generational filters that reconstruct the client in the coach's image and find him or her lacking.

This chapter sketches the key differences between Boomers and Xers to tease out the implications for coaches of both generations and to identify the special challenges of coaching down, when Boomers coach Xers, and coaching up, when Xers coach Boomers. Given the users of coaching services as high-potential up-and-comers or executives already in high-level positions, our portrait of Xers is restricted to what Rosen calls "elite" Xers and what Tulgan calls "high-achieving" Xers. It goes without saying that Boomer executives (and coaches) have already passed that hurdle, even if Xers frequently wonder how they ever managed. Our portraits of each group reflect the generally agreed upon, objective characteristics along with the value judgments that inevitably accompany these descriptions, because it's actually quite difficult to separate the two. What can look like a fact to one group can look like an accusation to the other. This is the consummate challenge for coaches of either generation: disaggregating the facts from the value judgments—the individual from the stereotype—to enable themselves and their clients to make constructive use of difference.

THE BOOMER GENERATION: 1945–1962

A staple of Boomer comedy is the lament "Oh my God. We are becoming our parents!" The generation that declared, "Never trust anyone over thirty" is now well over thirty itself and finding it hard to trust anyone who is under thirty. Underneath this comic revelation is the paradoxical inter-mingling among Boomers of the cultural revolution of hippiedom and the staid conservatism of their parents' generation. Much to Boomers' sur-prise, yesterday's flower children have indeed become today's parents, PTA presidents, homeowners, little league coaches, shoppers at Home Depot, community leaders, vacationers at Disneyland, voters, corporate execu-tives, and stewards of the social and economic institutions that embody our society. Though they have, and continue to, put their own stamp on business and cultural life, Boomers do so in a continuation of the tradi-tional work ethic that values self-sacrifice and loyalty to advance the com-mon good. But along the way, in the transformation from hippie to yuppie, many Boomers also manifest a narcissistic self-indulgence in which their youthful dedication to serving the underprivileged has morphed into a grown-up dedication to serving themselves.

The Boomer generation is a generation of limitlessness. Boomers grew up in a period of relative affluence and stability that engendered a view of the future as something that could be shaped for the better. Coming out of stable, traditional homes; extended the highest levels of education known to any previous generation; treated to an extended adolescence; and witness to the great social change movements in civil rights and women's rights against the backdrop of a great war for democracy, Boomers were able to view life itself as an extended experiment in the de-velopment of self and society. Once they entered the business world, Boomers brought with them a legacy from their parents of institutional loyalty combined with a self-appointed mandate to extend the participa-tory democracy of their youth to what looked like an autocratic business culture. Karp, Fuller, and Sirias (2002) argue that "team-based learning, participative decision-making, and shared reward systems are all facets of Boomer management ideals. Boomers have been waiting for years to undo the autocracy of the past and move into an enlightened and har-monious future" (p. 2). In the process, the "do your own thing" genera-tion has assumed that everyone's thing is more or less the same. Boomers' tunnel vision, along with their sense of entitlement to remake the world according to their own image, has led to the Xer contention that Boomers are "one of the most repressive and reactionary generations this country has ever produced" (p. 70).

Like any generation, the Boomers present a complex web of contra-dictions between lived values and espoused values, private morality and public morality, realism and idealism. One of the most striking differ-ences between them and the Xers, however, is the continuing presence of a clear and organizing worldview. However much Boomers may stray in their daily lives from an ideology of self-development, social justice, and participatory decision making, and however much or little individuals identify with that ideology, its origins, and their personal participation in shaping those origins, the ideology itself remains a common reference point that tends to unite Boomers in a sense of shared experience and values. This sense of commonality often becomes manifest in self-righteousness, in a conviction that one has paid one's dues, in a voice not just of experience but also of moral authority that overshadows lapses in personal conduct. Yet more than anything, the disconnect between what Boomers say they stand for and how they behave seems to be the source of the antipathy that Xers feel toward Boomers, while the lack of an articulated moral code, or at least one that even approximates Boomer values, fuels Boomers' belief that Xers are simply irredeemable.

THE XER GENERATION: 1965–1984

By the time the first Boomers turned eighteen, it was 1963, and Boomers witnessed the assassination of John F. Kennedy. By 1968, they were also witness to the assassinations of Martin Luther King Jr. and Robert Kennedy, along with the heights of the civil rights movement and the women's movement, the chaos of the Democratic National Convention in Chicago, cities looted and burning, military-enforced curfews in major population centers, student activism in the United States and abroad, flower power, and protests against the war in Vietnam. Historians largely agree that 1968 was a watershed year not just in U.S. history but internationally as well. It marked vast political and social change that swept up anyone who was paying attention in a self-conscious sense of destiny. In contrast, by 1988, when the first wave of Xers entered adulthood, the euphoria was gone, but the pace of change had accelerated to the point of being breathtaking and unnerving. Analysts agree that the sweeping economic, political, technological, and social changes of the mid-1970s, 1980s, and 1990s constitute a unique set of circumstances that set the Xer experience apart. Society was changing seemingly without much help from anyone, and survival in a complicated, confusing, and unstable world replaced the idealistic self-determination of the past.

The Boomer-Xer gap, therefore, is a study in contrasts. Xers grew up fending for themselves. Accounts vary as to why, but probably all of the following apply: the sharp rise in two-income families driven by both the weak economy of the 1970s and the women's movement, the increase in divorce rates during the same period that left more and more Xers in single-parent homes with working mothers and diminished economic well-being, and a philosophy of parenting among Boomers that allowed their children considerable independence. All these forces created a generation of latchkey children who spent significant time alone, taking care of themselves, or in tightly organized, care-taking activities such as day care and after-school programs. Tulgan (2002) concludes that Xers "have had few opportunities to witness or experience enduring affiliations of any kind—social, geographical, religious, or political. Our own family structures, and those of our peers, have not been reliable" (p. 46).

Xers also witnessed the wave of corporate downsizing, rightsizing, outsourcing, job elimination, benefit reductions, and corporate reengineering that, while it stunned their parents' belief in institutional loyalty, shaped a generation's expectations about what one could and could not expect from one's employers. In place of loyalty, Xers developed deep cynicism about what loyalty and commitment get you, distrust of both individuals and institutions, and anxiety in the face of continued economic and career uncertainty. The lessons of the workplace reinforced the lesson Xers were learning at home: the only person you can depend on is yourself. Accordingly, work serves as a means of continued self-development wherein you take what you can get, with specific jobs as short-term investments that are sustained as long as they are interesting and rewarding. It is no coincidence that studies cited by Michaels, Handfield-Jones, and Axelrod (2001) in *The War for Talent* identified such a high percentage of workers for whom opportunities for growth and development to bolster career prospects were the sine qua non of commitment to an organization. The authors note that "57% of the managers who intend to leave their current employer in the next two years cited insufficient development and learning opportunities as a critical or very important reason for leaving" (p. 98). It's reasonable to assume that most of these 57 percent are Xers intent on moving their careers forward.

Personal advancement, in Xer cosmology, is strictly based on individual merit. A pragmatic, Darwinian worldview leaves little tolerance for concerns about social justice, unequal distribution of wealth, or other inequities based on class, race, ethnicity, or gender. At the same time, Xers are the first generation to come of age with computers. The solitary and impersonal interaction of the individual and the computer complements and reinforces the lessons learned at home. They are comfortable with computers, more adept at using them, at learning from and with them, than their Boomer colleagues, and impatient with, perhaps even contemptuous of, those who don't embrace the information age as readily and negotiate the technology as easily as they do. Michaels, Handfield-Jones, and Axelrod conclude that "Gen-Xers are voracious learners. They grew up with the fast, self-paced learning of video games, computers, and the Internet. They were educated in schools that emphasized problem solving over rote memorization. If young managers don't get the kind of career development and learning they crave, they will simply go elsewhere to get it" (p. 58).

Thus, while Xers have achieved considerable technological savvy, some observers maintain that their human relations abilities are significantly underdeveloped. Bernard Rosen, whose comments open this chapter, offers the most complex analysis of Xers' interpersonal shortcomings. He, too, observes that Xers have developed a basic distrust of others, anxiety about the future, hostility toward authority, and a determination to succeed in a highly competitive, indifferent world. As a result, Rosen (2001) contends, Xers have developed a "chameleon personality." Being chameleonlike enables Xers to adapt superficially, and quite successfully, to the demands of a given situation while holding the real self apart—protected, suspicious, and cautiously disengaged. Chameleons, Rosen observes, have learned to please the people they need to please but "studiously avoid establishing relationships that would tie them down. Only a superficial bond, strong enough to sustain the wear and tear of business, is considered useful" (p. 14). Chameleonism allows the Xer to maintain a sense of superiority over others even while hiding underlying anxieties about one's abilities and worth. The strategy is one that works during a time of rapid change, unpredictability, intense competition, and high stakes.

Cross-Generational Coaching

These brief portraits of Boomers and Xers are rife with implications for coaching and being coached as the two reach across the generational divide. Left unexamined, the differences between the two groups set the stage for Boomer coaches who advise or pontificate to Xer clients, and Xer coaches who condescend or resent Boomer clients. This can occur just as easily in external coaching situations as in internal coaching between boss and subordinate. Issues of power and power differentials may cloud internal coaching relationships, but external coaching relationships can also become murky when the coach assumes, usually by dint of seniority in age, that she has the experience her client needs to hear. Coaches of both generations need to be honest with themselves about how their personal generational background plays into their values and attitudes and how it influences their preconceptions, prejudices, and stereotypes about the client.

We hope the sketches above are useful to coaches in beginning this process. As in any other coaching situation, self-knowledge allows coaches the distance they need to hear the client clearly and thus to make sound decisions about how to adapt to the client's needs. That said, the characteristics of these two generations and their experiences at work suggest some core themes, even if clients don't articulate them as such, that are likely to be at the heart of what Xers are looking for in coaching, and others that are of particular concern to Boomers. Particularly when coaching is programmatic in nature, it's often helpful to shape the long-term coaching dialogue around key themes in which specifics can be anchored. The assumption here is that Xers, though not quite at the dawn of their careers, are certainly somewhere around high noon, while Boomers are more likely nearing the twilight of their careers, not finished yet but seeing the end of the day approaching, perhaps with a mixture of relief and dread. Both have important decisions to make about how to handle themselves and others.

COACHING THEMES FOR
XER CLIENTS

The Meaning of Work

It's clear that Xers approach work differently than Boomers do. Questions of work-life balance may have more poignancy for Xers, not just because they are facing immediate decisions about marriage, family life, and dual career juggling, but also because the choices to be made are not already as narrowly prescribed for Xers as they were for Boomers. If the women's movement opened career doors for women, Xers of both genders are the ones who will be the architects of the new workplace now that they are inside those doors. The twenty-four-hours-a-day work environment made possible by the communications revolution adds to the urgency that work be reengineered so that workers can "have a life." Furthermore, Xers seem less likely to take family for granted and more drawn to making family life a more vital force in their adulthood than it was in their childhood.

Accordingly, coaches must beware of assuming that Xers who do not have an overriding commitment to work are somehow deficient or that a strong commitment to family life is a sign that the Xer doesn't "get it." It would not be unusual for a Boomer coach to assume that part of what an Xer client needs to learn through coaching is how to "get ahead" by sacrificing work-life balance for some period of time to demonstrate through extraordinary achievement that he is more promotable than others, but the Xer client may view this as the kind of foolish gesture his parents made and one that he not only has no interest in, but is unlikely to be rewarded for if he did it.

Balancing the Short and the Long Term in Career Development

Xers' desire to move ahead quickly in their careers creates one of the tensions that drives each generation crazy about the other. Coaches can be helpful in guiding high-achieving Xers to assess career patterns and engage in long-term career planning. Xers may not fully appreciate what it takes to reach the heights they aspire to or perceive the elements of a successful career strategy. Mentors, particularly champions, continue to be essential elements in a career path, and some Xer clients may need to develop the skills and attitudes to make a partnership with a more senior person authentic and mutually satisfying. A trusted coach can help an Xer client gain insight into how he or she comes across to senior people, to examine the attitudes that underlie perceptions, and to make good choices about what needs to change. In particular, Xers may grasp the opportunities but not know how to build and mobilize a supportive network to help them pursue those opportunities successfully.

Managing Anxiety over Work Performance

Performance anxiety is an outgrowth of Xers' Darwinian worldview. Failure lurks behind every success, and success may be only temporary and accidental. Small wonder Xers tend to be in a hurry to establish themselves and reap the rewards in a high-stakes game. Xers hold themselves to high standards; they don't approach work as a free ride. Perfectionism is often related to anxiety over work performance. Like anyone who experiences the dual pressures of performance anxiety and perfectionism, Xers can use coaching to clarify how these pressures affect their work and their need for balance. Chronic anxiety is something for a therapist to handle, but within the realm of coaching, Xer clients can explore and then test their assumptions and hypotheses about why they hold themselves to un-relenting standards. They can try out new behaviors to see when it might be better to relax the pressure they exert on themselves, or decide that the pressures are realistic and necessary, either for the short term or the long.

Interpersonal Relations

Perhaps the toughest work issue for Xers to grapple with has to do with developing the trust and authenticity necessary for enduring professional relationships. Chameleonism will take you only so far. The risk is that when others see it for what it is, they will feel exploited and manipulated and will likely question the ethical posture of someone who treats others as commodities for personal advancement. Executive careers are built on long-term relationships, not just on a fat Rolodex of fleeting acquain-tances or an impressive set of credentials. When colleagues vouch for each other, they know they are putting their own reputations on the line. The higher up the ladder you go, the more character counts and the smaller the circles in which people are known.

As experienced executives themselves, many Boomer coaches can offer a perspective on what those relationships look like and how they tend to be formed. The coaching relationship offers a safe haven for a cynical, alienated, or distrustful Xer to set aside defenses and experiment with the risk taking that goes hand in hand with trust. Coaching offers a sanctuary in which to explore self-disclosure, to process its effects in the workplace, and to realize limits that, while taking a client out of a familiar comfort zone, still aim toward the openness and authenticity that are characteris-tic of the best leaders. While the development of effective interpersonal relations is essential for anyone at any level to sustain a successful career, the particular circumstances of the Xer experience make this an especially compelling issue for this wide band of achievement-oriented workers.

COACHING THEMES FOR BOOMER CLIENTS

On the other side of the generational divide, Boomer clients are likely to have a different set of core themes as they confront the next generation.

Again, these themes may not be explicitly articulated, but they are very likely lurking just beneath the surface of a host of presenting problems involving Boomers' interactions with Xers.

Perceiving, Accepting, and Valuing Difference

If the research on difference in gender, race, class, culture, ethnicity, and generations has taught us anything, it's that you won't see what you're not looking for. For some people, it's simply not polite to talk about differences because difference is caught up in a host of other unmentionables such as superiority/inferiority; power differentials; and differences in economic, educational, professional, or social opportunity. For the peace and love generation, these continuing differentials are awkward and even painful to acknowledge, perhaps because of their youthful dedication to eradicating them. Even the staunchest supporters of diversity often express a preference for a gender-, color-, culturally, or generationally blind workplace. Despite the good intentions in these pronouncements, the reality is that this is really a way to say they wish the problems associated with difference would just go away, that everyone would just be like everyone else, and that if we were all more or less alike, we wouldn't have to deal with the troublesome problem of understanding and accommodating difference.

For Boomers, Xer differences are especially vexing because of the underlying sense of superiority that many Boomers hold toward their junior colleagues. When Boomer executives just can't get past the negative value judgments they hold toward Xers, coaching is a place to help surface these tensions and help Boomer clients evaluate them rationally. Both of us have coached senior partners in leading professional services firms and heard the complaint over and over that these partners are working way too hard because the junior people don't do the job right. They have to do it themselves, they say, or it's just easier to do it themselves than to redo their junior colleagues' work. They rarely perceive, let alone examine the assumption, that they are equating "the right way" with "my way"; nor have they thought about how to disaggregate the task or articulate the tacit knowledge they have acquired through years of practice to teach junior colleagues how to do it. These possibilities come as a real revelation. Is the issue really a performance problem or a stylistic difference? Are there merits in the way the Xer approaches things that the Boomer just can't see? Does a task really have to be done in a particular way? Just as we've tried to make a case in this book for the value of nondirective coaching for

adapting to a particular client's needs, Boomer executives may also benefit from learning how to coach their junior colleagues nondirectively to derive the benefits from Xers' ways of looking at problems and solving them.

Tackling Succession

The literature on succession planning is too vast even to attempt to summarize here. We will mention, however, that succession is ultimately
bound up in the transfer of power not just from one person to another
but from one generation to another. Business history is replete with tragic
stories of good companies whose leadership just couldn't face the idea of
succession or who confused succession with replacement, ensuring a status quo that could not be sustained in a changing business environment.
Good succession planning involves values and vision. It is a future-
oriented activity, not a present-oriented one. In *The Leadership Pipeline,*
Charan, Drotter, and Noel (2001) observe that "anyone attempting to des-
ignate a replacement now for a job that might open three years from
today will be basing their decision on specifications that will be woefully
out of date when the transition takes place" (p. 166).

Yet it's also clear that too often executives feel comfortable with people just like themselves, a phenomenon that accounts for much of the
stultifying sameness of the corporate world. An *HR Magazine* study concluded that "executives under pressure fall back on doing what they know
best—developing individuals like themselves. Too often, when asked why
they have been unable to identify, develop, and promote high-performing
nontraditionals, the response is that there are insufficient women and
people of color in the pipeline" (Ruderman, Ohlott, and Kram 1997).
This is, of course, an extension of the Boomer problem with difference
discussed above, but it's clear that problems with difference transform
into problems of succession from one generation to the next. The Xer
workforce is the most diverse group ever seen. Although at some point
the demographic reality will make it increasingly difficult for Boomers to
find people "just like me," succession must be affirmative and forward
looking, not a reactionary holdout against the future.

Particularly when coaches have an opportunity to work with executive
groups and corporate boards, they can be a powerful resource in uncovering generational biases that hinder thinking about succession. Coaches
can help Boomer executives explore the anxieties they feel about turning
over power, and even help them find common ground with Xers, since
Boomers were also the "barbarians at the gates" at the same stage in their

career. As thought partners, coaches can be extremely valuable helping Boomer clients think about the company's future needs and the kind of people it will take to meet them.

Making One's Mark

No matter how tarnished their ideals have become, Boomers began their careers with high aspirations. They saw themselves as challengers of the status quo and change agents of a repressive system. For some Boomers, these ideals now look like youthful naïveté, but for others, the rhetoric of justice, equality, and betterment still stir old allegiances. For still others, their careers have been guided in any number of domains by these basic values. Having achieved positions of power and authority, and as they contemplate the final stages of their career, many Boomers are ready to evaluate their achievements and use their influence to make their mark. This calls for honest soul-searching and big-picture thinking—the very things that coaches are uniquely positioned to facilitate.

Too many people end their career bitter and resentful. They may retire on the job. They may quietly undermine the organization in all sorts of passive-aggressive ways. They may become embittered that their experience has gone unrecognized, their contributions unappreciated. They may simply hate coming to work because their younger colleagues seem alien and self-absorbed. A coach can hold up a mirror and help Boomer clients see themselves for what they have become. They can help them decide whether they like what they see and, if not, what they would like to see instead. They can be a sounding board for the kind of action plan that will take clients where they want to go. Coaching, like teaching, is ultimately one of the most optimistic of professions, and a good coach can help able and talented senior people navigate through the dangerous waters of late career stages to sustain, perhaps even regain, the vision that enables people to make their mark.

COACHING DOWN AND UP

The pitfalls of coaching, as we've shown throughout this book, generally have to do with giving unsolicited or inaccurate advice, not listening or not hearing the real problems, and not letting clients find their own way. Repeatedly, we've found that coaching needs to be an invitation to clients to examine the choices they are making and, if they don't like those choices or their consequences, to use a coach to help them develop the alternatives, plans, and skills they need to pursue a different course. In coaching across generations, these pitfalls manifest themselves differently, depending on whether the coaching situation is one of coaching down or coaching up.

Coaching Down

The themes we've discussed above allude to the risks that arise when Boomers coach Xers. The tendency is to lecture based on the coach's experience. In *Primal Leadership*, Goleman, Boyatzis, and McKee (2002) conclude,

> *Unfortunately, we've found that many managers are unfamiliar with—or simply inept at—the coaching style, particularly when it comes to giving ongoing performance feedback that builds motivation rather than fear or apathy. For example, leaders who are also pacesetters—focused exclusively on high performance—often think they're coaching when actually they're micromanaging or simply telling people how to do their jobs.* (p. 61)

Though managers are not necessarily Boomers, when they are, generational differences can only compound this tendency.

Our experience is that in internal coaching situations, the Boomer coach has to be especially transparent at separating the authority relationship of superior/subordinate from the coaching relationship. Xer clients in these relationships need to participate from the start in shaping the rules of engagement for coaching; otherwise, the coach can look and feel like the boss in disguise. Conducting coaching conversations outside the office, outside working hours, or in a more social location such as a restaurant or bar are some of the ways to signal a different dimension to the relationship. Letting Xer clients know that you are willing to share your experience but won't do so unless they ask helps to undercut the paternalism inherent in coaching down. Assuring clients that what worked for the coach may not work for the client also reduces the tendency to lecture or appear to be lecturing.

It is also true, though, that in spite of all these safeguards, some younger clients will not be able to get past the authority relationship if the coach is also the person who is responsible for promotions, performance evaluations, raises, job assignments, and other working conditions. And some older coaches may not be able to let go of their convictions that they really do know more than the client and the client needs to profit from their experience. External coaches do not carry the baggage of supervisory relationships, but the same risks of paternalism and transference still apply. The paradox is that coaching down can be a highly productive relationship for all the same reasons that make it difficult. The key is to keep the dialogue focused on the client's needs and not the coach's.

Coaching Up

Coaching up entails quite a different set of pitfalls. Xer coaches, for all their Xer bravado, may question whether they have the right to coach someone older and more experienced. There is a tendency to put oneself in a subordinate position, to be overly deferential, and thus not to coach. Avoiding the term *coaching* altogether can be useful in a situation like this. It can be a loaded term, often carrying connotations of correcting problems and therefore evoking defensiveness. It is also becoming an overused term, losing its distinctive meaning because it is applied to just about any conversation about work. Another way to coach up is to ask, "Would it be helpful to think through several options?" or, "Would it be helpful to try out some other perspectives?" Xer coaches need to maintain the self-confidence that they can have a helping relationship with someone more senior at the same time that they maintain an element of humility that they don't have all the answers. Again, the key is to stay focused on what the client needs, not what you need. It's not about proving yourself; it's about helping the other person.

Beyond self-confidence and overcoming the sense that they "don't have the right to coach older people," Xer coaches face a real dilemma in coaching Boomers who do in fact have more on-the-job and life experience and who may find the Xer's perspectives and suggestions naïve or uninformed. The solution in most cases is to coach nondirectively and not offer advice that may appear naïve, no matter how well founded it might be. Xer coaches coaching up need to bear in mind that the older client may feel intimidated—or even embarrassed—at being coached by a young person. The question of age differential does occur. An Xer coach we were working with told the story of coaching a much older Boomer manager. Startled by their age difference, the Boomer asked, "How old are you anyway?" "Twenty-seven," the Xer replied. "Well, hell," the Boomer exclaimed, "my son is older than that. I wouldn't take advice from him. Why should I take it from you?" The quick-thinking Xer coach responded by saying, "I may be only twenty-seven, but if it's any consolation, I'm aging rapidly at the moment." His humor dispelled the tension, and the coach and client got along well after that.

What makes an older person open to being coached by a younger one? Generally, Xers coaching up must establish that they have the experience or expertise to offer help the client will benefit from. This is no different from the trust and credibility all coaches must establish. When coaching up, however, it's important to establish that trust and credibility early in the relationship. When you are coaching down, there is a presumption of greater experience, which may not be true; however, in coaching up, there is no such presumption, and the trust and credibility must be established.

Whether you are a Boomer coaching down a generation or an Xer coaching up a generation, the key is to maintain what psychologist Carl Rogers called "unconditional positive regard" toward the people you are coaching. By this, Rogers meant accepting clients for who they are and not imposing your worldview, values, or assumptions upon them. To do this, you must first be self-conscious about the cultural views you hold, and you must understand that your perspective is just that, a *perspective*, and not the *truth* about life, business, career goals, or ways of being. To coach up or down effectively, you need to appreciate the values and worldview of the people you are coaching and to a great degree accept them for who they are and how they perceive the world. Of course, it is helpful to point out to them when and where their worldview may clash with the values, beliefs, and assumptions of the organization in which they are working. However, it is not helpful to simply impose your own views and assume that these represent truth.

As in our earlier discussions of difference involving gender, race, class, and culture, understanding generational difference involves exploring a host of generalizations that can be more or less empirically supported but that still must be applied with care to specific individuals. While there is good reason to believe that the workplace reverberates with generational tensions just as it does with tensions over gender, culture, and the like, these tensions may or may not be related to the concerns of any specific client. Likewise, some coaches may be entirely unidentified with the generational markers of their time, some may be quite self-conscious about them, and others may be influenced without really knowing it, perhaps until a particular client pushes all the right buttons. Our purpose here has been to give coaches enough of a picture of what these generational tensions are all about to see if the shoe fits—and if it does, to help figure out what to do about it.

15

Coaching C-Level Executives

Few chief executives will talk about it. But more and more, they're turning to counselors for help in navigating the current corporate turmoil.

MICHELLE CONLIN, "CEO COACHES"

I absolutely believe that people, unless coached, never reach their maximum capabilities.

BOB NARDELLI, CEO OF HOME DEPOT

C-level executives are expected to be good coaches themselves. After all, leadership is intimately bound up with involving, motivating, inspiring, encouraging, teaching, developing, influencing, and rewarding people, whether in an up-close and personal way with immediate members of an executive group or at a distance with junior executives, managers, and staff. Although current business literature is questioning the godlike omnipotence expected of C-level executives (see, e.g., Khurana 2002 and Collins 2001), it's still clear that in the transformation from command-and-control leadership to leadership grounded in inspiration and influence, these top leaders are presumed to be able to execute their responsibilities in part by developing others. When they fail, it's not for lack of technical skill but the inability to establish effective human connections—upward, downward, and outward—that motivate and inspire people, build effective teams, and make organizations work through people, which, when one thinks about it, is the only way organizations can work. As a *BusinessWeek* article so succinctly puts it, "CEOs get hired for their skills but fired for their personalities" (Conlin 2002, p. 99). So who coaches these C-level coaches?

THE UNIQUE WORLD OF C-LEVEL EXECUTIVES

The language associated with topmost executives is replete with terms ranging from *royalty* to *deity*. For instance, a recent Booz Allen Hamilton study proclaims, "CEOs are the emperors of global business" (Lucier, Spiegel, and Schuyt 2002, p. 2). In the current culture of the celebrity CEO, many come to believe that they are, in fact, superheroes, the titans of industry, the kings or queens of commerce. The difficulty posed in such characterizations is twofold. First, C-level executives and their constituents can regard the executives as having reached the pinnacle of success, with nothing left to learn and nothing to change. Second, the executives themselves can either come to believe their own press or assume they must act as if they believe it, taking on a façade of invincibility, self-importance, and omniscience. In both cases, the isolation that ensues for C-level executives unleashes a chain of detrimental consequences that contributes to the increasingly short tenure or suboptimal performance of too many top-level executives. In this chapter, we explore these perils and discuss how coaching can help to mitigate them. To begin, we will discuss some metaphors that describe the unique world in which C-level executives live: in quarantine, alone at the helm, in a glass house, in a kindergarten, and inside their own head.

Living in Executive Quarantine

There's an old joke that goes: "What are the two things a CEO never gets?" Answer: "A bad meal and the truth." First, of course, no one is going to take the CEO to lunch at a mediocre restaurant. Everyone wants the CEO's experiences with them to be first-rate, so the CEO is going to be feted in the finest ways. Second, everything the CEO hears is going to be spun in one way or another. Even the financial numbers CEOs see are unlikely to reflect "objective reality," if there is such a thing. It isn't that people deliberately lie to the CEO. Most assuredly, that rarely happens.

However, people will tell the "truth" as they see it. Everyone *inside* the organization and most people *outside* it have an agenda when they talk to the CEO. They are trying to cast themselves in a good light. They are trying to position themselves and their business unit in a way that is most favorable, given the circumstances. If an executive's unit is failing, for example, the individual nonetheless wants the CEO to know that it's not entirely his fault and he's doing all he can to turn the situation around. If another executive's unit needs more funding for R&D than has been allocated in the budget, she will try to position her unit's work as more deserving of the money because it has the greatest potential, and so on. *Everyone* who talks to the CEO has an agenda. Insiders want to stay in good standing or want the CEO to think or act in a particular way. Outsiders want the CEO to value them and keep employing them or talking to them. The result is life in executive quarantine.

This takes us back to the bad meal part of the joke and lets us see that the point is really subtler than it appears at first. Providing the CEO with a fine meal is just one way of painting reality in a particular way. The fine meal creates an aura of success that the two of you share. You are a winner and so is the CEO. Day after day of fine meals, metaphorically speaking, builds a cocoon in which the CEO is effectively quarantined. The CEO participates in the quarantine process as well. James Maxmin, former head of Laura Ashley, UK Volvo, and the consumer-electronics branch of Thorn EMI, observes: "Being a CEO is really a lonely job. With your subordinates and with your peers, you need to have a degree of detachment. There's some detachment from your board, too, because they are evaluating you. So you become cocooned in your own self-importance" (Hammonds 2002, p. 81). If others are trying to cast themselves in a good light with the CEO, the CEO is likewise trying to cast himself or herself in a good light, regularly providing the great meals as well as receiving them. Maintaining that façade is another contributor to CEO isolation. In effect, life becomes a stage play—and all the participants are actors in a drama—in which impressions are carefully crafted to maintain an illusion of success and the continuing expectation of it. Failing to maintain that illusion can cause doubts among important stakeholders, including customers, employees, the board of directors, and Wall Street.

The value of outside coaching should be clear. Yes, the coach is also an external "employee" who is motivated to remain employed. But if the CEO's coach is behaving ethically, she is obligated to speak the truth as she sees it. In fact, the coach is probably the only one who talks to the

CEO with no agenda except to be helpful. Speaking the truth sometimes means saying to the CEO, "You are the problem." If that's what the coach believes, that's what she has to say, even if the CEO doesn't want to hear that message and fires her. The value an outside coach can provide is absolute integrity, and clients, for the most part, value that candor and honesty greatly. You can imagine, given what we've said about C-level quarantine, what a relief it can be for a CEO to have an unbiased outsider who is willing to speak candidly, listen to the CEO's thoughts and questions, and respond in a thoughtful way that helps the CEO escape from the quarantine, however briefly.

Living Alone at the Helm

Like the captain of a ship, the CEO is alone at the helm, and this metaphor reveals another aspect of the C-level executive's isolation. The fact of organizational life is that the higher you go, the more isolated you become. Everyone else on a ship has someone to talk to if he needs help, guidance, or just someone with whom to "let his hair down." But the captain can't go to a member of the crew and say, "I'm having doubts about the direction I'm taking. I'm not sure what to do. What do you think I should do?" The captain is expected to have no problems and no doubts; otherwise, the ship and crew could be in peril. So the captain is isolated, and not just in terms of whom he can or cannot talk to. In most corporations, the CEO is never really aware of what's happening "down below," because most people are afraid to tell him. They may not want to appear incapable of handling the situation themselves, or they simply don't want to be the bearer of bad news. Too often, people want to "protect" the CEO from problems that "should not concern him," so they don't tell him. When the CEO finds out, it's usually because the situation has gotten out of control and can no longer be managed down below. We have been speaking only of the CEO, incidentally, but COOs, CFOs, and other C-level executives experience the same isolation.

The value of an outside coach is immeasurable, because the captain can express doubts to the coach, knowing that the coach is not evaluating him and won't spread rumors throughout the crew. Goleman, Boyatzis, and McKee (2002) describe the executive coach as "an antidote to the peril of the information quarantine that too many leaders suffer. . . . To be really helpful, a coach will understand the leader's dilemmas from multiple perspectives: the individual level (what's going on for the person); the team level (the group dynamics of the executive staff or staff teams); and the organizational level (how all of this fits with the culture, systems, and strategy)" (p. 165).

Beyond helping C-level executives gain an accurate perception of what's going on in their organization, coaches are uniquely suited to act as thought partners precisely because they do not (or should not) have an agenda. Being agenda-less is liberating for both the coach and the client. Because you don't have an agenda to push, you can listen openly to the executive's issues or problems and ask thoughtful questions that help the executive think through her problems and examine her alternatives. The executive doesn't have to worry about how to frame the issue with you and doesn't have to think about whom you might talk to regarding the information you're being given. If you are acting responsibly as a coach, *everything* you hear from the CEO is confidential and will not go anywhere else. So the CEO can speak freely, admitting to doubts and misgivings, and can explore alternatives and the consequences of potential decisions without having a listener who is reacting overtly or covertly to what's being said and is worrying about his position or the success of his personal agenda.

To appreciate how valuable this kind of dialogue is for C-level executives, just consider how rare it is for them to have such dialogues. In *all* their normal conversations with the people around them, they cannot speak freely; must consider the impact of what they say, which is frequently greater and farther reaching than they imagine; and do not have objective listeners. For this reason, we believe that C-level coaches should always come from outside the organization. Inside coaches bring too much baggage with them and cannot be objective, no matter how much they might try.

Living in a Glass House

Still another way to understand the isolation of C-level executives is the glass house metaphor. Because they operate in such a public spotlight, C-level executives must become highly circumspect about what they say and how they say it. The celebrity culture surrounding CEOs, even in the smallest, most local organizations, makes this a pervasive phenomenon, spilling over from the job itself into their personal lives as well. You are never not the CEO—not even at the grocery store. Says Anne Mulcahy of Xerox Corporation, "There's a lot you can't share with anyone. I've tried to be fair and honest in my approach, letting people know what to expect. But there's information that you have to retain while keeping up the image that you're feeling no anxiety inside" (Hammonds 2002, p. 81).

Part of the glass house phenomenon is that C-level executives cannot be themselves. Their words and actions take on a greater than normal meaning, and their behavior is often interpreted in ways they could not have foreseen. We worked with one person who had recently been promoted to the C level. He was a "regular guy" and had previously been a member of a rock band within the company. After being promoted, he hoped to continue in his role as the group's lead singer and guitarist, and when he played with the group he kept joking with them and making the same kind of irreverent comments he'd made while in his previous role. In his mind, nothing had changed except his position in the company, but to everyone else he was a new person. His joking comments were now taken seriously, and he soon found that he could longer "be himself" because everyone interpreted what he said in ways he did not intend and often couldn't predict. It forced him to be much more circumspect about what he said and did with the people who were previously just friends. For him, the new C-level role was interesting and rewarding in most ways, but it came at considerable personal loss.

One of the challenges, therefore, that await new C-level executives is developing a trustworthy and effective public persona that remains consistent with private values and ethics. The transition from living and controlling one's private life to becoming a public figure that one is able to define only to a limited extent is a wrenching experience for some and is filled with challenges for anyone new to this level of an organization. A coach can help an executive learn to live with the new persona. Unlike the media relations people who help organizations craft public messages for the CEO to deliver, the coach is the sounding board for the tensions that inevitably arise between what the CEO must say and what she wishes she could say, between who the CEO is in public and who the CEO really is.

Living in a Kindergarten

This metaphor evokes images of what we might call the tattletale conspiracy—a common but annoying occurrence in some organizations that isolates C-level executives in still another way. In these highly politicized environments, there is an unspoken agreement among lower levels of executives to protect one another and not to "tattle" to the CEO if one of them is having problems. The contract is: "You scratch my back, and I'll scratch yours." This sort of conspiracy of silence undermines the effectiveness of the organization because candor and the flow of information are inhibited. The CEO can't know what is truly going on, because no one will be forthright. Problems aren't addressed or fixed, employees become exasperated with poor leadership, the CEO's effectiveness is called into question, and the whole organization is destabilized. The behavior is childish, hence the kindergarten metaphor, and the results can be disastrous.

Another manifestation of the tattletale conspiracy has the children vying for the teacher's attention. In this version, some executives become confidants of the CEO and tell the CEO in secret what's going on with the other executives (who's okay, who's making mistakes, who needs to be fired, etc.). Of course, people learn that this is happening and begin to distrust one another. Every executive then wants to have the CEO's ear but also knows he has to watch his back while ensuring that others don't win more of the CEO's favor. This type of political environment is also clearly dysfunctional. Assuming the CEO catches on, the result is often detachment from *everyone* because *no one* can be trusted. The result is a passive-aggressive culture that infects everyone within it.

One of the values of outside coaches is that they can be unbiased and apolitical truth tellers. Effective outside coaches discover what's going on in the organization and can help the CEO see it (without the coaches themselves becoming complicit in the political shenanigans). If there is a dysfunctional executive culture, and the CEO is wittingly or unwittingly contributing to it, the coach should have the courage and professionalism to say so—and to say it bluntly. Coaches can also work with the entire executive group to help them confront the problem and find more productive ways of dealing with one another.

Living Inside Their Own Head

The ultimate kind of executive isolation is what we might call psychological isolation, when the executive comes to believe that he or she is the invincible, all-knowing, take-charge public persona that has been created. C-level executives tend to overestimate their abilities, perhaps because they lack good feedback. Michelle Conlin (2002), in *BusinessWeek*, describes research that shows that "the higher up the ladder they climb, the more likely senior execs and CEOs are to think their performance is much better than their underlings do" (p. 98). In *Good to Great*, which chronicles his study of more than one thousand business organizations, Jim Collins (2001) reports the implications of this overestimation of one's talents: "In over two thirds of the comparison cases, we noted the presence of a gargantuan personal ego that contributed to the demise or continued mediocrity of the company" (p. 29).

Accordingly, some senior executives have the sense that they "have arrived," that they don't need coaching, that they've reached the pinnacle of professional success and have nothing they need help with. This self-deception occurs, we believe, because of an inherent narcissism that some people develop as they gain more power, position, and privilege. They've been successful most of their lives (and probably rationalize any times when they weren't). They've been told over and over how great they are. They have, in fact, accomplished a great deal in their lives, and now they are at the peak. They're making a lot of money. Most if not all of the people around them treat them as though they are special. They control thousands or tens of thousands of people and their futures. They know politicians, entertainers, and other highly successful people. They are sought after by the press. Articles (and sometimes books) are written about them. It's no wonder many of these chief executives develop the mind-set that they are perfect or that their imperfections are the reason for their success ("Sure I'm tough on people. How do you think I got here?").

It's easy to understand how some senior executives can develop egos that prevent them from seeking coaching help or acknowledging that they might need it. On our coachability scale, these executives might be C1s (narcissistic) or C2s (defensive and reject feedback). They rarely seek outside coaching and will hear feedback only if it validates their inflated self-concept. For them to agree to coaching, they typically need to be forced by some power greater than themselves (the board, for instance). Often, they will agree to coaching only if it's done by someone they know they can control. Of course, by the time they agree to accept coaching, much of the damage has been done, and the turnaround effort is considerably more difficult because the people around them have already formed their opinions and may be reluctant to give the "reformed" executives a chance to show that they've changed.

It's also clear that C-level executives sometimes don't want to show or admit vulnerabilities—to themselves or anyone else. The way to protect yourself is to appear perfect, especially to your peers (who are often rivals for the next promotion) and to your boss (the CEO, perhaps, or the board). In our work with C-level executives, we frequently confront the fear that they will appear "broken" if they have a coach: "Gee, you need a coach? What's wrong with you?" When we work with such executives, we often have to negotiate carefully the language we will use in talking to other people in the organization so the executive doesn't look like she needs help or is in trouble. The situation can cause a real crisis in confidence: "Our CEO can't handle the job. She needs a coach! Oh my God, there goes my 401(k)!" The way we handle this, by the way, is to call the coaching something else, such as "transitional consulting." This is not a cop-out. If the euphemism is helpful and does not detract from the real coaching taking place, then it may serve a useful public purpose.

Sometimes the executive is quite right about his reaction, because in many companies coaching has been provided only for executives who were demonstrably "broken," and many of those executives wound up leaving the company anyway. A pattern is thus established in which if you need a coach, you're on your way out. No wonder so many executives, even when they recognize the need, resist coaching or want to do it "under the table." In the long run, the solution to this problem is to create a developmentally minded organization in which coaching, mentoring, and assessment are routine parts of what everyone receives, including the most senior people. But in truth there are very few companies with such cultures, and some senior executives, recognizing that they need coaching but afraid to ask for it, seem to hope that bravado, real or imagined, will carry them through.

MAKING COACHING WORK WITH C-LEVEL EXECUTIVES

Despite the internal and external pressures that work against C-level coaching, the odds are that many senior executives will need coaching either in their transitions into new positions or to prevent derailment. In his study of good-to-great leaders, Jim Collins (2001) and his research team identified only eleven CEOs of the 1,435 companies in their initial sample as Level 5 leaders—the type of leader "who builds enduring greatness through a paradoxical blend of personal humility and professional will" (p. 29). Few of these, Collins notes, are recognizable names: "They were seemingly ordinary people quietly producing extraordinary results" (p. 20). If one accepts Collins' conclusion that very few CEOs qualify as Level 5 leaders, then there is a considerable need for C-level coaching, especially when leaders are promoted to C-level positions or assume those positions from another organization. In our experience, the first three months or one hundred days is the most critical, because this is the honeymoon period, during which new executives need to establish their leadership within the new organization or in the new position and when people inside the organization are apt to be most forgiving as new executives learn to "get it right."

Executives in Transition: The First Hundred Days

The most immediate challenge for a new C-level executive is to read the culture and politics of the organization accurately. The first hundred days in a C-level position is the critical time period. It is typically a honeymoon period full of goodwill, perhaps even relief, throughout the organization, a time when new chief executives are accorded unusual latitude for their initiatives and raise expectations that they will make something good happen. But the honeymoon is also highly conditional, and any number of critical missteps can end the romance. Employees don't know what is in store for them, so the new person must ease everyone's fears, demonstrate that she is competent and will be a good leader, understand what to preserve from the past and what not to, and give hope to the organization that things under this new leader will be good. Forming alliances with the wrong people, acting on bad advice, alienating key supporters, moving so quickly as to seem precipitous or reckless or so slowly as to seem hesitant and fearful, behaving in ways that appear inconsistent with the person the organization thought it was bringing in, managing with a style that simply doesn't fit the organization's expectations or culture—all these are among the land mines that can explode a promising start.

Coaching the C-level executive, particularly someone new to the organization, means asking a lot of questions throughout the company about what people expect from this new leader and interpreting and passing on those expectations. It means looking for the critical success factors and uncovering critical obstacles. It means helping the executive assess her leadership style to see how it can be an asset or a liability in the new culture. Once in office, new executives typically cannot ask the kinds of questions that an objective outside coach can ask. As coaches during the first hundred days, we like to think of ourselves as interlopers who can ask questions such as the following.

✓ We know what the brochure says, but how do things *really* work around here?

✓ What can get you in trouble here? And how do you avoid it?

✓ Where are the bodies buried and who buried them?

✓ What do people expect to see changed? And what do they pray won't be?

✓ We've read the statement of operating principles and corporate values. What is really valued here? What's really important and what isn't?

✓ If you were stepping into this role, what would you do first? What would you avoid?

C-level executives coming into a new position typically can't ask these kinds of questions. If they do, they generally receive polite and carefully measured responses, because people are worried about why the questions are being asked. We have found that, as outside coaches who promise confidentiality, we are able to get a remarkable amount of "inside" information in response to these questions that is invaluable to the incoming executives we are coaching.

It's not difficult to understand why transitions are challenging for many new senior executives. Just consider what successful executives who are tenured in senior positions already know.

▪ They know the organization intimately. They understand the culture, the people, the products, the markets, and the customers.

▪ They know how things work. In particular, they understand both the formal and informal structures of power, influence, and authority.

▪ They know how to get things done, because they know how things work. They know where to find resources, how to gain cooperation from other people and groups, and how to ensure that progress is being made.

▪ They have already built an infrastructure that supports their style of leadership and management, along with the systems and processes that make the infrastructure function more or less smoothly. This infrastructure needs to be built anew with each new C-level executive, because it is not just about structural relationships but about personal connections and networks.

▪ They know what the organization's values and beliefs are; in fact, the incumbents may have been largely responsible for shaping them.

They know how to work within those values in a way that gains the cooperation and support of the people who work for them.

- They know what their boss, peers, direct reports, and other employees need and expect from them, and these people know what to expect from the incumbent executives.

- They know enough of the history of the place and the people in it to know what leads to success and what leads to failure. They know how to avoid the hidden obstacles, pitfalls, and dead ends.

When C-level executives move into new positions, especially in organizations that are new to them, they have little or none of this knowledge at the very time when expectations for their performance are probably higher than they will ever be. New CEOs are expected to act quickly and decisively—and of course, brilliantly. They are expected to play out what Rakesh Khurana (2002) described in "The Curse of the Superstar CEO": "CEOs acquire their hold over others by meeting certain socially constructed criteria about what constitutes a great leader. One of the most powerful of these constructs is the idea that outsiders are particularly well qualified to lead" (p. 64). Thus, new to the job and new to the organization, new CEOs can err without knowing they have done so. Not knowing the real operating values, new senior executives can be quickly relegated to the category "not one of us." They can lose supporters and potential allies easily if they violate the unspoken edicts of the organization or behave in ways that are culturally unacceptable. Yet top-level executives consistently tend to underestimate the magnitude of the challenges before them—perhaps because their confident and authoritative public persona spills over into the personal sphere, causing executives to overestimate their abilities to effect change all by themselves. A key expectation for an executive coach is to render this covert organizational knowledge and culture transparent so that the new person can make astute, knowledgeable decisions.

C-Level Coaching to Prevent Derailment

The high turnover and increasingly short tenure of C-level executives is routinely acknowledged. A 2001 study by Lore International Institute of 2,171 executives found that 47 percent have either derailed already or are on their way out (Singer 2001). This figure is consistent with a 1992 finding that between 33 percent and 66 percent of high-potential executives will fail (Kessler 1992). Interpersonal shortcomings are at the heart of executive derailment. The author of the Lore study, Barbara Spencer Singer, concludes that "as executives advance in their careers, these interpersonal deficiencies are magnified" (p. 4). The tragedy of executive derailment is not just about personal loss but about the organizational destabilization that can affect thousands of lives as well as the fortunes of thousands of shareholders.

It's clear that timely coaching interventions, if treated as a routine part of executive development, can prevent many of these derailment crises, ultimately saving organizations vast sums of money in the costly process of transition. Whether it's the spectacular crash and burn of a sensational new appointment or the long, slow fizzle of a more established leader, C-level coaching has an important role to play in reducing the disturbingly high incidence of derailment. However, one of the painful patterns of behavior among the most senior people is the denial or rationalization that they are in trouble; hence the tendency to miss the warning signs or to wait too long before seeking help—if they seek it at all. A C-level coach, through a careful assessment of the client's real needs, can help identify problems that can cause derailment if not corrected. However, senior executives must be open to the coaching process, must accept the assessment that is part of it, and must ultimately be willing to admit that they need to change their behavior before the behavior becomes critically problematic.

THE PITFALLS OF THE CELEBRITY COACH

We have spoken about the risks inherent in C-level executive positions, particularly the narcissism that can blind executives to the need for coaching. Coaches who coach C-level executives are also at risk. It's all too tempting, in a climate that *Fortune* describes as the "celebritization of the CEO" (Useem 2002, p. 90) for the person behind the celebrity to step out of the shadows and into the spotlight, and to think of himself as a *celebrity coach.* If your client is a "god," a "king," or a "titan" and you are that person's trusted advisor, then you must be pretty special. If you have joined the ranks of the $10K- to $15K-a-day coaches, and articles are being written about you, if aspiring coaches are hanging on to your every written and spoken word, if you are keynoting big conferences, if publishers are clamoring for you to write the next big book, and if celebrity buddies of your celebrity client are coming to you for your help, then you, too, can all too easily see yourself as having joined the pantheon of business celebrities.

The downside is all too obvious. You begin to think of yourself as a celebrity whose advice should be followed because, after all, it is *your* advice. In fact, you come to see yourself as a *dispenser of advice* because listening, reflecting, and guiding don't seem sufficient to justify your worth, and more and more people are asking you for advice. And if you are being paid a disproportionately high fee for your services, you can develop a sense of entitlement that says, "I work only with celebrity CEOs myself, and I work only for top dollar." In short, you develop an arrogance that can distort your sense of self-worth, making you act more and more like the CEO and less and less like the CEO's coach.

Here, as we see them, are the dangers in viewing yourself as a celebrity coach:

- You can come to believe that you deserve to coach only in the highest circles with the most renowned CEOs. Your arrogant attitude can become evident to the "underlings" you won't work with, and they come to resent you and the influence you are having on their boss. They may start to undermine your efforts or poison your name throughout the organization. The executives below the CEO level may begin to talk about how to counter what they perceive (rightly so) as an outside influence that could be detrimental to the organization (and to them personally). In short, by your attitude and influence, you can create a political situation that begins to damage the CEO's credibility among the senior management team and can create active opposition to you. Very soon, this becomes a dysfunctional environment.

- You may start to identify with the CEO's mission and position and begin, psychologically, to assume responsibility for it. We have seen coaches and consultants do this time and again. They get to know an organization well and develop a deep understanding of its strengths and weaknesses—at least from their perspective. They lose sight of the fact that they are coaching a person and start coaching the organization. Soon, instead of coaching the CEO on his leadership style and effectiveness in the role, they are coaching the CEO to reorganize the management team, to put more emphasis on one product and less on another, and so on. In other words, they are trying to *be* the CEO instead of coaching the CEO, without bearing any of the responsibilities or consequences of actually having chief executive authority. We've known a number of senior coaches who evolve to this position and ultimately wind up being fired because they've lost their perspective on the role they should have been playing for the organization. It is exceedingly dangerous to lose sight of your mandate as a coach and assume that you can cure all the ills of the organization—if only they will listen to you.

- The role of celebrity coach can be intoxicating and distorting. Once you have a relationship with a CEO, especially a renowned or highly visible CEO, you may want to keep that relationship so badly that you become willing to tell the CEO whatever he wants to hear. In short, you can lose your objectivity, your courage, and your integrity. Wanting to keep a relationship because it serves your own financial or ego needs is often how professionals lose their professionalism and compromise their values.

- The trap of the celebrity CEO takes us back to the psychodynamics of the coaching relationship. In *Executive Coaching*, Richard Kilburg (2000) cautions that the mere fact of paying increased attention to someone, as a coach does with a client, presents "a two-edged sword," because while people can "thrive when attended to properly," attention can also be "based on voyeurism, an unconscious desire to demonstrate superiority, needs for power and control, and a host of other motivations" (p. 227). When coaches become managers of their clients, it's clear that the relationship has strayed into the netherworld of attending that Kilburg describes.

In his essay on the very real dangers of executive coaching, psychologist Steven Berglas (2002) tells the story of a CEO who fell under the sway of an executive coach. Initially hired to coach an athletic shoe company's CEO during a time of fiscal downturn, the coach went on to become the CEO's close advisor, a kind of shadow-CEO, who wound up suggesting a number of disastrous personnel changes that eventually undermined the entire organization. The CEO, Berglas concludes, had been placed "in the role of an information-dependent child vis-à-vis an expert parent" (p. 92). It took another consulting firm, hired when the company faced a second major decline in sales, to ferret out the problem, ending the coach's relationship with the company.

To avoid the pitfalls of the celebrity coach, here are some points to keep in mind as you coach C-level executives.

- You are not the CEO. Don't imagine that you are, even for a moment. Don't assume the executive's role or responsibilities. Don't say, "If I were you, I would do [this or that]."

- Keep the focus of your coaching on the CEO's personality, leadership, and effectiveness in the role. If the CEO asks, "What should I do about this division?" answer with, "It wouldn't be for me to say. That's your call. But I can help you think through the issues."

- Be careful how you frame advice. Remember that what you advise could have a disproportionate impact on people's lives and on the fortunes of the company. What if you're wrong? Be very circumspect about advice giving while coaching at the C level. Generally, it's best to confine yourself to nondirective coaching. CEOs have a disproportionate amount of power in the organizations they run. As the CEO's coach, therefore, you can acquire a disproportionate impact on people's lives. Even if you were once a CEO yourself and feel experienced and qualified to wield that kind of influence, as a coach you should refrain from it. You need, instead, to help the CEO think through issues and make decisions, not to advise on those issues and decisions. Remember that the focus of the coaching is generally on the CEO's leadership and effectiveness in the role, not on how the corporation is running.

- Don't let it go to your head. If you do, it will distort your perspective and close your mind. Pride goeth before the fall.

Avoid Being Trapped in the Fun House

Throughout this book, we have used the image of the mirror to describe what coaches do for their clients. By providing a clear reflection for the client to see himself as others see him, the coach enables the client to see his leadership for what it is, not what he wishes it were, thinks it is, or wants others to think it is. To hold up that mirror, the coach must be equally clear in her vision of herself. The pitfall of the celebrity coach is that it becomes all too easy for the images of both coach and client to become distorted. You both become trapped in the fun house, where you can't see beyond the trick mirrors that show you to be something other than what you really are. The two sets of distorted images—the coach's and the client's—keep reinforcing each other, locking the two people in a mirage of grandiose self-deception.

If you can keep your wits about you, coaching C-level executives can be tremendously rewarding as a coach. Generally, you need to follow the nondirective method, even when clients ask for more directive advice. Keep in mind that the executive responsibilities are theirs, not yours. You can help them think through the issues and the implications of various decisions, behaviors, and courses of action, but you are not accountable for the consequences of their actions and so should refrain from wielding undue influence on their decisions.

To C-level executives, the principal value of coaching is in having an unbiased, objective thought partner, someone who can listen to the executive's doubts without ringing the alarm bell, someone who can discuss the alternatives without having a stake in the outcome, and someone who can offer feedback and suggestions without passing judgment.

Epilogue

Helping Clients Change

Make more effort to explore the coachee's feelings, motives, and ambitions, and stay closer to these while you are coaching.

You are quick to understand behavior, but you could be more effective by pushing people to find their own insights and need for action.

I have always liked the way you refuse to give "the answer." You coach until you feel like the other person finally understands things.

SUGGESTIONS TO COACHES FROM THE "COACHING EFFECTIVENESS SURVEY,"
LORE INTERNATIONAL INSTITUTE, INC.

The purpose of coaching is to help people change. Of course, a particular coach may be giving performance feedback, teaching an employee how to use equipment, brainstorming with a group on how to improve quality, advising a colleague about improving customer relationships, or counseling a young person about her career options and helping her think through them. Whatever the specific coaching task in each of these cases, fundamentally, the coach is trying to help the other person change—improve performance, make better choices, do something differently, avoid ineffective behaviors, or change an attitude or perspective.

The problem is that change is difficult for most people, and data from Lore's (1997) "Coaching Effectiveness Survey" show that most coaching is only moderately effective. Forty-five percent of clients report that their sessions with their current coach have not had much positive impact on their work performance, and 60 percent of those surveyed said they would like better coaching than they are currently receiving. The irony, of course, is that coaches can't make people change; they can only offer guidance and help. Change is the client's responsibility, and no change will occur, no matter how helpful or brilliant the coach, if the client isn't able to make it happen.

Change is difficult, mysterious, and uncertain, which creates an enormous challenge for us when we try to coach others. The fact that people fear even the smallest change was poignantly illustrated by the late Eric Hoffer—migrant worker, longshoreman, street philosopher, and author. In his 1963 book, *The Ordeal of Change,* he tells the story of how a slight change in his life precipitated a feeling of foreboding:

> *Back in 1936 I spent a good part of the year picking peas. I started out early in January in the Imperial Valley and drifted northward, picking peas as they ripened, until I picked the last peas of the season, in June, around Tracy. Then I shifted all the way to Lake County, where for the first time I was going to pick string beans. And I still remember how hesitant I was that first morning as I was about to address myself to the string bean vines. Would I be able to pick string beans? Even the change from peas to string beans had in it elements of fear.* (p. 3)

We fear change because it undermines our security. It threatens to upset our routine and eliminate (however temporarily) the comfort zone we create around the behaviors and habits we have become accustomed to. We aren't certain the change will be better for us. We don't know whether we will adapt well to it. It may require new skills we don't have and can't master. It will be uncomfortable for us because it's not part of our routine. We may have to think harder about what we're doing; we won't be able to go through the motions, because we aren't sure which motions to go through. Change is difficult. If it were easier, no one who knows how bad smoking is for them would smoke cigarettes, average life expectancies would rise because fewer people would be overweight, there would be no need for Alcoholics Anonymous, and more New Year's resolutions would be kept.

To explore the idea that personal change is difficult, try this experiment on yourself. On a blank piece of paper, map your daily routine. Think about all the small details of your daily life. When do you usually get up? What do you typically do next? Where are the things in your bath-room that you use in the morning? In what order do you shower, brush your teeth, take your pills—or whatever you do after you get up? What do you typically start reading in the newspaper? How do you typically get to work? What are your normal work routines? How is your office or work-space organized? *What* needs to be *where* for you to be happy? Map your entire, normal workday. No matter how frantic or unpredictable your working life might be, there will be certain routines and rituals you ob-serve and are uncomfortable without.

Now imagine totally changing your routines—not just doing a few things differently, which we all like to do now and then, but completely changing the normal way you live. Better yet, actually do it. Along with changing what you do now, try introducing some new elements. If you don't exercise in the morning, try adding thirty minutes of jogging, walk-ing, or another aerobic exercise. If you always eat breakfast in your house, start eating breakfast somewhere else. Try changing your morning bath-room routines. If you brush your teeth before showering, start doing it af-terward. Find a different way to get to work. Alter your work routines. Then pause to reflect on this experience. How does it feel? Are you stressed? Anxious? Are you unhappy about how this new routine is work-ing for you? Does it feel inefficient or uncomfortable? If not, change your routine again. And again. And again. (Incidentally, this is how it feels to people in companies undergoing frequent mergers, acquisitions, reorga-nizations, or other disorienting shifts in *how things work*.)

Radical life changes are even more difficult. Eric Hoffer (1963) speaks of this in his book: "In the case of drastic change the uneasiness is of course deeper and more lasting. We can never be really prepared for that which is wholly new. We have to adjust ourselves, and every radical ad-justment is a crisis in self-esteem: we undergo a test, we have to prove ourselves. It needs inordinate self-confidence to face drastic change with-out inner trembling" (p. 3). Drastic changes could include the following.

- Changing your work life so you spend more time with your family

- Changing your management style so you are less of a command-and-control manager and more of an empowering manager

- Changing your approach to your projects so you are more creative, more open to new ideas, and more innovative in your solutions

- Changing your personality so you are less emotionally volatile and have more composure when things go wrong

▓ Changing the way you relate to others so you build trust sooner and are better able to create sustained, trust-based relationships

These kinds of changes are drastic because they require very different routines and ways of behaving, and the capacity to accomplish such change may not be within us. To successfully accomplish these changes—not only immediately but forever—we would have to radically alter the way we behave, make decisions, set priorities, and perhaps relate to other people. This is not easy. Now imagine trying to coach other people to make these changes:

▓ Coach an ambitious, career-oriented direct report who is working too many hours and starting to have problems at home to change his work habits so he spends more time with his family. (What if he doesn't want to change?)

▓ Coach a manager whose department is suffering because of her rigid, hierarchical, command-and-control management style so she becomes more of an empowering manager. (Is she truly capable of releasing control?)

▓ Coach a professional whose work is no longer acceptable, because she seems to have fallen into a rut, to change her approach to her projects so she is more creative, more open to new ideas, and more innovative in her solutions. (How easy is it to help someone else become more creative?)

▓ Coach a supervisor whose abrasive personality is grating on people and causing high turnover to be less emotionally volatile and have more composure when things go wrong. (Maybe his personality is part of who he is. Is it even possible for him to be more composed? How emotionally intelligent is he?)

▓ Coach a struggling salesman who can't sustain customer relationships to change the way he relates to people so he is better able to create sustained, trust-based relationships with customers. (Do you understand enough about human relationships to know how to help him become better at sustaining relationships with his customers?)

Without a doubt, most of us could coach others in these situations and have at least *some* positive impact, but would it be lasting? Can you honestly say that you'd be certain to help the person you're coaching permanently change his or her behavior? Changing yourself is hard; coaching others to change is even harder because you can't be present all the time. You can't know the external and internal pressures on them. You can't help them manage their moment-by-moment priorities, decisions, trade-offs, and temptations. More important, you can't manage their commitment to change or their persistence in doing things differently.

Some coaches fail to have impact with people because they either don't understand human change or lack the patience to see it through. For example, a command-and-control manager might think that coaching is giving feedback and orders. If you point out what people are doing wrong and tell them how to do it right, isn't that enough? An empowering manager, on the other hand, might think that just helping people think about their performance, encouraging them to do things differently, and providing resources for them is enough to make a difference. If you take off the handcuffs and empower people to do it themselves, and if you discuss it with them and give them the resources they need, isn't that enough? Sadly, it usually isn't. Human change is complicated, as anyone who's successfully completed an AA twelve-step program can confirm. Permanent change in people over twenty-one years of age is usually a monumental struggle.

It reminds us of the story of the physicist and psychologist who are arguing. The physicist contends that psychology is too soft and touchy-feely. It's not even a science, the physicist asserts. On the other hand, physics is a difficult field that deals with the most fundamental questions in nature—the elemental particles that form the physical world, the laws that govern how the world works, the formation and death of stars, and the creation of the universe. The psychologist says, "You're right. By your definition, psychology is not a science. It deals with human beings and how they work, and that's so much more complicated than physics."

A HUMAN CHANGE PROCESS

Given that human change is difficult and coaching people to change is even more difficult, what can coaches do to help others change? The most important thing to understand is that change rarely happens instantaneously. It usually takes time, in part because it means rewiring the brain, and the older people get, the longer the rewiring can take. Human change is a process, not an event. Consequently, it's helpful for coaches to think in terms of process as they try to help the people they're coaching.

Figure 8   The Human Change Process

Figure 8 shows a coaching sequence that's been very helpful in our work with others. Before discussing it, we should mention several important caveats.

- The process shown here is a rational one. In our experience, it applies in most business settings with people who are rational, well-functioning adults. It does not necessarily apply in circumstances in which people are not rational or have psychological issues that should be treated by a therapist, not a coach.

- Although the process appears as a series of steps, in fact change is often messy and the process is really iterative.

- Even this rational coaching process will not work unless the client is able to change. As we said earlier, the responsibility for change lies with the client, not the coach. The coach is a helper, not a driver.

People begin the change process when they become aware of the need for change. However, being aware of the need will not result in change unless they also feel a strong sense of urgency. That urgency must be enough to compel them to decide that they need to do things differently. Following the decision must be some problem solving around what, specifically, they need to do differently, what barriers they might encounter, and how they will overcome them. If they can successfully problem-solve, they know what to do. The next step is commitment—having the will to act, to start following the new path. Down the road, they will need to have their new behaviors reinforced or they risk lapsing back into their old, familiar habits. If you wish to have impact as a coach, you must make sure that the people you're coaching go through each step. It would be nice if there were simple shortcuts, but there aren't.

AWARENESS

First, the person you're coaching must become aware of the need to change. This can be more difficult than it sounds because people tend to disregard or sublimate disconfirming information—something that contradicts what they already believe—especially if it disconfirms their self-image. John may believe he's a good manager, for instance, so if he gets feedback that he's not, he may resist hearing that message. He may ignore it, blame the problems on someone else, or attack the messenger. It may take repeated messages or feedback from someone John respects for him to hear what others are saying. This is the value of a coach. If you have built a good coaching relationship and are skilled at giving feedback so that even tough messages are delivered with obvious caring, then you can help John and people like him hear and accept disconfirming messages.

A useful tool for thinking about how you can help others become more aware of the need for change is the Johari Window (see figure 9). This framework was developed by professors Joseph Luft and Harry Ingham. The four boxes of the window indicate what both you and John know or don't know about him. The **arena** is the area of shared knowledge. You know that John is a manager; he knows that, too. You know that John's latest performance assessment shows that his management skills are among the lowest rated in the company. He now knows that, too, because he's seen the report. Though he may be in denial about the results, they are indisputably what they are, and you both know it. This information is in the arena.

Where you can help John most is with his **blind spot**—the area of things you know about John that he doesn't know. Maybe you have talked to some of John's direct reports and you have more insight into what's been happening. Perhaps you've observed John yourself, so you can tell him what you've observed and enlarge his arena by sharing your

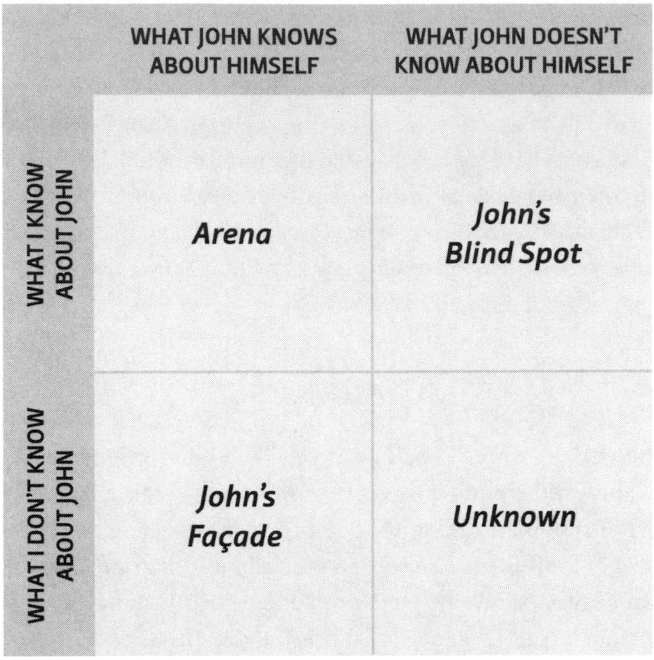

	WHAT JOHN KNOWS ABOUT HIMSELF	WHAT JOHN DOESN'T KNOW ABOUT HIMSELF
WHAT I KNOW ABOUT JOHN	*Arena*	*John's Blind Spot*
WHAT I DON'T KNOW ABOUT JOHN	*John's Façade*	*Unknown*

Figure 9 Johari Window

perceptions. Or maybe you have other information—from customers, performance measures for his department, or observations of his peers—information you can provide that may help John develop a better understanding of how his management skills and style are viewed. Reducing the blind spot is one of a coach's important roles.

Where you need John's help is regarding his **façade**. This includes the things John knows about himself that you don't know. Maybe he's actually had more direct feedback on his management style and he hasn't shared it with you yet. Or maybe he's been having some misgivings himself. Maybe he's more aware of the issues than you realized. You help him reduce his façade by asking questions. For example:

✓ John, how is it going? What's working well in your department and what isn't?

✓ Where do you think you're strong as a manager? Where do you have developmental needs?

✓ If you could be doing two or three things better as a manager, what would those be?

✓ What do your people think about your management style?

How much John tells you is usually a good indicator of how self-aware he is and how willing he is to acknowledge his developmental needs. As coaches, we find these kinds of questions extremely useful.

Often, a very useful area to explore with people like John is the **unknown**—the area in which neither of you has any insights. You do this, again, by asking questions. You might also ask John to do a 360-degree management skills assessment and then look at the results together. You could do a roundtable discussion with John and his direct reports—so both of you can hear their observations and ask questions. This kind of roundtable may be high risk for John, but it usually has high returns if it's handled well and his direct reports have no fear of retribution.

Your purpose in building awareness is to help the person you're coaching understand what needs to be changed. Clearly, no change is possible unless the person first accepts that something should be changed. These are the kinds of questions you ask yourself as a coach as you reflect on the other person's level of awareness:

- ✓ How do you need to change?
- ✓ What could you be doing better?
- ✓ What is the source of the need to change—is it within you or is it coming from external pressure?
- ✓ What problems are you having? *Or,* What opportunities are being missed?
- ✓ What is wrong that needs to be fixed?
- ✓ What are you doing that is dangerous, ineffective, or inadequate?
- ✓ Do you recognize this?
- ✓ To what degree are you aware of any developmental needs? To what degree do you accept responsibility for them?
- ✓ Where are your blind spots? What are you missing?
- ✓ What kinds of things have you already tried to do?

URGENCY

Of course, nothing whatsoever will happen just because people are aware of the need to change. How many times in your life have you been aware of something you needed to do differently but were not able to do it—or

at least weren't able to sustain it? The fact is that people won't change unless they feel a compelling need to do so. Their *felt need* must be urgent
enough to prompt them to act. Furthermore, it must be urgent enough to
help them overcome their fear of change. Millions of smokers are no
doubt aware of the dangers of cigarette smoking. The medical establish-
ment, the courts, the government, the media, and educators have made it
abundantly clear to anyone who's listening that smoking is harmful.
Awareness is not the issue. Urgency is. People won't feel compelled to stop
smoking until they feel an urgent need to do so. They may *decide* to stop
smoking. They may even buy the patch or the nicotine chewing gum or
find some other aid to help them stop. But they won't follow through on
their decision and make a permanent change unless their sense of urgency is strong enough to overcome the physical and psychological de-
pendencies smoking creates.

Similarly, a manager with an abrasive style may become aware of the
need to change but will not act on it unless she feels an urgent need to do
so. What could create a sense of urgency for her? Fear is one of the primary motivators. She may fear that if she doesn't change she will lose her
job or won't be promoted. But even if her manager tells her she needs to
change, she is still likely to weigh the other pressures on her and think, "Is
it *that* serious? They promoted me to this position. I've done well so far.
I keep making my numbers. Besides, they don't know my people. My people *have* to be pushed. If you don't set tough standards and weed out the
nonperformers, then you won't meet the goal. Is that what they want? No
way. At the end of the day, they'll accept who I am because I hit the tar-
gets." In her case, the threat may still not be strong enough for her to fear
the consequences sufficiently.

Fear is one of the primary motivators because it reflects the deep-
seated human need for safety and security. As Abraham Maslow noted in
his famous hierarchy of needs, beyond physiological needs, humans need
to be safe and secure (see, e.g., Maslow 1998). We need to feel that we are
safe from harm. When fears arise that threaten our safety, we are compelled to act and have a far stronger sense of urgency. So, what are we
afraid of? Certainly death and lesser forms of physical harm. We also fear
punishment. We fear losing ground, losing face, or being left behind (social exclusion). We are afraid of failure.

Suddenly faced with the prospect of failure or social exclusion, we will
feel a stronger sense of urgency to change what we're doing. A smoker, for
instance, may have a physical checkup in which the doctor notes a spot on

his lung or sees the early signs of emphysema. Or the smoker's father may die of lung cancer after a long, wasting illness. Sometimes such events are sufficient to create a strong sense of urgency based on fear. If the abrasive manager is sent to an interpersonal skills program and told that she has ninety days to become less abrasive and improve the morale and productivity in her group, she may have a strong enough sense of urgency to change. In these examples, the person's felt need is based on fear—a negative emotion—and the tools for increasing the felt need are based on real or implied threats. However, while fear can be a powerful motivator, a person's sense of urgency can also derive from fulfillment, fellowship, followership, or faith.

Fulfillment reflects the common human need for achievement. Virtually all human beings need to feel that they have accomplished something, that they are valuable, that their efforts result in something they and others can be proud of. People with a high need for achievement push themselves to excel in some way—to get an advanced degree, to win the competition, to achieve higher status, to be recognized as an expert, to become certified in some important field, or to use their hard-earned expertise in some way that benefits others. Maslow felt that the desire for achievement and recognition underlie the two highest needs on his hierarchy—self-esteem and self-actualization. One way to increase a person's sense of urgency, therefore, is to appeal to her need for achievement, to help her attain a higher level of self-esteem or self-actualization through change. Most Olympic and professional athletes are driven, largely, by an inner desire for fulfillment through the accomplishment of something difficult and demanding.

Another of the needs in Maslow's hierarchy is social inclusion, the need for fellowship. We are social creatures and are driven in part by our need to affiliate with other people. This manifests itself in our desire for acceptance and belonging, by our responses to peer and group pressures, and by our conformance to the cultural norms of the societies, families, organizations, clubs, and other groups we belong to. People may feel the urgent need to change because they want the approval of their peers, because they want to be admired and loved, or simply because it's the fashion (it's what their friends are doing). You have only to look at how teenagers respond to fashion changes to see how powerful a force this can be.

Sometimes the urgent need to change comes from followership—from being inspired or motivated by a leader. For some people, an inspirational leader represents a cause, a movement, a philosophy, a passion, or a direction they lack. Following the leader enables them to find meaning and passion in what the leader represents and how he or she can motivate them to act. Martin Luther King Jr., Gandhi, Susan B. Anthony, John F. Kennedy, Eleanor Roosevelt—these are leaders whose ability to inspire moved millions of people, generally as a force for good. Clearly, it is also possible for leaders to move scores of people as a force for evil—Adolf Hitler, Josef Stalin, David Koresh, Jim Jones. Followership can become so consuming a force for change in some people that they lose themselves completely in the leader's destructive aura.

Finally, some people may feel an urgent need to change because of their need to believe in something greater than themselves. The search for meaning in their lives, the desire for universal truth and understanding, or the sense of connectedness with God, nature, or revered persons—these can be powerful incentives for change. People can come to embrace certain principles—justice, truth, righting wrongs, improving lives—and be driven by a vision that changes how they see the world and thus how they behave. Occasionally we see profound midlife changes in someone who has come to embrace a particular religious faith late in life. In this regard, the missionary is a coach who builds the sense of urgency through faith.

It is virtually certain that change will not occur unless a person feels a strong enough sense of urgency. However, urgency can be preempted by *necessity* when a radical event necessitates change whether the person likes it or not. If a person is fired or laid off after a long term of employment with the same company, for instance, necessity may force him to change regardless of how urgently he felt the need for change prior to losing his job. Similarly, a right-handed person who loses the use of her right hand has no choice but to change and learn how to be left-handed. Traumatic, life-changing events are usually the vehicles of necessity. They can include the death of someone dear, a catastrophic illness, becoming a victim of crime or war, being displaced from one's home, and so on. It should be apparent that these kinds of circumstances compel change through a kind of shock treatment.

In the absence of such traumatic events, people feel a less-compelling need for change. Fortunately, most coaches work with people who aren't faced with catastrophic situations, but this means that developing a sense of urgency may be challenging. To succeed, you have to know what would be most compelling to the person you are coaching. What would cause him or her to feel a greater sense of urgency? Fear? Fulfillment? Fellowship? Followership? Or faith? As coaches, we devote most of our time to this area—helping the people we're coaching explore their sense of urgency. The questions you might ask are these:

✓ How important is this?

✓ What will happen if you don't change? What would be the negative consequences?

✓ What could you lose? What will happen if you continue doing what you are doing now? How much worse could it get?

✓ What will happen if you do change? What are the positive consequences? What could you gain? How much better could it be for you?

✓ What would have to be different for you to be able to change?

These are implication questions. They are some of a coach's most powerful tools.

DECISION

The decision to change is both pivotal and fragile—pivotal because it represents the point at which the person decides to change, fragile because that decision can evaporate in an instant. A common, mistaken belief is that the decision to change is the most important part of this process, that once people have decided to be different, they will be. In fact, the decision is the weakest link in the chain. The journey after the decision is fraught with pitfalls and barriers in the form of habits, temptations, diversions, problems, and daily life—the rituals and noise of which can dissolve even the staunchest resolve.

The decision is fragile because nothing yet has happened—nothing concrete to test the person's resolve, nothing specific in the form of new behaviors, nothing challenging in terms of barriers, skill gaps, resource deficits, and resistance from other people, all of which can weaken the person's resolve and erase the decision. People who decide to do something differently often experience a psychological release when the decision is made. It seems like a climactic moment: "There, I've done it! I'm going to change." Yet until the decision is tested, until it is acted upon, until the challenges have been faced and overcome, the decision is as fragile as a newly born calf in a stampede.

Nonetheless, it is crucial for coaches to help the people they're coaching reach this fragile point. Once they've reached the decision, most people have enough commitment to it to continue—at least for a while. Among the key questions a coach can ask at this stage are these:

- ✓ What have you decided to do differently?

- ✓ Why are you doing this? What do you expect to gain from it? What will it do for you?

- ✓ What will be different for you afterward?

- ✓ What's the ideal outcome?

- ✓ What are your new goals?

- ✓ When will you start? When do you expect to be finished (with the change)?

Problem Solving

In problem solving, we ask people to explore how they will change, what they will have to do differently, what barriers they might encounter and how they will get around those barriers, what skills they need to have and how they will develop those skills, what the next steps are, and so on. In short, we ask them to think through what change will actually mean for them.

Problem solving is the roll-up-your-sleeves grunt work in the human change process. It's where you become pragmatic, specific, and action oriented—and it's where many people falter as they confront what change will actually mean to them and how they will have to be or act differently. In some ways, it is the toughest part of making personal change, because it's where the rubber meets the road, as they say. It's where the dream becomes real, where the goal is transformed into the often-harsh reality of what the person must now do differently. There are three parts to this problem solving. First, the person needs to envision and think through the alternate future (what he needs to do differently to achieve the change goal). Then he needs to explore potential barriers. Finally, he needs to develop an action plan, with specific next steps. Your role as the coach is to guide people through this problem solving. You might use these questions:

ALTERNATE FUTURE

✓ What do you need to do differently?

✓ Specifically, what would that look like? How could you do it?

✓ What options do you have?

✓ What must you do to get the job done?

✓ When will you have to do it?

POTENTIAL BARRIERS

✓ How and why could this change be difficult for you?

✓ What could get in your way?

✓ What barriers could you face? Externally? Internally?

✓ How will you overcome these barriers?

✓ Do you have the skills to do this?

✓ Do you have the resources?

ACTION PLANS

✓ What is your plan?

✓ What, specifically, should you do?

✓ Do you need anyone else's buy-in? Support? Encouragement? Cooperation?

✓ If so, how will you bring them on board?

✓ What are your next steps?

✓ How will you make those next steps happen?

In our experience, when people fail to improve or change in some other way, it is often because they haven't thought through what they must do differently or really considered the implications of the change. In other words, they haven't problem-solved. People sometimes ask for coaching because they haven't been able to do something they've wanted to do and they don't understand what's keeping them from doing it. In 90 percent of the cases, they have failed either because they didn't have a strong enough sense of urgency or because they didn't problem-solve.

Problem solving is not a particularly strong area for many coaches. In Lore's survey of coaching effectiveness, 38 percent of the client respondents said that their coach was not effective at identifying the barriers or situational constraints that interfered with their performance or ability to change, nor was their coach effective at helping them set action plans so they would know specifically what they had to do to accomplish their goals. Problem solving is an area where many coaches need to improve their own skills.

COMMITMENT AND ACTION

If people have truly completed the preceding steps, then making the commitment to the change and initiating action is the logical next step. This is not to say that it's always easy, but it can be easier—*if* they've truly taken themselves through the preceding steps. Commitment falters, however, if they don't feel a strong enough sense of urgency, if their decision was halfhearted, and if they haven't problem-solved. So the coach's role at this point is to test those preceding steps. What you're testing is the person's will. Is he committed to this change? Does she have the will to do it? The kinds of questions you might ask include the following.

✓ Now that you've thought through your plan, are you committed to doing it?

✓ Do you have the will to do it?

✓ How strong is your commitment?

✓ What will happen to your commitment over time?

✓ What if this is harder than you imagined?

✓ What if things don't turn out the way you wished?

Note that there are two important parts to this step: expressing the commitment and then taking action. It's important that the commitment be expressed. Saying "I will do this" is a crucial early step in *acting* on the change the person is committed to making. It's best if that commitment is made publicly, because people have a deep psychological desire to appear consistent to others and to live by their commitments. As Robert B. Cialdini (1993) observes in his book *Influence: The Psychology of Persuasion,* "Once we have made a choice or taken a stand, we will encounter personal and interpersonal pressures to behave consistently with that commitment. Those pressures will cause us to respond in ways that justify our earlier decision" (p. 57).

The second important part of this step is taking action. A plan is still a plan until it is acted upon; then it starts to form the new reality. One of the most helpful things you can do as a coach is to help your clients take those important first steps. After they start taking action, they are no longer thinking about improving; they *are* improving. If it's going well for them, their success will reinforce their decision, and they are likely to build momentum to keep going. Conversely, if they have some early failures, they'll need your help to work through them and maintain their resolve. In fact, it is often best to plan for some relapses, or at least the possibility of relapse, and then develop a plan that minimizes the damage or loss if and when a relapse occurs. Rather than encourage relapses, this actually minimizes the impact of a slip and allows clients to feel successful, to feel that they've handled it well. If the setbacks are not planned for, it leads to feelings of failure and discouragement, which could snowball into complete failure.

REINFORCEMENT

Until the change becomes the new reality, it remains difficult, because even though the person may have changed, his environment is likely to be the same. Tomorrow, the office will look the same as it did yesterday. The same quality problems will exist on the production line. There will still be an urge to get angry when things go wrong. The temptations will still be there. So will the habits and accoutrements of the old routines. The brain will still be wired the same way and will urge people to think, behave, and respond as they have in the past. In short, it will be "business as usual."

So it's crucial that people undergoing change have the positive aspects of change reinforced in their environment and by the people around them, including their coach. You should reinforce every little step, which helps build momentum. Enough small steps will eventually create a critical mass, and the new reality will be established. Lasting change is generally not possible unless the person receives support and encouragement from others and unless the reasons for and benefits of the change are reinforced repeatedly during the period in which the changed behaviors are still unusual and the old, usual behaviors are still habitual. The diagram shown in figure 10 illustrates the dynamic process of integrating new learning into one's normal behavior.

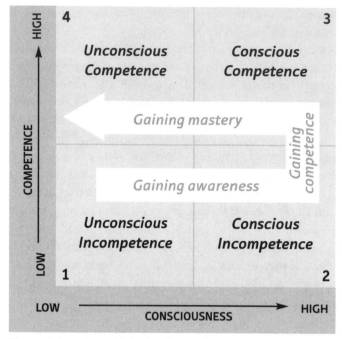

Figure 10   Learning and Behavioral Integration

Everyone begins in the lower left, the area of unconscious incompetence. They don't know that they aren't skilled. They move to box 2 (conscious incompetence) by developing *awareness* of their lack of skill. Coaches help them move from box 1 to box 2 by giving them feedback about their performance or otherwise helping them understand that they need to develop greater skill. Being in box 2 is generally unsettling for people, especially if having the skill is important to them. If their *sense of urgency* is high enough, they will *decide* that they need to change (to develop their skills). *Problem solving* and *commitment and action* take them from box 2 to box 3 (conscious competence). While they are highly skilled at this point, box 3 is also an unsettling area to be in, because they have to continue to consciously practice the skills in order to build and maintain their competence. Finally, through the processes of *practice* and *reinforcement,* they attain the highest level of learning—unconscious competence or, better yet, *mastery.* At this point, they have integrated the new skills into their normal behavior and no longer have to consciously think about what they are doing.

Consider the relatively straightforward process of learning a new sport, such as golf. When you take up the game, you are initially unaware of how unskilled you are. The game may look easy, but it's not, which you discover when you start to play. At that point, you become conscious of your incompetence. So you take lessons. Over time, you develop the skills but still have to think about your swing, your putting, your club selection, and so on. Now you are consciously competent, probably even hyperconscious about every little piece of the new routine. This phase of the change is so difficult because it's mentally taxing to have to think about everything, and it feels uncomfortably unnatural. You often have to talk yourself through each step or make up various memory aids to help you translate what you know into what you do. You feel a little silly, even incompetent. If you continue playing for a while and continue developing your skills, you will eventually stop thinking about what you're doing and do it naturally and instinctively, though there is nothing natural and instinctive about it. At that point, you will have integrated the skills into your normal behaviors and will be unconsciously competent.

This learning and behavioral integration process applies whether you are learning to play golf, learning to lose weight and keep it off, learning to be a more empowering manager, learning to be more creative, or learning to improve your ability to build strong relationships with your customers. In short, this process applies to anything that you could be coached on or coach someone else on. It should be apparent, then, how critical reinforcement is. It is the process where the behavioral integration occurs; it helps clients become unconsciously competent. Surveys of people being coached indicate that this is also a weak area for many coaches. Nearly 40 percent of clients report that their coach does not consistently follow up after coaching to help ensure that they are making the progress they wanted. To better help the people you are coaching, follow through on your coaching sessions and ask these kinds of questions:

✓ Are you doing what you said you would do?

✓ Are you sticking with it?

✓ How does the change feel? What's going well?

✓ Is it working? If not, what more could you do?

Incidentally, the coach should not be the only source of continued support for people trying to change. People need as broad a support network as they can reasonably get, including friends, colleagues, spouses or significant others, children, other coaches and mentors, and so on. They need other people who believe in them when they may not fully believe in themselves, and they need the positive aspects of their change reinforced and encouraged by other people in their environment. If the going gets tough, they need others who will empathize with the difficulty they're having and continue to provide positive support and reinforcement through the most difficult days of change. As their coach, you should help clients build this support network and teach them how to use it.

DIAGNOSING CHANGE FAILURES

When coaching fails to result in the improvements or changes you wanted, what has gone wrong? First and foremost, remember that improving is the client's responsibility, not the coach's. The coach's ability to influence the client will always be limited. Nonetheless, here is a quick diagnostic checklist for identifying the problem.

1. **Did the person have sufficient awareness of the need for change?** If not, can you or anyone else do anything to help increase awareness?

2. **Did the person feel a strong enough sense of urgency?** If not, can you or anyone else help increase the person's sense of urgency? What would motivate this person most? Fear? Fulfillment? Fellowship? Followership? Faith? If the sense of urgency isn't strong enough, change is unlikely to happen.

3. **Did the person make the decision to change—and express that decision?** If not, was the person's sense of urgency truly high enough? Maybe it wasn't. Revisit the sense of urgency by asking implication questions. If the *felt need* is strong enough, then ask the person to make a firm decision.

4. **Did the person do enough problem solving? Did she identify and remove the barriers? Did she create a specific action plan?** If not, reengage in problem solving. Don't stop until the person seems to have a clear sense of what must be done, has thought through and removed the barriers, and has a clear sense of the path forward, including next steps.

5. **Did the person commit to the change and then start taking action?** If not, then the sense of urgency may not be strong enough or the person still may not have done enough problem solving. Return to these steps.

6. **Finally, did the person have adequate reinforcement following action?** If not, you may need to help the person you're coaching build greater awareness or urgency. Or you may need to help her reenter the process at some subsequent step and, in essence, start over. Remember that the weakest link is the decision and that the two points where someone is most likely to falter are urgency and problem solving.

As a self-test, think back to a key change you wanted to make in your life or work but were not able to—some skills you wanted to develop but didn't, something you resolved to do differently or better but couldn't, or something new you wanted to learn but haven't. Go back through this diagnostic checklist and ask yourself, "Where did I falter? Why wasn't I able to follow through?"

Try the same test with someone you coached in the past or are coaching now, someone who is not improving as you'd hoped or who intended to make a change but didn't. Use the diagnostic checklist to ask the same questions as above: Where did this person falter? Why wasn't he or she able to follow through? What happened that prevented the change? Where in the human change process did the breakdown occur?

Coaching would be less challenging if it were easier for people to change, but it's not. There are no shortcuts except traumatic ones. Nearly all the time, you need to follow the steps outlined in this human change process—and even this will not guarantee success, because human beings are complicated and the coach's powers are limited. Ultimately, the only people who can change your clients are themselves.

Nonetheless, following the human change process described here will help you be a better coach. Remember that each step requires the one before it. There can be no sense of urgency without first having awareness. There can be no decision without a sense of urgency. And there will be no lasting commitment and action unless problem solving has taken place. This process is often iterative, which means that steps may need to be repeated. Problem solving may require a return to urgency. Faltering commitment may necessitate a return to the decision or to problem solving, and so on. The process is iterative, but it always begins with awareness and should always end with reinforcement.

The coach's work is to guide people through this process. It may be simple or complex, quick or tedious. It may involve simple skill development or complicated personal issues. But whatever your particular challenge or opportunity to help someone, your coaching will be more successful if you follow the principles of this six-step process for helping people change. Coaching people is hard because old habits are hardwired into people's brains. They become complacent, comfortable in familiar patterns and routines. Being creative and following a new, uncharted path are just plain difficult.

REFERENCES

American Psychiatric Association. 1994. *Diagnostic and Statistical Manual of Mental Disorders.* 4th ed. Washington, D.C.: American Psychiatric Association.

Austin, Linda. 2000. *What's Holding You Back?: Eight Critical Choices for Women's Success.* New York: Basic Books.

Belenky, Mary, Blythe Clinchy, Nancy Goldberger, and Jill Tarule. 1986. *Women's Ways of Knowing: The Development of Self, Voice, and Mind.* New York: Basic Books.

Berglas, Steven. 2002. "The Very Real Dangers of Executive Coaching." *Harvard Business Review* (June).

Blanchard, Ken, and Don Shula. 1995. *Everyone's a Coach.* Grand Rapids, Mich.: Zondervan Publishing.

Bohm, David. *On Dialogue.* London: Routledge, 1996.

Bohm, David, Donald Factor, and Peter Garrett. 1991. "Dialogue: A Proposal." Accessible at http://world.std.com/~lo/bohm/0000.html.

Business Women's Network. *Women and Diversity: Wow Facts.* Washington, D.C.: The Business Women's Network, 2001.

Catalyst. 2000. *Cracking the Glass Ceiling: Catalyst's Research on Women in Corporate Management, 1995–2000.* New York: Catalyst.

Caver, Keith A., and Ancella B. Livers. 2002. "Dear White Boss." *Harvard Business Review* (November).

Chambers, Elizabeth, Mark Foulon, Helen Handfield-Jones, Steven M. Hankin, and Edward G. Michaels III. 1998. "The War for Talent." *McKinsey Quarterly* 3.

Charan, Ram, Stephen Drotter, and James Noel. 2001. *The Leadership Pipeline: How to Build the Leadership-Powered Company.* San Francisco: Jossey-Bass.

Cialdini, Robert B. 1993. *Influence: The Psychology of Persuasion.* Rev. ed. New York: William Morrow.

Collins, Jim. 2001. *Good to Great: Why Some Companies Make the Leap . . . And Others Don't.* New York: HarperCollins.

Conlin, Michelle. 2002. "CEO Coaches." *BusinessWeek,* November 11, 98–104.

Coutu, Diane. 2002. "How Resilience Works." *Harvard Business Review* (May).

Duran, Eduardo, and Bonnie Duran. 1995. *Native American Postcolonial Psychology.* Albany: State University of New York Press.

Egan, Gerard. 1998. *The Skilled Helper: A Problem-Management Approach to Helping.* 6th ed. Pacific Grove, Calif.: Brooks/Cole.

Fletcher, Joyce. 1999. *Disappearing Acts: Gender, Power, and Relational Practice at Work.* Boston: MIT Press.

Flick, Deborah L. 1998. *From Debate to Dialogue.* Boulder, Colo.: Orchid Publications.

Fuentes, Carlos. 1992. *The Buried Mirror: Reflections on Spain and the New World.* Boston: Houghton Mifflin.

Glazer, Penina, and Miriam Slater. 1987. *Unequal Colleagues: The Entrance of Women into the Professions, 1890–1940.* Camden, N.J.: Rutgers University Press.

Goldsmith, Marshall, Laurence Lyons, and Alyssa Freas, eds. 2000. *Coaching for Leadership: How the World's Greatest Coaches Help Leaders Learn.* San Francisco: Jossey-Bass/Pfeiffer.

Goleman, Daniel. 1995. *Emotional Intelligence.* New York: Bantam.

Goleman, Daniel, Richard Boyatzis, and Annie McKee. 2002. *Primal Leadership: Realizing the Power of Emotional Intelligence.* Boston: Harvard Business School Press.

Goodlad, John. 1984. *A Place Called School: Prospects for the Future.* New York: McGraw-Hill.

Hammonds, Keith H. 2002. "The Secret Life of the CEO: Do They Even Know Right from Wrong?" *Fast Company* 63 (October).

Hart, Vicki, John Blattner, and Staci Leipsic. 2001. "Coaching Versus Therapy: A Perspective." *Consulting Psychology Journal* 53, no. 4 (fall).

Hay Group. 2001. "The Retention Dilemma: Why Productive Workers Leave." Working paper no. 1. Hay Group.

Helgeson, Sally. 1985. *The Female Advantage: Women's Ways of Leadership.* New York: Doubleday.

Hirsh, Sandra Krebs, and Jean M. Kummerow. 1998. *Introduction to Type in Organizations.* 3rd ed. Palo Alto, Calif.: CPP, Inc.

Hoffer, Eric. 1963. *The Ordeal of Change.* New York: Harper and Row.

Hooks, Bell. 2000. *Where We Stand.* New York: Routledge.

Kampa-Kokesch, Sheila, and Mary Z. Anderson. 2001. "Executive Coaching: A Comprehensive Review of the Literature." *Consulting Psychology Journal* 53, no. 4 (fall).

Karp, Hank, Connie Fuller, and Danilo Sirias. 2002. *Bridging the Boomer Xer Gap: Creating Authentic Teams for High Performance at Work.* Palo Alto, Calif.: Davies-Black Publishing.

Kessler, Bernard. 1992. "How to Prevent Executive Derailment." *Human Resources Professional* 5, no. 1: 44–47.

Khurana, Rakesh. 2002. "The Curse of the Superstar CEO." *Harvard Business Review* (September): 60–66.

Kilburg, Richard. 2000. *Executive Coaching: Developing Managerial Wisdom in a World of Chaos.* American Psychological Association.

Laing, R. D. 1970. *Knots.* New York: Pantheon.

Lipman-Blumen, Jean. 1996. *Connective Leadership: Managing in a Changing World.* New York: Oxford University Press.

Lore International Institute. 1997. "Coaching Effectiveness Survey." Durango, Colo.: Lore International Institute.

———. 2000. "Survey of Influence Effectiveness." Durango, Colo.: Lore International Institute.

Lucier, Chuck, Eric Spiegel, and Rob Schuyt. 2002. "Why CEOs Fail: The Causes and Consequences of Turnover at the Top." *Strategy and Business* 28 (3d quarter).

Lyons, Laurence. 2000. "Coaching at the Heart of Strategy." In Marshall Goldsmith, Laurence Lyons, and Alyssa Freas, eds., *Coaching for Leadership: How the World's Greatest Coaches Help Leaders Learn.* San Francisco: Jossey-Bass.

MacFarquhar, Larissa. 2002. "The Better Boss." *The New Yorker,* April 22–29.

Mama, Amina. 2002. "Gender, Power, and Identity in African Contexts." *Wellesley Centers for Women Research and Action Report* 23, no. 2 (spring/summer): 6–15.

Maslow, Abraham. 1998. *Toward a Psychology of Being.* 3rd ed. New York: Wiley.

McCall, Morgan, Michael M. Lombardo, and Ann M. Morrison. 1988. *The Lessons of Experience: How Successful Executives Develop on the Job.* New York: The Free Press.

McCracken, Douglas M. 2000. "Winning the Talent War for Women: Sometimes It Takes a Revolution." *Harvard Business Review* (November–December).

McIntosh, Peggy. 1985. "Feeling Like a Fraud." Working paper no. 18. Wellesley, Mass.: Stone Center.

Merriam-Webster's Collegiate Dictionary. 1999. 10th ed. Springfield, Mass.: Merriam Webster.

Meyerson, Debra E. 2001. *Tempered Radicals: How People Use Difference to Inspire Change at Work.* Boston: Harvard Business School Press.

Michaels, Ed, Helen Handfield-Jones, and Beth Axelrod. 2001. *The War for Talent.* Cambridge, Mass.: Harvard Business School Press.

Milken Institute Research Summary. 2000 (October).

Morrison, Ann M., Randall P. White, Ellen Van Velsor, and the Center for Creative Leadership. 1992. *Breaking the Glass Ceiling: Can Women Reach the Top of America's Largest Corporations?* Cambridge, Mass: Perseus.

O'Reilly, Charles A., III, and Jeffrey Pfeffer. 2000. *Hidden Value: How Great Companies Achieve Extraordinary Results with Ordinary People.* Cambridge, Mass.: Harvard Business School Press.

Ritchey, Karen. 1995. *Marketing to Generation X.* New York: Lexington Books.

Rodriguez, Richard. 1982. *Hunger of Memory.* Boston: D. R. Godine.

Roland, Alan. 1988. *In Search of Self in India and Japan: Toward a Cross-Cultural Psychology.* Princeton, N.J.: Princeton University Press.

Rosen, Bernard Carl. 2001. *Masks and Mirrors: Generation X and the Chameleon Personality.* Westport, Conn.: Praeger.

Rosener, Judy B. 1995. *America's Competitive Secret: Women Managers.* New York: Oxford University Press.

Ruderman, Marian N., Patricia J. Ohlott, and Kathy E. Kram. 1997. "Managerial Promotion: The Dynamics for Men and Women." *HR Magazine* (April).

Said, Edward. 1993. *Culture and Imperialism.* New York: Alfred Knopf.

Saporito, Thomas. 1996. "Business-Linked Executive Development: Coaching Senior Executives." *Consulting Psychology Journal* 48 (spring): 96–103.

Seligman, Martin E. P. *Learned Optimism.* 1990. New York: Pocket Books.

Sellers, Patricia. 2000. "The Fifty Most Powerful Women in Business: Secrets of the Fastest-Rising Stars." *Fortune,* October 16.

Singer, Barbara Spencer. 2001. "Recovering Executives at Risk of Derailing." Lore Executive White Paper Series. Durango, Colo.: Lore International Institute.

Spear, Karen. 2001. "Understanding Executive Development: A Framework from Adult Learning Theory." Lore Executive White Paper Series. Durango, Colo.: Lore International Institute.

Sue, David, and Derald Wing Sue. 1999. *Counseling the Culturally Different: Theory and Practice.* 3rd ed. New York: John Wiley and Sons.

Tobias, Lester L. 1996. "Coaching Executives." *Consulting Psychology Journal: Practice and Research* 48, no. 2 (spring): 87–95.

Trompenaars, Fons, and Charles Hampden-Turner. 1998. *Riding the Waves of Culture: Understanding Diversity in Global Business.* 2nd ed. New York: McGraw-Hill.

Tulgan, Bruce. 2000. *Managing Generation X: How to Bring Out the Best in Young Talent.* Rev. ed. New York: W. W. Norton.

Unseem, Jerry. 2002. "Tyrants, Statesmen, and Destroyers: A Brief History of the CEO." *Fortune,* November 18.

White, Steven. 1999. *Privileged Information.* New York: Kensington Publishing.

Working Mother magazine. 2000 (June).

Young, Jeffrey E., and Janet S. Klosko. 1994. *Reinventing Your Life.* New York: Penguin.

INDEX